Reading this book leads to deeper and more secret levels of the psychoanalytic experience, those that allow a contact with the Unconscious and its fantasies which, from obscurity, steer and powerfully influence the destiny of individuals, groups and sometimes entire nations. The path of exploration chosen by the authors is the most effective and convincing: the clinic, presented here at a high-quality level and complemented by refined and harmoniously consistent theoretical reflections. This publication has a decidedly international flavor and provides the most up-to-date and comprehensive view on the subject of unconscious fantasies, a dimension of the human psyche about which Psychoanalysis has developed a specific and absolutely unparalleled expertise.

Stefano Bolognini, *President, International Psychoanalytical Association*

Nancy Goodman and Paula Ellman propose a creative structure for revisiting the concept of Unconscious Fantasy. A dialogue is developed among excellent clinicians/authors belonging to different psychoanalytic cultures, based on clinical presentations. They focus on "finding the unconscious fantasy in the psychoanalytic encounter" which "brings processing and meaning to what was previously unrecognized" in my words an "as yet situation" – even in situations of trauma or physical pain. This book generously opens multiple perspectives, so the readers continue this dialogue exploring how they create in their own work the best conditions with their patients for the unspoken to be heard. I highly recommend this book.

Haydée Faimberg, *author of* The Telescoping of Generations

An essential text book for all psychotherapists and psychoanalysts on how to discover the unconscious fantasy in psychoanalytic treatment. This book may be read as a mystery novel with two smart detectives, Nancy R. Goodman and Paula L. Ellman, in search of discovering the unconscious fantasies of the clinical cases of body pain and trauma with colleagues from across the globe of analytic thinking.

David Rosenfeld, *M.D., Ex Vice President IPA, Professor for Buenos Aires University, recipient of Sigourney and Hayman Awards and author of* The Body Speaks: Body Image Delusions and Hypochondria

Character is destiny, and unconscious fantasies form the mind-molding DNA that pattern each person"s unique character. In these engaging and remarkably candid contributions, clinicians of diverse theoretical backgrounds offer clinical reports alive in their actuality, each account followed by a dialogue of serious questions and reflections. These frank discussions expose and explore the rocky paths by which those hidden soul-shaping fantasies can be uncovered. This is analysis *in vivo*. Reading this work offers the stimulation and learning that comes from taking part in a seminar with master clinicians. Here, analysis lives.

Warren S. Poland, *M.D., author of* Intimacy and Separateness in Psychoanalysis

Paula Ellman and Nancy Goodman have produced a most unusual book that functions at one and the same time on a number of different levels. The book itself can perhaps be best considered as scholarly research in action. It brings together writers from varying clinico-theoretical orientations, asking each to consider the concept of unconscious phantasy not as a theoretical concept but as something discovered, a living evolving phenomenon in their clinical work. The editors in their scholarly introduction, foreground a tension in psychoanalysis that takes it origin at the earliest beginnings of our discipline – a kind of clinico-theoretic bifurcation between the concepts of "trauma" and "unconscious fantasy". The editors are to be congratulated on having done much to repair this split and in so doing show how different ways of thinking can enrich each other. The book will be a most valuable research and clinical reference, a real "workbook" for all psychoanalytically oriented clinicians.

David Bell, *author of* Psychoanalysis and Culture: A Kleinian Perspective

Finding Unconscious Fantasy in Narrative, Trauma, and Body Pain

Finding Unconscious Fantasy in Narrative, Trauma, and Body Pain: A Clinical Guide demonstrates that the concept of the unconscious is profoundly relevant for understanding the mind, psychic pain, and traumatic human suffering. Paula L. Ellman and Nancy R. Goodman (editors) established the book to discover how symbolization takes place through the "finding of unconscious fantasy" in ways that mend the historic split between trauma and fantasy. Cases present the dramatic encounters between patient and therapist when confronting discovery of the unconscious in the presence of trauma and body pain, along with narrative.

Unconscious fantasy has a central role in both clinical and theoretical psychoanalysis. This volume is a guide to the workings of the dyad and the therapeutic action of "finding" unconscious meanings. Staying close to the clinical engagement of analyst and patient shows the transformative nature of the "finding" process as the dyad works with all aspects of the unconscious mind. *Finding Unconscious Fantasy in Narrative, Trauma, and Body Pain: A Clinical Guide* uses the immediacy of clinical material to show how trauma becomes known in the "here and now" of enactment processes and accompanies the more symbolized narratives of transference and countertransference. This book features contributions from a rich variety of theoretical traditions illustrating working models including Klein, Arlow, and Bion and from leaders in the fields of narrative, trauma, and psychosomatics. Whether working with narrative, trauma or body pain, unconscious fantasy may seem out of reach. Attending to the analyst/patient process of finding the derivatives of unconscious fantasy offers a potent roadmap for the way psychoanalytic engagement uncovers deep layers of the mind.

In focusing on the places of trauma and psychosomatic concreteness, along with narrative, *Finding Unconscious Fantasy in Narrative, Trauma, and Body Pain: A Clinical Guide* shows the vitality of "finding" unconscious fantasy and its effect in initiating a symbolizing process. Chapters in this book bring to life the sufferings and capacities of individual patients with actual verbatim process material demonstrating how therapists and patients discover and uncover the derivatives of unconscious fantasy. Finding the unconscious meanings in states of trauma, body expressions, and transference/countertransference enactments becomes part of the therapeutic dialogue between therapists and patients unraveling symptoms and allowing transformations. Learning how therapeutic work progresses to uncover unconscious fantasy will benefit all therapists and students of psychoanalysis and psychoanalytic psychotherapy interested to know more about the psychoanalytic dialogue.

Paula L. Ellman, Ph.D., ABPP, is a Training and Supervising Analyst in the Contemporary Freudian Society, Washington, DC Program and the International Psychoanalytical Association. She is Vice President of the CFS Board, a Member of the Committee on Women and Psychoanalysis of the IPA (COWAP), a Board Member of the North America Psychoanalytic Confederation (NAPsaC) representing CFS, and Visiting Professor at the Sino-American Continuing Training Project for Wuhan Hospital for Psychotherapy, Wuhan, China. She has a private practice in psychotherapy and psychoanalysis in North Bethesda, Maryland and Washington, DC.

Nancy R. Goodman, Ph.D., is a Training and Supervising Analyst with the Contemporary Freudian Society, Washington, DC Program and the International Psychoanalytic Association. She publishes on the topics of psychic trauma, female development, sadomasochism, and witnessing processes and is Director of the Virtual Psychoanalytic Museum, www.virtualpsychoanalyticmuseum.org. She maintains a psychoanalytic practice in Bethesda, MD.

Finding Unconscious Fantasy in Narrative, Trauma, and Body Pain

A Clinical Guide

Edited by Paula L. Ellman and
Nancy R. Goodman

Routledge
Taylor & Francis Group

LONDON AND NEW YORK

First published 2017
by Routledge
2 Park Square, Milton Park, Abingdon, Oxon OX14 4RN

and by Routledge
711 Third Avenue, New York, NY 10017

Routledge is an imprint of the Taylor & Francis Group, an informa business

British Library Cataloguing in Publication Data
A catalogue record for this book is available from the British Library

Library of Congress Cataloging in Publication Data
Names: Ellman, Paula Lisette, editor. | Goodman, Nancy (Nancy R.), editor.
Title: Finding unconscious fantasy in narrative, trauma, and pain : a clinical guide / edited by Paula L. Ellman and Nancy R. Goodman.
Description: Abingdon, Oxon ; New York, NY : Routledge, 2017. | Includes bibliographical references and index.
Identifiers: LCCN 2016054951| ISBN 9781138955004 (hardback : alk. paper) | ISBN 9781138955011 (pbk. : alk. paper) | ISBN 9781315666631 (e-book)
Subjects: LCSH: Fantasy. | Psychic trauma. | Psychoanalysis. | Psychotherapy.
Classification: LCC BF175.5.F36 F56 2017 | DDC 154.3–dc23
LC record available at https://lccn.loc.gov/2016054951

ISBN: 978-1-138-95500-4 (hbk)
ISBN: 978-1-138-95501-1 (pbk)
ISBN: 978-1-315-66663-1 (ebk)

Typeset in Times New Roman
by Wearset Ltd, Boldon, Tyne and Wear

Contents

Contributors

Editors

Paula L. Ellman, Ph.D., ABPP, is a Training and Supervising Analyst in the Contemporary Freudian Society (CFS) and the IPA, Vice President of the CFS Board, past institute director of the Washington Program of CFS, a Member of the Committee on Women and Psychoanalysis of the IPA (COWAP) and a Board Member of the North America Psychoanalytic Confederation (NAPsaC). She is Visiting Professor at the Sino-American Continuing Training Project for Wuhan Hospital for Psychotherapy, Wuhan China. She has written and presented in the areas of female psychology, enactment, terror, sadomasochism, and unconscious fantasy. Recent publications include: "Donald Winnicott Today: Book Review" (co-authored with Nancy Goodman) *Division Review* (2014); *Battling the Life and Death Forces of Sadomasochism: Clinical Perspectives* (co-edited with Harriet Basseches and Nancy Goodman, Karnac, 2013); and *Courage to Fight Violence against Women: Psychoanalytic and Multidisciplinary Perspectives* (co-edited with Nancy Goodman in the *Psychoanalysis and Women* series (Karnac, 2017)). She has a psychoanalytic practice in North Bethesda, Maryland and Washington, DC.

Nancy R. Goodman, Ph.D., is a Training and Supervising Analyst with the CFS and the IPA. She is on the permanent faculty of the CFS and has served as Institute Director of the CFS Washington, DC Program. She writes on female development, analytic listening, Holocaust Trauma, enactments, sadomasochism, and unconscious fantasy. Her most recent publications include: "Donald Winnicott Today: Book Review" (co-authored with Paula Ellman) *Division Review* (2014); *Battling the Life and Death Forces of Sadomasochism: Clinical Perspectives* (co-edited with Harriet Basseches and Paula Ellman, Karnac, 2013); *Psychoanalysis: Listening to Understand, Selection of Readings of Arlene Kramer Richards*, ed. Nancy R. Goodman (IPBooks, 2013); *The Power of Witnessing: Reflections, Reverberations, and Traces of the Holocaust – Trauma, Psychoanalysis, and the Living Mind* (co-edited with Marilyn B. Meyers, Routledge, 2012); and *Courage to Fight Violence against Women: Psychoanalytic and Multidisciplinary Perspectives* (co-edited with

Paula Ellman, in the *Psychoanalysis and Women* series (Karnac, 2017). She is Director of The Virtual Psychoanalytic Museum (www.virtualpsycho analyticmuseum.org, IPBooks). Dr. Goodman has a psychoanalytic practice in Bethesda, Maryland.

Contributors

Marilia Aisenstein is a Training Analyst with the Hellenic Psychoanalytical Society and the Paris Psychoanalytical Society. She has been President of the Paris Society and the Paris Psychosomatic Institute, member of the editorial board of the *Revue Française de Psychanalyse*, and co-founder and editor of the *Revue Française de Psychosomatique*. She has been Chair of the IPA's International New Groups. She was the European representative to the IPA's Executive Committee and to the Board. She presently works in private practice and gives seminars in both the Hellenic and the Paris Societies and is the President of the Executive Board of the Paris Society's Psychoanalytical Clinic. She has written chapters and books on psychosomatics and hypochondria, and numerous (150) papers in French, Greek, English, Spanish, and Portuguese in international reviews. She received the Maurice Bouvet Prize in 1992.

Nanette C. Auerhahn, Ph.D., is a Clinical Psychologist and Psychoanalyst in private practice in Beachwood, Ohio. She has taught at Stanford University, the California School of Professional Psychology in Berkeley, and Case Western Reserve University and is the author of numerous articles on trauma.

Harriet I. Basseches, Ph.D., ABPP, is a Training and Supervising Analyst in the Contemporary Freudian Society (CFS). She was a Trustee on the Board of the International Psychoanalytical Association (IPA), the North America Chair to the Program Committee for the 2015 IPA Congress. She is currently serving on the Task Force for IPA and Constituent Organizations, and on the IPA Education and Oversight Committee. In 2014, she received the American Psychoanalytic Presidential Award for service to the IPA. Formerly, she served as: President, the New York Freudian Society, President of the Independent Psychoanalytic Societies of the IPA in North America (CIPS), and Chair of the North American Psychoanalytic Societies Confederation of North America (NAPsaC). She was a board member of ABPsaP, and held numerous positions in the Division of Psychoanalysis of the American Psychological Association (Division 39). Dr. Basseches was also on the editorial board of the APsaA Newsletter, *The American Psychoanalyst (TAP)*. She has studied and written on the subjects of femininity, psychoanalytic listening, and response to terror, and has written book reviews for TAP and publications of Division 39. In 2013, she, Paula Ellman and Nancy Goodman edited: *Battling the Life and Death Forces of Sadomasochism: Clinical Perspectives* (CIPS Book Series, Karnac).

Werner Bohleber, Dr. Phil, is a psychoanalyst in private practice in Frankfurt and a Training and Supervising Analyst. He was former President of the German Psychoanalytical Association (DPV) and a former member of the Board of Representatives of the International Psychoanalytical Association (IPA). He served as editor of the German psychoanalytic journal *Psyche* and was a recipient of the Mary S. Sigourney Award 2007. Dr. Bohleber is the author of several books and numerous articles. His most recent book in English is *Destructiveness, Intersubjectivity, and Trauma. The Identity Crisis of Modern Psychoanalysis* (Karnac, 2010).

Catalina Bronstein, MD, is visiting Professor in the Psychoanalysis Unit at University College London. She is a Fellow and Training and Supervising Analyst of the British Psychoanalytical Society. She trained as a child psychotherapist at the Tavistock Clinic and as an analyst at the British Psychoanalytical Society. She works as a child, adolescent, and adult psychoanalyst in private practice and also at the Brent Adolescent Centre. She is on the Board of the *International Journal of Psychoanalysis* (IJP), and until recently she was the London Editor of IJP. She lectures in Britain and abroad, and has written numerous papers, chapters in books, and monographs on a wide variety of topics. She edited *Kleinian Theory: A Contemporary Perspective* (Wiley, 2001) and co-edited *The New Dialogues Klein-Lacan* (2015, Karnac). With Edna O'Shaughnessy she has co-edited *Attacks on Linking Revisited* (Karnac, in press). She is the current President of the British Psychoanalytical Society.

Irene Cairo, MD, received her medical training in Buenos Aires, Argentina. She is a board certified psychiatrist in New York State. She is a member, Training Analyst and faculty of the Contemporary Freudian Society, and is a graduate, member, and faculty of the New York Psychoanalytic Institute. She is the author of "My Colleague, that Other" (*Psychoanalytic Dialogues*, 2005). She has published a chapter in *Immigration in Psychoanalysis* (Routledge, 2015), and a chapter in *The Bion Tradition* (Karnac, 2015). For the past 20 years Dr. Cairo has co-chaired with Rogelio Sosnik a discussion group on the work of Bion, at the biannual meetings of the American Psychoanalytic Association, where she also coordinates a clinical workshop on process and technique. She has participated in many meetings devoted to Bion both nationally and internationally. She is currently the North American Chair of the Ethics Committee of the International Psychoanalytic Association. She is in private practice in New York.

Carolyn S. Ellman, Ph.D., is a Training and Supervising Analyst (Fellow) at the Institute for Psychoanalytic Training and Research (IPTAR) and the Contemporary Freudian Society. She is also an Adjunct Clinical Professor and Supervising Analyst at the New York University Postdoctoral Program in Psychotherapy and Psychoanalysis and a Clinical Associate Supervisor at the City University Clinical Psychology Department. She is the senior editor, with Joseph Reppen, of *Omnipotent Fantasies and the Vulnerable Self* (Aronson, 1997) as well as *The Modern Freudians: Contemporary*

Psychoanalytic Technique (with Stanley Grand, Mark Silvan, and Steven Ellman) (Aronson, 1999). She has co-edited with Andrew B. Druck, Aaron Thaler, and Norbert Freedman, *A New Freudian Synthesis: Clinical Process in the Next Generation* (Karnac, 2011). She has written several articles and taught and lectured extensively on the topic of envy.

Ilany Kogan, MA, is a Training and Supervising Analyst of the Israel Psychoanalytic Society. She works as a teacher and supervisor at the Generatia Center in Bucharest, Romania, and in various places in Germany, especially in Munich and Aachen. For many years Dr. Kogan worked extensively with Holocaust survivors' offspring, and published papers and books on this topic. She was awarded the Sigourney award (2016) and the Elise M. Hayman Award for the Study of the Holocaust and Genocide (2005). She is author of *The Cry of Mute Children* (Free Association Books, 1995); *Escape from Selfhood* (IPA Publications, 2007); *The Struggle Against Mourning* (Rowman & Littlefield, 2007); and *Canvas Of Change – Analysis Through the Prism of Creativity* (Karnac, 2012).

Dori Laub, MD, was born in Cernauti, Romania, on June 8, 1937. He is currently a practicing psychoanalyst in New Haven, Connecticut, who works primarily with victims of massive psychic trauma and with their children. He is Clinical Professor of Psychiatry at the Yale University School of Medicine and co-founder of the Fortunoff Video Archive for Holocaust Testimonies. He obtained his MD at the Hadassah Medical School at Hebrew University in Jerusalem, Israel, and his MA in Clinical Psychology at the Bar Ilan University in Ramat Gan, Israel. He was Acting Director of the Genocide Study Program (GSP) at Yale in 2000 and 2003. Since 2001, he has also served as Deputy Director for Trauma Studies for the GSP. Dr. Laub has published on the topic of psychic trauma, its knowing and representation in a variety of psychoanalytic journals and has co-authored a book entitled *Testimony: Crises of Witnessing in Literature, Psychoanalysis, and History* with Professor Shoshana Felman (Routledge, 1992).

Janice S. Lieberman, Ph.D., is a psychoanalyst in private practice in New York City. She is a Training and Supervising Analyst, faculty member at IPTAR (Institute for Psychoanalytic Training and Research) where she teaches a course on The Contemporary Dream. She has served on the Editorial Boards of *JAPA*, the *PANY Bulletin*, and *The American Psychoanalyst*. She chairs an annual discussion group on Masculinity at the winter meetings of the American Psychoanalytic Association. She has written two books: *The Many Faces of Deceit: Omissions, Lies and Disguise* (with Helen Gediman) (Aronson, 1996) and *Body Talk: Looking and Being Looked at in Psychotherapy* (Aronson, 2000), and has published and presented numerous papers on gender, body narcissism, deception, greed and envy, art and psychoanalysis, loneliness, and the digital age and its effects on relationships.

Batya R. Monder, MSW, BCD, is a Training and Supervising Analyst at the Contemporary Freudian Society (CFS) and a member of the Institute for Psychoanalytic Training and Research (IPTAR). She also serves on the IPA Committee on Perspectives on Aging. She teaches in the CFS psychotherapy program and has given electives on aging at CFS and at the Confederation of Independent Psychoanalytic Societies (CIPS). She was the Editor of *The Round Robin*, a psychoanalytic newsletter of Section I of Division 39 of the American Psychological Association, from 2002 to 2007. She has written and presented on enactment, shame, perversion, and sexual abuse. She maintains a private practice in Manhattan.

Robert Oelsner, MD, is a Training and Supervising Analyst of the Northwestern Psychoanalytic Society, the Psychoanalytic Institute of Northern California and guest faculty of the Child Analytic Training Program of the San Francisco Center for Psychoanalysis. He is the editor and co-author of the book *Transference and Countertransference Today* (New Library of Psychoanalysis, 2013), as well as the author of over 150 articles on technique and psychopathology and numerous book chapters. He teaches regularly in the U.S., Europe, and South America. Dr. Oelsner is a graduate of the Institute of the Buenos Aires Psychoanalytic Association in Argentina where he lived and practiced until 2002. Since 1999 he has been the organizer of an annual international clinical seminar in London, UK. His special interests are the works of Donald Meltzer, Wilfred Bion, and the contemporary Kleinian authors. He has a private practice in Seattle, Washington, where he offers consultation, psychotherapy, and psychoanalysis for children, adolescents, and adults.

Arlene Kramer Richards, EdD, is a psychoanalyst and a poet. She is a Training and Supervising Analyst with the Contemporary Freudian Society and the IPA and Fellow of IPTAR. She is faculty at the Contemporary Freudian Society and Tongji Medical College of Huazhong University of Science and Technology at Wuhan, China. Her psychoanalytic writings clarify issues of female development, perversion, loneliness, and the internal world of artists and poets. Her book of poetry (IPBooks, 2011) is titled: *The Laundryman's Granddaughter: Poems by Arlene Kramer Richards*. Her most recent books are: *Myths of Mighty Women: Their Application in Psychoanalytic Psychotherapy* (with Lucille Spira), (Karnac, 2015); *Psychoanalysis: Listening to Understand. Selected Papers of Arlene Kramer Richards* (Nancy Goodman Ed) (IPBOOKS, 2013); *Encounters With Loneliness: Only the Lonely* (with Arthur A. Lynch and Lucille Spira Eds.) (IPBOOKS, 2013). She serves as elected representative to the IPA and practices in New York City.

Elias M. da Rocha Barros, Training Analyst and Supervisor at the Brazilian Psychoanalytical Society of São Paulo, Fellow of the British Psychoanalytical Society and of the British Institute of Psychoanalysis, past Editor for Latin America of the *International Journal of Psychoanalysis*, Latin American

Chair of the Task Force for the International Encyclopedia of Psychoanalysis (IPA); recipient of the Mary S. Sigourney Award 1999.

Elizabeth L. da Rocha Barros, Training Analyst and Supervisor at the Brazilian Psychoanalytical Society of São Paulo, Fellow of the British Psychoanalytical Society and of the British Institute of Psychoanalysis, Child Analyst – British Psychoanalytical Society and Tavistock Clinic, DEA in Psychopathology Sorbonne University (Paris), Co-Chair for Latin America for the Clinical Comparative Methods Groups.

Rogelio Sosnik, MD, is a Training and Supervising Analyst, Buenos Aires Psychoanalytic Association, Training and Supervising Analyst and faculty, Contemporary Freudian Society, and a member of the American Psychoanalytic Association and the IPA. He is a member of the Editorial Board of the IJP. He has published papers in Argentina, Uruguay, Italy, and the U.S., on the relationship between Ferenczi and Bion, on the British School, and on the work of Bleger. He has written on the Ethical Texture of Psychoanalysis and co-chaired a workshop on the death penalty at the meeting of the American Psychoanalytic Association. For many years he has chaired a discussion group on the Clinical Value of Bion's ideas at the meetings of the American Psychoanalytic Association. He is in private practice in New York City.

Acknowledgments

We are grateful to all of the contributors to this volume. We experienced each of you willing to show us the intimacy of your work and willingness to open your minds to work with us to reveal the intricacies of showing the process of "finding unconscious fantasy." We thank Routledge Press and Kate Hawes for her receptivity to our ideas and her encouragement, and Charles Bath and Aiyana Curtis for responding to our many questions and welcoming our work. Hannah Riley, with Wearset, has been careful and thoughtful with our work, and we are grateful.

Paula L. Ellman, Ph.D., ABPP. I extend my loving appreciation to my husband, Douglas A. Chavis, my children, Jennie Chavis, Sam Chavis and Anna Chavis, and Karl Rodger, for their ongoing support of my work. I appreciate my co-editor and collaborator, Nancy Goodman, for our thinking, learning, and working together. I am grateful for my colleagues in our many year-long Bion Study Groups: Harmon Biddle, Elizabeth Fritsch, Nancy Goodman, Nancy Griscom, and Shelley Rockwell for our continued studying and deepening our work together. I have much appreciation to Harriet Basseches and Nancy Goodman for our Study Group of many, many years. And, lastly, I thank my many Contemporary Freudian Society colleagues for serving as my analytic home.

Nancy R. Goodman, Ph.D. I thank my husband, Louis W. Goodman, my children, and my grandchildren for supporting me as I have taken time to think deeply and write about unconscious fantasy. I am grateful to my co-editor, Paula Ellman, my friend and partner in thinking and writing together over the years. We feed each other's minds. I thank the teachers I had in the New York Freudian Society, DC Program, who emphasized the importance of unconscious fantasy. Thank you, Edwin Fancher. Thank you, Harriet Basseches for all of our work together with Paula on research projects. Arlene Kramer Richards has brought the thinking of Jacob Arlow to me, enriching my thinking in so many ways. My Bion Study Group (Harmon Biddle, Paula Ellman, Elizabeth Fritsch, Nancy Griscom, and Shelley Rockwell), my CIPS Enactment Group (Raquel Berman, Batya Monder, and Elizabeth Reese), and my co-creators of the Virtual Psychoanalytic Museum (Paula Ellman, Marilyn Meyers, and Batya Monder, www.virtualpsychoanalyticmuseum.org) enliven my mind with creativity.

Chapter 1

Finding unconscious fantasy

Paula L. Ellman and Nancy R. Goodman

Psychoanalysis views unconscious fantasy as foundational in the understanding of psychic realities.

This volume is about "finding unconscious fantasy" in psychoanalytic treatment. We use "finding" to mean the uncovering, discovery, and creative imaginings of derivatives related to unconscious fantasies, the psychic reality. Finding unconscious fantasy brings processing and meaning to what was previously unrecognized. Finding unconscious fantasy arises from the engagement of analyst and analysand as they work with narrative, body pain, and trauma. The work evolves in the mind of the patient, the analyst, and the unconscious communications between them. Sometimes the fantasy appears in the analysis as narrative, sometimes as interaction, or sometimes in the transference and countertransference, articulated by the patient or the analyst or both. We see both activity and receptivity as necessary for finding to take place within the conscious and unconscious communications between analysand and analyst.

We are proposing the emphasis on process, that is, the "how" of our psychoanalytic work with patients. We consider how unconscious fantasy becomes known layer after layer, elaboration after elaboration. The patient brings in free associations, dreams, body experience, enactments, and self-reflection; the analyst brings in listening to the patient and her own mind, containing, holding, countertransference enactments and affects. As reveries are exchanged, the patient and the analyst find unconscious fantasies together. We think of unconscious fantasy in an expansive way inclusive of stories, metaphors, images, beliefs, scenes, affects, trauma, and body sensations. Analyst and analysand can see, hear, feel, and enact elements of unconscious fantasy derivatives that are multilayered, have gone through secondary revision and originally arise from instinctual desires. Uncovering the wishes, fears, constellations of object relations, traumas, and meaning of enactments is the work of psychoanalysis.

While our contributors differ with their use of "ph" or "f" (phantasy or fantasy), we find that all consider unconscious fantasy to be the core of psychic life and central to their function as analysts in addressing the workings of the mind. The writers/analysts in this volume follow thinking that fantasies (inborn primal fantasies, baby and infant fantasies and oedipal constellations) link to instinctual life and death forces. We primarily use "fantasy" without the intent of adhering to any implicit theoretical tradition. We may use alternative spellings depending on the contributor we reference. Our book intends to stay close to clinical process and bring the voices of many theoretical traditions to a careful consideration of the process of "finding unconscious fantasy."

We apply finding unconscious fantasy to the understanding of psychic realities appearing both in narrative, the symbolic, and in the concrete nature of the traumatic, yet to be symbolized. Thus, our focus on finding emphasizes a unitary view of the mind, all that is in the psyche. When trauma and somatic pain are in the psyche, unconscious fragments of the traumatic mind have yet to emerge and often come to be known through enactment processes. The finding of unconscious fantasy brings a symbolizing process to areas of the mind that have been inaccessible either due to repression or because contents are in a pre-symbolized form. In considering clinical cases where there is both the symbolized and unsymbolized in the mind, as in the more extreme circumstances of psychic life, this guide offers the means for finding unconscious fantasy as it evolves through uncovering and creating what could not previously be known.

The clinical focus on cases with trauma and somatic pain

To allow for a full view of the processes involved in finding unconscious derivatives in psychic realities, we asked our contributors to write about clinical cases in which traumatic and somatic problems were part of their patients' psychic lives. In the clinical arena of instances of both trauma and somatic expression, there can often be the experience of frozenness in the analytic dyad as translation of body pain and the psychic deadness of severe trauma resist revelation and meaning. Trauma and somatic expressions can be disturbingly concrete and frightening to approach. When Freud discovered the significance of the fantasy and the way something in the present (such as a traumatic event) can bring a past hidden conflict of mind, a theoretical split formed between traumatic helplessness and unconscious fantasy. Watchfulness for the sequelae of actual seduction or other trauma slipped into the background, often leading analysts to minimize actual trauma while emphasizing the power of the forbidden wish. We recognize that psychic realities are likely to carry history of both trauma and fantasy and their interconnections, all to be uncovered and symbolized through a finding process.

How the work of finding unconscious fantasy takes place is crucial for understanding analytic process with all psychic pain and conflict. We find both narrative and trauma in the minds of most patients. The dyad translates manifest into latent and latent into deeper levels of mind that include revisions from all stages of psychic development. We view the daydream, night dream, narrated wishes and fears, and enactment processes as means for developing metaphor thereby connecting with unconscious fantasy even in the traumatic places of the mind. We see a connection between unsymbolized trauma and the pervasive anxieties from unconscious beliefs in annihilation/castration, both female and male forms. Through affects and images becoming known, metaphor and symbol become possible and meaning is created.

"Finding" involves the creation of space in the mind of the patient and the analyst, and within the treatment dialogue. In cases where there is narrative and trauma we have the opportunity to recognize and listen to symbolized and unsymbolized material, and investigate the process of uncovering of networks of fantasy between analyst and patient. Sometimes fantasy is discovered and sometimes it is created as imagination enters the dead places of trauma in the mind. We are interested in reflecting on ways that analysts work with unconscious fantasy material in these cases and see the nature of the mind as unitary with derivatives of trauma, unconscious fantasy, and their intermingled influences.

An edited book: our exploration of "finding"

We invited psychoanalytic practitioners/thinkers to write about clinical work with patients who bring trauma and somatic concerns. These are the patients with blank spaces in their psyches, who have overwhelming experiences of help-lessness, and suffer wrenching pain. Each contributor presents clinical material and reflections on the process of uncovering derivatives indicative of uncon-scious fantasy in the mind. Some contributors present the cases, some serve as commentators of the cases, and some write individual chapters with clinical material and their reflections. In order to accomplish the task of being a clinical guide, each chapter stays close to the case material and to ideas about finding unconscious fantasies. Our book contributors come from diverse theoretical tra-ditions; many are major writers in the areas of trauma and psychosomatics. We ask our contributors to present their thinking through associations and reflec-tions. With the types of cases presented this entails engaging with concreteness, states of trauma, somatic pain, and countertransference. The engagement is both direct, for the analysts in the actual treatment, or from a once removed place for the commentators. Each chapter shows how the work proceeds, how the finding of unconscious fantasy is taking place. Four full clinical cases are presented with in-depth descriptions of the actual work. Each case has two commentators pre-senting their associations and their understanding of finding unconscious fantasy.

Our invitation to contributors

In order to investigate how our contributors find unconscious fantasy, we gave directions asking that they remain close to clinical material including their own countertransference awareness and their thinking about unconscious fantasy.

Directions to case writers and chapter writers (verbatim)

Focus on process – the "finding" of unconscious fantasy. The clinical is the most important aspect of our book, *Finding Unconscious Fantasy* – the true demonstration of analytic work. How you and your patient create ways to "find unconscious fantasy" will be shown in the process that you each will highlight in your case. We want to show how "finding" unconscious fantasy takes place in the analytic exchange even when there are unsymbolized places in the analysand's mind. The importance of the unsymbolized makes for our requesting case material about either trauma patients (can be through generational transmissions) or patients with somatic pain where the body speaks what cannot yet be narrated. Often somatic pain accompanies trauma. It is these types of cases where the potency of analytic finding of the unconscious fantasy can be demonstrated.

Working in the transference/countertransference arena is often the way to find the unconscious fantasy. We ask that you stay close to the process. You may also comment on how you think of "finding unconscious fantasy" in your work and particularly in the context of your case. Most importantly, we want a clinical focus. We have invited two contributors for each of your cases whose chapters will discuss your clinical case with a focus on finding unconscious fantasy.

For discussants: as we have been thinking about the purpose of the book, to ultimately gain insight about how "finding of unconscious fantasy takes place," we have solidified our thinking about how to bring this rich topic into focus. We want you to feel free to associate to the case material – really free – with thoughts, your own fantasies, your own counter-feelings, your subjectivity as analysts. Please make some comments about how you think the process of finding unconscious fantasy evolves often through ideas about the transference and countertransference and through a symbolizing process taking place over time. How do the somatic issue and the traumatic enter a symbolizing process?

Conceptual history of unconscious fantasy

Forces of the unconscious were first articulated with early consideration of hysterical symptoms. Unraveling the paralysis of the hysteric led to a new theory and a metapsychology, the topographic model of the mind (Freud, 1896). Focus on soma and trauma take us back to the very beginning of psychoanalysis, the discovery of depth of mind and of the talking cure. Laplanche and Pontalis (1973) attribute the development of major psychoanalytic concepts to these early studies of hysteria.

> It was of course in the process of bringing the psychical etiology of hysteria to light that psychoanalysis made its principal discoveries: the unconscious, phantasy, defensive conflict and repression, identification, transference, etc.
>
> (p. 195).

As early as 1893, Breuer writes the following with regard to discoveries on hysterics:

> We describe as conscious those ideas which we observe as active in us, or which we should so observe if we attended to them. At any given moment of time there are very few of them; and if others, apart from those, would be current at the time, we should have to call them *unconscious* ideas.
>
> (1893–1895, p. 221)

And in the "Two principles of mental functioning" (1911), Freud presents his thinking about the inherent connection between instinctual life and "phantasying":

> With the introduction of the reality principle one species of thought activity was split off: it was kept free from reality-testing and remained subordinated to the pleasure principle alone. This activity is phantasying which begins already in children's play, and later, continued as day-dreaming, abandons dependence on real objects.
>
> (p. 221)

Here developed the theoretical and clinical necessity for the concept of unconscious fantasy making possible an understanding of anxieties, symptoms, and traumatic affects. As seen in the chapters of this book, psychoanalysts from differing theoretical orientations validate the continued usefulness and potency of the concept in current analytic thought and practice.

Scenes of seduction in the mind were at the center of psychic pain, both in traumatic memories and repressed wishes. At first the presence of trauma and seduction were considered the root of symptoms. Then came the development of the idea of an internal scene of seduction involving forbidden wish. While catharsis may ease paralysis, the acknowledgment of the forbidden wish and the need for punishment may free conflict and inhibition, and facilitate growth. A theoretical split ensued between the validity of traumatic impact from the environment and psychic realities of unconscious fantasies/wishes. It was as if only one could be the most true.

Additionally, along with the early ideas on the place of unconscious fantasy was another ground-breaking idea that the trauma of the present brings back the full force of historic trauma and forbidden desire. This is evident in Freud's early letter to Fleiss, September 21, 1897: "It seems once again arguable that only later experiences give the impetus to fantasies, which (then) hark back to childhood" (Masson, 1985, p. 265). This is about the "fiction which has been cathected with affect" – *Nachtraglichkeit* – deferred action – the core aspects of Freud's idea of unconscious fantasy. The concept *Nachtraglichkeit* helps us understand what happens "here and now" in treatment; how the present relates to past experience through fantasies that are embedded in the mind. Finding unconscious fantasy involves listening for connections with the past unconscious including primal fantasies and infantile fantasies.

Early on there were theoretical differences about the notion of "phantasy," "whether or not it is identical or near-identical with hallucinatory wish fulfillment, and whether it is or is not primary mental content" (Hayman, 1989, p. 110). Isaacs (1948) retains the word "phantasy" to emphasize the genetic continuity between the earliest and the latest levels. "Phantasy is (in the first instance) the mental corollary, the psychic representative, of instinct. There is no impulse, no instinctual urge or response which is not experienced as unconscious phantasy" (p. 81). Therefore unconscious phantasy is actually the mind's content underlying the entire structure of mental functioning throughout life, psychic reality.

Jacob Arlow highlights the idea of an ongoing stream of fantasy accompanying and influencing perceptions at all times. He sees unconscious fantasy as connected to instinctual life of childhood and is elaborated throughout life in compromises and development of myths in the individual mind and in culture. There is a fantasying function in the psyche. After seeing a cartoon being played on a translucent screen from outside of his home, Arlow (1969) develops a metaphor of the showing of dual films: the idea of two images simultaneously being shown, an inner one and an outer one. This metaphor captures the idea that there is always unconscious activity streaming in the mind. In his numerous papers he writes of the crucial centrality of unconscious fantasy in the psyche and in psychoanalysis.

> Unconscious daydreaming is a constant feature of mental life. It is an ever-present accompaniment of conscious experience. What is consciously apperceived and experienced is the result of the interaction between the data of experience and unconscious fantasying as mediated by various functions of the ego.
>
> (1969, p. 22)

In "The Madonna's Conception through the Eyes," Arlow (1964) traces his patient's somatic symptoms, headache and pain and sensitivity in the eyes, to a symbolic equivalent set of compromises concerning a wished-for penetration and pregnancy in the transference. The wishes and strictures of a harsh superego create the symptom formation expressed in body pain. Arlow demonstrates the central importance of listening for the stream of unconscious thought and affect throughout, in perceptions and in soma.

Steiner in his edited collection (2003) considers the development of the concept of unconscious phantasy through revisiting the historical papers of Freudians, Kleinians, Lacanians, and neuroscientists and the central position unconscious phantasy occupies in psychoanalysis. "I have tried to remind the reader briefly of some of the historical vicissitudes of the concepts of fantasy and phantasy and their cultural context in some of the European languages" (2003, p. 3).

Furthering efforts to understand the development of psychoanalytic concepts through the lens of diverse schools, the International Psychoanalytic Association (IPA) launched studies of conceptual integration of key concepts in psychoanalysis. In their article, "Unconscious Phantasy and its Conceptualization: an attempt at conceptual integration" (2015), Bohleber, Jimenez, Scarfone, Varvin, and Zysman bring together concepts of unconscious fantasy from the major theoretical views. Interestingly, the authors find Klein and Arlow similar in belief in the presence of unconscious fantasies at all times and in their identifying drives as the "instigator" of unconscious fantasy:

> For Freud unconscious phantasies can only be partially known. They are to be inferred from the derivatives of the unconscious itself. Kleinians agree that, while unconscious phantasies must be inferred from the patient's clinical material, their existence is independent of the inference. Arlow thinks similarly on this matter. He speaks of an unconscious fantasy function. The stream of inner stimulation is organized by fantasy thinking.
>
> (2015, p. 727)

Recent emphasis on transference and countertransference and the "here and now" bring focus to what Joseph (1985) calls the total situation, the projections of the unconscious fantasy into the analyst. From work on the traumatic mind authors have added understanding to how fantasy comes into existence from the work of witnessing (Goodman & Meyers, 2012; Laub, 1992a, 1992b; Poland, 2000). Intersubjective analysts find unconscious fantasy and describe the dyadic creation of fantasy where it was previously unformulated (Stern, 2010). Ferro (2006) and Baranger and Baranger (2008) find the unconscious and trauma in the "field" where story in need of containment and transformation are discovered. Nonetheless, many contemporary analysts bring Freud into their formulations. For instance, as David Bell (2012) writes about unconscious phantasy he refers to Freud's basic idea of unconscious fantasy as the remnant from the reality principle curtailing pleasure:

> Phantasy as scene, Phantasy as representation of drive; Phantasy as representation of wish as its fulfillment; Phantasy as split off activity of the mind functioning under aegis of the pleasure principle; Phantasy as representation of the minds' own activities; and lastly as the basic function of all mental life, including drives, impulses, all anxiety situations and defences.
>
> (p. 8)

The realm of unconscious fantasy has been and continues as a primary focus of psychoanalysis in pursuing the underpinnings of the working of the mind.

The analyst's position and centrality of countertransference

Our focus on the way "finding the unconscious fantasy" in clinical work takes place brings attention to expressions as they become crystallized in the transference/countertransference. In fact it is often only through the elaboration of the transference/countertransference that the unconscious fantasy is defined and becomes accessible. In his 1905 paper on Dora, Freud first observed *in vivo* the presence of unconscious fantasies in the transference. Now psychoanalysts from all theoretical schools would agree that the countertransference accompanies the transference in the "here and now" of sessions. Through narrative, but more relevant to working with trauma and somatic expression, through enactments, we see the powerful place of the countertransference that allows for the coming to know unconscious fantasy. The focus on the analytic dyad becomes the means of bringing together work with trauma and the continued idea that mental representations are key to understanding the mind. Experience occurs and the fantasy function is always present making meaning out of experience.

In the context of Bohleber et al.'s work on conceptual integration, attentions to the powerful tool of the countertransference becomes an emphasis (2015). Bohleber et al. write:

> ... the description of the process whereby the analyst's mind embraces the idea that an emerging phenomenon in the relationship with the patient can be defined as unconscious fantasy is important. Monitoring countertransference has become a key tool in this process.
>
> (p. 710)

Bohleber et al. describe beautifully the process of finding in the context of the dyadic relationship:

> The analyst is oriented to going beyond the explicit words of the patient in an endeavour to unveil what we may call unconscious experience.... Sooner or later, both analyst and patient will face a discontinuous, somewhat fragmented and inconsistent reality.... We select those facts that appear closest to our own world, thus allowing us to participate in the patient's world. A shared world begins to take shape ...; this shared world "appears" in the analyst's mind as a fantasy, that is, as a complex visual image – a short figurative narrative – which simultaneously describes multiple dimensions in the patient (and in the analyst), within the "here and now" of the analytic relationship. The unconscious fantasies we "find" during the process of "discovering" the patient's inner world constitute a way of describing the experience of the unconscious as it emerges at the interface of the analyst's and patient's interpersonal/intersubjective contact.
>
> (p. 711)

The analytic dyad uncovers layers of experience and accesses the substrate of unconscious fantasy. Birksted-Breen (2016) describes "reverberation time" where the back and forth within the dyad and in time brings a symbolizing process. Understanding countertransference enables the analyst to speak to the seam of analyst/patient – where psychic reality lives. The interface carries access to unconscious fantasy.

Trauma and body

We choose cases in which trauma and body pain are part of the psychic makeup of the patient for two basic reasons: (1) to show how finding unconscious fantasy comes about in these treatments; and (2) to help bring together the historical trauma/fantasy split. Trauma and fantasy no longer must be an either/or, they accompany one another in the unconscious mind. Somatic expression and trauma are present in all of the cases in which the contributors show how "finding" unconscious fantasy occurs. We emphasize that we think of unconscious fantasy in an expansive way that includes the primal inborn fantasy and the derivatives over time, and also infantile fantasies from each developmental phase. The here and now of transference/countertransference is where the fantasies are most often felt and become known.

We see the mind as whole, a unitary mind, in which traumatic fantasy, likely unsymbolized, is present and interacting with that which is symbolized. Finding unconscious fantasy is often finding traumatic affects and associated images and scenes. Trauma and narrative interact, growing each from the other as affects get into internal stories and as internal imaginings develop around the psychic helplessness of trauma. Primitive unconscious fears can bring about helplessness and debilitating compromises, and traumas can cause psychic devastation and obstacles to resilience and growth. Examining the way trauma and body pain exist in the mind is essential to our view of psychic realities. We review here some of the literature related to soma and trauma to bring further richness to understanding clinical processes.

The body

How the body speaks can lead the way for the process of finding unconscious fantasy. Body pain can make for a debilitated life. We see body pain inviting opportunity to pursue underlying unconscious fantasy. McDougall (1974) states that the capacity for symbolic functioning that enables the binding and coping with physical or mental pains breaks down in adults in instances of massive psychic trauma or in individuals who experience traumatic events in childhood. Whether or not one's view is of a capacity for symbolization in somatic expression, the transference/countertransference provides the arena where accessing even the rudimentary unconscious fantasy and its meaning allows for making contact with the internal world. "A primitive psychically unprocessed conflict is relived in the transference relationship via the psychosomatic symptom"

(Bronstein, 2010, p. 63). In his book, *The Body Speaks: Body Image Delusions and Hypochondria*, David Rosenfeld (2014) demonstrates with case material how soma representations carry multiple meaning about unconscious fantasy, internal objects, and transferences. Perelberg (2017) describes how bodily symptoms may present themselves as a solution to the conflict between longing for and fear of fusion with the mother. It is through the transference to a female analyst that can allow for an identification with a primitive maternal imago which then "explodes more vividly" transferentially.

We understand unconscious fantasies to be connected to the body in ways that include both metaphoric expression and unsymbolized forms. Bronstein (2015) shows:

> ... the different symbolic forms that unconscious phantasies can adopt *and* the important role played by sensory experiences, semiotic dispositions and their articulation with symbolic forms in the analytic situation and how their coexistence can propel and enrich one another.... The analyst's receptivity to this coexistence in the patient facilitates the process of symbol formation.
>
> (p. 96)

Importantly, the analytic situation may allow for the development from the unsymbolized in body expression into metaphoric representation. Early life fantasies are closely connected with the body and carry yet to be processed emotions. These are apt to be projected into and identified with by the analyst, and experienced in a bodily fashion, becoming a key source of data in the countertransference. Through the elaboration and exploration of the transference/countertransference, the emergence of the unconscious fantasy originally held in the body begins to take shape thereby providing access to psychic reality (Bronstein, 2015). The publication of papers and edited books with the psycho-soma focus (Aisenstein & Aisemberg, 2010; Sloate, 2016) is a testament to the relevance and richness of analytic work in this arena, and the importance of the emphasis on "finding unconscious fantasy."

Trauma

Severe trauma often leaves a non-symbolized wound in individuals' psychic realities. Something occurs that overwhelms and cannot yet be known. Thus, finding the unconscious fantasy in these cases highlights the capabilities of analytic work to bring to light the intertwining of trauma and fantasy. This often means that the patient and analyst are creating what needs to be put into words. Scenes of seduction were the prototypic traumatic events in early psychoanalytic thinking. The traumas of World War I, World War II, the Holocaust, the Vietnam War, Rwanda, the Gulf War, and Afghanistan, and the recognition of child abuse and sexual abuse challenge psychoanalytic treatment to work with the overwhelmed traumatized mind.

The word "trauma" comes from a Greek word referring to a wound, a break through the skin that fits with the idea of a break through the psychic barrier. Anna Freud (1967) reserves the term "trauma" for that which is truly overwhelming and catastrophic. In his writing on trauma and vicissitudes of affects, Krystal (1978) states: "In the traumatic state there is a psychological paralysis which starts with a virtually complete blocking of the ability to feel emotions and pain as well as other physical sensations" (p. 101). Contemporary writers about trauma (Bohleber, 2010; Davies & Frawley, 1994; Frosch, 2012; Goodman, 2012; Kogan, 1995, 2007; Krystal, 1978; Laub, 1998; Shengold, 1989) create a variety of terms depicting psychic helplessness such as the black hole, dead places, the empty core, "toomuchness," and soul murder. Psychoanalytic attention to extreme trauma such as in Holocaust survivors and intergenerational transmissions brings emphasis to enactment (Ellman & Goodman, 2012; Kogan, 1995, 2007) and intersubjective processes (Bohleber, 2010; Stern, 2010). Bohleber (2007) speaks of the necessity to "find" phantasy and remembrance in order to approach the "foreign body" of trauma:

> They … [traumatic memories] … constitute a kind of foreign body in the psychic-associative network, but rather than forming an exact replica of the traumatic experience they undergo specific remodellings.… Resolving its predominant dynamics and extricating phantasy from traumatic reality requires a remembrance and reconstruction of the traumatic events in the analytic treatment.
>
> (p. 329)

Enactments produce a convincing "here and now" that lead to affects being connected to remembrance and reconstruction.

Instinctual wishes and fears are often embedded in the psyche and spoken of by way of traumatic transmissions; and, in turn, aspects of trauma (terror, symbolic fragments, and affects) can become instinctualized, creating renditions of unconscious fantasy. Much of this process takes place in the transference/countertransference and is discovered in a witnessing process (Goodman, 2012; Goodman & Meyers, 2012; Laub, 1992a, 1992b). Witnessing creates space for knowing the traumatic affects and fantasies expressed in enactments in sessions bringing process to the 'as yet unknown' (Faimberg, 2005). It is often the break in the empathic bond, no one helping to absorb and contain, that is the greatest initiator of annihilation terror. Bion (1962) reminds us that the mother provides a specific function he calls alpha function to metabolize the infant's distress, and Ferro (2006) identifies the function of the analyst in similar ways. Once witnessing is brought to trauma, once the therapist experiences the affect about the trauma, the traumatized individual is no longer alone thereby reinstating connection and creativity.

In turn, I have come to think of the power of witnessing as the force providing a clearing away and lighting for a living surround near the dead space where an opening, the new space, develops and takes hold.… There can now be communication between the trauma and the living mind.

(Goodman, 2012, pp. 5–6)

In the living surround grief can be felt and resilience can grow. It is crucially important for the analyst and patient to comprehend that "finding" fragments of the traumatized mind along with metaphor and affect is possible. The opening of new space enables the "finding" of unconscious fantasy derivatives which have been infused with the feel of trauma.

Observations: clinical guide for "finding" unconscious fantasy

By using the chapters as a research base, our intention is to develop an overview that serves as a clinical guide. The guide is relevant to the working mind of all psychoanalysts viewing unconscious fantasy as the core of their efforts. We follow the way sequelae of trauma, somatic symptoms, and repressed conflict are inevitably intertwined. All of the cases presented in this book include elements of the unsymbolized mind where psychic trauma and/or somatic expression are present. With this emphasis, we bring together all aspects of the psyche thereby mending former splits in the consideration of narrative and trauma and between conflict and defect. When following the processes of the finding of unconscious fantasy we discover the mind as unitary and whole. What is analyzable is expanded. This perspective, of the unity of the mind, is relevant to finding unconscious fantasies in the case of this volume.

This section is an overview considering our contributors' chapters and the observations we find in the full compilation of this book. We discovered more than we anticipated in vitally significant areas of psychoanalytic thought and practice. We divide observations into two sections: summaries of the way each chapter discovers finding of unconscious fantasy, and identification and observations of methods for discovering unconscious fantasy, both differences and commonalities among our contributors. In this way our guide provides a way to think about unconscious fantasy and psychic realities in which narrative, symbolic thinking, trauma, body pain, and the unsymbolized can all be found and understood.

Summaries of each chapter's finding unconscious fantasy process

Werner Bohleber in "The psychoanalytic treatment of an adult patient traumatized in early childhood" presents a case of an analysis that illustrates early trauma and its influences on the development of personality structures in adolescence and adulthood. Bohleber describes the horror of his patient at 18 months old who is hospitalized for 9 months and confined to a plaster bed for hip luxation without any adult attachments present for him. The patient's life has been one of trying to avert catastrophe by being perfect as he struggles with fantasies of confinement and abandonment. In his effort to find unconscious fantasy, Bohleber looks to his countertransference and the enactments in the analysis. The experience of timelessness and the patient's compulsion to break away, including from the analysis, involve the analyst in enactments full of affect and the writing of a letter. These countertransference attempts to hold the patient differently from the cast open arenas for finding unconscious fantasy. Recurring dreams of being in very small rooms, unable to leave, along with symptom recurrence of urinary retention, become "royal roads" to unconscious fantasy. The discussants, Nancy Goodman in "The impossible and the possible: finding unconscious fantasy dimensions in Werner Bohleber's case of Mr. A." and Elias and Elizabeth da Rocha Barros in "Unconscious phantasy: discussion of Werner Bohleber's case," bring their focus to the enactments, calling attention to finding a scene. The da Rocha Barroses speak of the "scene fragments," the "engram," the "template" for how the patient organizes emotional experience that make for "kernels of meaning" in the unconscious fantasy. Goodman emphasizes the finding of unconscious fantasy in Bohleber's countertransference enactments that break into the patient's fantasy of timelessness and relate to the helplessness of the hospitalization, the constraining plaster bed and the dead internal objects, his parents. As Goodman emphasizes the "witnessing process" in the finding, the de Rocha Barroses bring focus to a "metabolizing process." Both speak to the need for "imaginings." The da Rocha Barroses discuss the unconscious phantasy of the patient being the cause for all his sufferings, the idea of "rightful punishment for being a bad baby operating as an engram that immobilizes his adult self" – his "traumatic immobilization." Goodman takes the reader to the place in the unconscious of loss of contact as she writes letters to the analyst, including them in her discussion much like the analyst's writing to his patient. Both discussants emphasize the incapacitation in mental functioning, the frozenness, and the attention brought to dreams, symptoms, and countertransference that lead the way to finding unconscious fantasy in order to bring a capacity for symbolization and the creation of metaphor.

Paula Ellman titles her clinical case, "A Soma case of pain" signaling to the reader that pain is the central feature of the analysis with Margaret. The analyst's clinical process material and the two discussions demonstrate that even in the most traumatic painful concrete expressions of pain there can be contours of unconscious fantasy. Ellman presents a case of early life trauma where the patient was treated as a doll and a dog, inhumanely, as if inanimate. Margaret brings her constant efforts to please into all her relationships. The treatment relationship carries attempts and failures at making contact. Ellman finds unconscious fantasy derivatives in elements of the pain of her patient and in her own reactions, her emotions and feelings of helplessness. From their first contact the analyst experienced that someone was hitting someone and she imagined herself throwing the punch. The clinical material presents narratives and dreams, and also shows the continuous enactments of torture in the transference and counter-transference where Ellman finds elements of unconscious derivatives underlying the constant searing tortures. Marilia Aisenstein finds unconscious fantasy in Ellman's case of Margaret in her chapter, "Painful transference and pains of transference: discussion of Paula Ellman's case." She focuses on the many ways that the analysis reveals the meanings of suffering in the body. Aisenstein finds unconscious fantasy in the transference and what Margaret wants to do to her analyst. She sees Margaret immobilizing her analyst's effectiveness as an attack on the internal mother, but also as a way to keep the mother alive. Aisenstein writes of the patient unconsciously seeking to paralyze the analyst and others with her pain in order to maintain the sadistic and living mother inside. In her commentary titled "Discussion of Dr. Paula Ellman's case," Batya Monder notes how Ellman stays with her patient, providing needed containing for Margaret so that she might eventually be able to use metaphor and to express her own angry emotions. Monder reminds us of Isaacs' emphasis on unconscious fantasy as the makeup of the patient's relation to the analyst. Monder shows the ways that Margaret brings stories of her wordless body pain to Ellman by doing to Ellman what was done to her, by creating psychotic descriptions of pain as a retreat, and by demonstrating the soul murder and brainwashing as described by Shengold (1989). Monder describes the assertiveness and capacity to mourn as evidenced in the process material and relating to the close availability of Ellman to stay with her patient. Pain is the event and a psychic retreat is returned to again and again. The finding of symbolization in the constant presence of raw pain takes place in the evolution of the transference/countertransference.

Irene Cairo, in "Babette, interrupted," presents a case of a patient well versed in many languages where the primary symptom bringing her into treatment was her stammering. There is a history of trauma with two early experiences of hospitalizations at 2 and a half years old (infection) and 6 years old (tonsillectomy), both involving separations and abandonments from parents. Cairo describes the stammering as repetitions of "something interrupted." Cairo writes about the use of words associated with destructive phantasies contained in the patient's variations of speech and silences. Clinical material shows the finding process in the transference of idealization of the analyst cloaking a history involving generational persecution. Along with the idealization is contempt, the question of whether to trust, and the rescue fantasy. Money transactions in the analysis carry meanings and unconscious fantasy derivatives. Cairo engages in the finding with consideration of the symptom of stammering that comes to be associated with unconscious phantasies. The action of interruptions in and outside the treatment, the sending of the sister for treatment, the bringing of the baby to the first session, become means of developing the finding process. Harriet Basseches, in "Discussion of Dr. Irene Cairo's case: Babette, interrupted," explains that our theory informs our way of listening. She speaks of being the outside third, working to catch a "glimpse" of the underlying fantasy

in the transference/countertransference. Basseches presents the idea of a "hierarchy of underlying fantasy," allowing her to see multiple layers of wishes and
fears and compromises. She presents a basic wish/fantasy in Babette: "Perhaps
the wish would be that she had omnipotent control over who came and who went
and that she would be the queen of leave-takings, and the belief that with that
control, she would never be hurt." Basseches articulates the many ways she went
about finding fantasy: transference/countertransference, manifest and latent
content, conscious wishes like daydreams, repetition compulsions, of escaping,
screen memories and symptoms. Catalina Bronstein in "Noises and voices: discussion on Babette, interrupted" closely follows the course of Cairo's clinical
process:

> While the content of the patient's discourse can carry symbolic meaning,
> early phantasies can affect the rhythm, the prosody, the "semiotics" that
> accompany the account. In the case we are discussing, it seems to me that
> this rhythm is compounded by the stammering – the interruption in the
> formulation of words.

Interrupted speech is about words not reaching their natural ending. The treatment is interrupted, not terminated, based on the early anxiety of phantasy of
death to infant or object. Babette's phantasies of the analyst change from a safe
object into an unsafe one as the perception of the analyst's voice changes to one
of noises. Bronstein suggests that Babette's work with Cairo reaches different
levels of phantasy bringing the development of a coherent ego.

Janice Lieberman, the case writer, and the two discussants, Carolyn Ellman
and Ilany Kogan, find unconscious fantasy in the transference and countertransference tensions of the case – the demeaning, the devaluing, the fears of closeness, the attempts to defeat, and the turning passive to active. Lieberman titles
her case "Not quite a princess," referencing what happens to the princess who
feels the pea through 20 mattresses. This is a case illustrative of the presence of
trauma, being tied to the crib to keep her in the crib and having her mouth
washed with soap when in protest. Later traumas include an abortion and cervi-
cal surgery. Karen is often in states of "too much" arousal and "too much" deadness. Lieberman finds derivatives of fantasy and unconscious wishes in her
counter-reactions to her patient's continual complaints about what she has not
received from her mother and analyst. The patient brings an array of sadomasochistic fantasies to the transference. Carolyn Ellman, in "Mirror, mirror on the
wall: who's the fairest of us all? Comments on Janice Lieberman's case: 'Not
quite a Princess'," finding evidence of envy of the brother and his genitals that
she is missing. C. Ellman then finds the aggressive envy of the mother's body
that the patient turns against herself. There is soon recognition that femininity is
pleasing to the patient but she is filled with unconscious fantasies of attacking
the insides of her mother's procreative body or of being attacked. She tends to
enact self-abortion in various forms that Carolyn Ellman is able to identify as

related to unconscious fantasies. C. Ellman uses K's symbolizing dreams to understand the presence of unconscious fantasy and trauma in K and the attacking enactments with her analyst. Kogan writes about Lieberman's case in her paper, "The broken doll: discovering the unconscious fantasy in the case of Karen." Kogan sets out to find fantasy according to Jacob Arlow's ideas – in the "interaction between fantasy thinking and the perception of reality." Kogan finds unconscious fantasies in the patient's association to symbols and in the sadomasochistic enactment of the transference. She finds a fantasy of dissociation, of deadness, at the core of Karen's psychic reality. Kogan finds unconscious fantasies in the active and passive forms of sadomasochism and in the defensive moves found in Lieberman's patient. The patient's dreams and descriptions provide fertile ground for associative processes that "find" wishes and fears and the unconscious fantasies connected to their compromises. Trauma and unconscious fantasy are knit together in this case. The analyst and commentators refer to ways the trauma of having been tied to the crib is a major feature of the transference being enacted with the analyst.

Dori Laub and Nanette Auerhahn title their chapter "Unconscious traumatic fantasy," indicating that finding of the way trauma is seared into the mind. Their view of extreme trauma is that it blacks out the mind, erases the functioning of the mind, and that it is unknown until a series of enactments bring it into being. As they state, "We start to imaginatively enter the gas chambers but emotionally refuse to stay." They raise the question, is the unconscious fantasy in the traumatic erased mind or is the erasure sometimes complete? And they answer that the traumatic fantasy is inevitably discovered in transference/countertransference enactments. The analyst is the witness to the traumatic scenes, to the absolute psychic helplessness. Repetitions leaving the analyst stunned and often helpless eventually bring about imaginings of what is not known. A process of witnessing between analyst and patient puts fragments of images in the "here and now" in the room. The myth of Philomela conveys trauma and silence. Philomela is raped and her tongue is cut out. She weaves a tapestry revealing her story. Her sister Procne then kills her own son (fathered by the perpetrator) boiling him and serving him as a meal to her husband (the perpetrator). There are further iterations of this story indicating the way trauma is so often silencing thereby forcing the victim to re-absorb it alone. Their cases are wrenching in the trauma they carry – repetitive rape, betrayal, abuse, Holocaust generational traumas, war and horrendous deaths. Some treatments remain in the enactments of the relentless trauma and other treatments progress, creating regeneration of an imagining mind.

In addition to providing a rich review of the literature in his chapter entitled "The dawn of unconscious phantasy," Robert Oelsner presents clinical material where there is a failure in the development of the capacity for forming unconscious phantasies. One case struggled against the bombardment of the external world, clinging to the mother. Here words lost meaning, and phantasies became mechanical motions. In a second case where the mother withheld engagement, the child resorted to hallucinations as an autistic retreat. Oelsner distinguishes between phantasy and hallucination of a non existent world of retreat. A discussion of the developmental conditions that bring unconscious fantasy into existence addresses the need for there to be a mother to allow for the creation of an idea, that which makes for a projective-introjective process. Oelsner importantly raises the question whether interest in the external world can be recuperated, and the relevance this has for the place of unconscious fantasy. In his clinical work Oelsner describes the oscillations between developmental arrest and dawn of unconscious phantasy. His "finding" considers transference processes as manifestations of early phantasies. These are never given up, but are overridden by new modes of thoughts and relations. With his work with young children, Oelsner accesses the process of unconscious phantasy that is closer to its origins. He finds unconscious phantasy in play or the absence of play where exploring textures and reciting lists take central stage. Countertransferences are crucial, as Oelsner works with his feelings of being dropped by his patient and not existing. Finding is also carried out in drawings and action in the session and between sessions as in breaks in continuity.

In her chapter, "Fantasy and trauma," Arlene Kramer Richards presents the idea that "the inevitable losses and damages of infancy" are the motivation for development of fantasy. External events precipitating trauma and the metaphors depicting internal life (wishes, fears, and moral values) work together creating "kernels of fantasy." She believes there is no need to choose between fantasy and trauma, stating:

> The new idea that has come out of my thinking on this complex issue of whether mental conflict comes out of trauma or out of fantasy is that the inevitable potentially traumatizing events of infancy and childhood are the breeding ground of fantasy.

Richards illustrates her ideas in her clinical understanding of two cases, showing the finding of unconscious fantasy in each. A case from China demonstrates the way enactments of elements at work and with roommates arise from fantasies related to an historic event, one she sees appearing in the form of a Hamlet story. During the Cultural Revolution the patient's father was likely turned against, shamed, and spat at and he committed suicide. The patient could not make eye contact, was in a state of shame, and was sure others would spit on him. Transmissions of trauma were enacted in all aspects of his life. The second case is a male patient who experiences himself as excrement and relates to fantasies arising from seeing his mother's genital as she demonstrates how to make a bowel movement to enhance the little boy's toilet-training. Richards emphasizes the therapeutic action of "finding unconscious fantasy" as the patient expands his web of associations enabling him to actively master trauma.

Rogelio Sosnik entitles his chapter "Searching unconscious phantasy" where he writes on the history of theory of unconscious fantasy and emphasizes the two-person psychology where the development of unconscious fantasy involves the idea of the mother and baby and primitive states. He describes the central place of the body as unconscious phantasies are held in the body, relating closely to the early mother–baby relationship. He writes of his patient having had a history of a struggle in making contact and the analytic work where contact between analyst and patient is difficult to create. Sosnik speaks to the counter-transference in his process of "finding" using free floating attention to open the mental space, thereby allowing for the possibility of unveiling unconscious fantasy. In his description of the clinical process Sosnik emphasizes the patient's style of communication in a family with secrets. His patient's efforts at detachment bring his interpretations of her terror of proximity and connection. His countertransference in his feeling alone and hopeless guides him to notice a loss of internal equilibrium and wish to connect with a maternal object who would take care of her need to develop. Dreams along with bodily experiences guide the finding, leading to an understanding of the patient's expectations of reproach. Unveiled is the idea that the patient's body is a repository making for a sense of physical fragility. Trauma is related to early losses and unresolved mourning. The "finding" brings a differentiating process that includes the transference to a more whole object, fewer evacuative and avoidant reactions and more symbolic thinking.

Discoveries

This clinical guide offers an understanding of the rich and varied ways that psychoanalysts and their patients "find" derivatives of unconscious fantasy. In the clinical descriptions and commentaries, the work of "finding" takes place as metaphor and meaning become available, deciphering symptoms and increasing knowing of traumas. There are multiple roads to the unconscious fantasy: narrative, daydream, night dream, body feelings and movement, associative processes, transference, countertransference, and the enacted interactions of analysand and analyst. Discovery takes place along a continuum from revealing repressed scene and narrative to imagining the unsymbolized. In the finding of unconscious fantasies, the analysts/writers show their use of all of these pathways demonstrating a view of the psyche as a complex array of fantasies, trauma, somatic expression, symbolic equivalences, and concreteness.

By asking the contributors to speak to their finding process with patients who have some trauma and/or body pain in their psychic life, we are able to observe clinical work with the symbolized and unsymbolized mind and the mutual influences. The clinical work shows the way trauma and body pain hold psychic unconscious stories found in the transference/countertransference, primal fantasies, and unconscious fantasies from all stages of development. For patients whose pain stems from trauma or whose manifest symptoms reside in body concreteness, unconscious fantasy is less accessible until the therapeutic exchange unfolds with meaning leading to metaphor and symbolic presence. The historic either/or split of conflict versus deficit limits the capacity to fully integrate the forces of the mind. The study of "finding" shows how what presents as concrete becomes a symbolic story creating and revealing unconscious fantasies.

We see analysts dreaming, imagining, and feeling their way to unconscious fantasies. The analysts/writers use countertransference awareness in their writing about their clinical cases and their theoretical thinking. Both micro and macro (global) transference/countertransference interactions lead to recognition of unconscious derivatives of bits, fragments, and nascent fantasy development of patients' psychic realities that reach back to infancy.

All contributors view enactment as a major mode for finding unconscious fantasy when there is trauma and bodily expression, and are attuned to recognizing and working with enactments. Attention to enactment processes and intersubjective aspects of psychoanalytic discovery helps reveal finding of the unconscious fantasy. With trauma and somatic pain there may be affect overload and "erasure" of thinking that makes for the global enactments in the transference. Even in the more extreme circumstances of somatic pain and trauma, psychoanalytic work can be accompanied by the presence and exploration of the symbolized as well. In fact, there is across cases a continuum of the presence of trauma and the presence of repression.

With our invitation for contributions by psychoanalysts from a diversity of theoretical traditions, we expected there might be vast differences in ways of working and thinking. We found a profound commonality among analysts in their belief that their therapeutic task is to find unconscious fantasy, and that this is pivotal to their ideas about therapeutic action. While some writers speak to the centrality of the thinking of Freud, Klein, Arlow, or Pontalis, and some focus on the importance of the traumatic, the clinical presentations all value attention to finding unconscious derivatives that are organizing the psychic realities and pain of their patients. Revealing countertransference feelings and imaginings show the finding of unconscious derivatives in the affect-laden psychic experience of the analysts and through enactments. Also, most contributors place an emphasis on work with primal fantasies, such as oral, anal, oedipal derivatives that are universal and date back to the infancy of our species rather than to one's individual childhood. Contributors appear to work with the symbolized and the unsymbolized in their discovery and creation with their patients of the unconscious fantasy. The mind of the analyst is ready to receive derivatives of fantasy and theoretical discussions of our contributors suggest that the mind in general is organized to produce fantasy, ready to create symbolized narratives.

Our compilation of case presenters and discussants clarifies and supports that Unconscious Fantasy is central to psychoanalysis and that the Finding Process is robust, alive, and flourishing. We thank all of our contributors for their assistance with creating this guide.

References

Aisenstein, M., & Aisemberg, E. (Eds.). (2010). *Psychosomatics today: A psychoanalytic perspective*. London: Karnac Books Press.

Arlow, J. A. (1964). The Madonna's conception through the eyes. *Psychoanalytic Study of Society, 3*, 13–25.

Arlow, J. A. (1969). Unconscious fantasy and disturbances of conscious experience. *Psychoanalytic Quarterly, 38*, 1–27.

Baranger, M., & Baranger, W. (2008). The analytic situation as a dynamic field. *The International Journal of Psychoanalysis, 89*, 795–826.

Bell, D. (2012). Unconscious phantasy: Historical and conceptual dimensions. *Paper given to conference "Unconscious Phantasy Today."* University College London.

Bion, W. R. (1962). *Learning from experience*. London: Karnac.

Birksted-Breen, D. (2016) *The work of psychoanalysis: Sexuality, time and the psychoanalytic mind*. London: Routledge.

Bohleber, W. (2007). Remembrance, trauma, and collective memory. *International Journal of Psychoanalysis, 88*, 329–352.

Bohleber, W. (2010). *Destructiveness, intersubjectivity, and trauma: The identity crisis of modern psychoanalysis*. London: Karnac.

Bohleber, W., Jimenez, J. P., Scarfone, D., Varvin, S., and Zysman, S. (2016). Unconscious phantasy and its conceptualizations: An attempt at conceptual integration. *International Journal of Psychoanalysis, 96*, 705–730.

Breuer, J. (1893–1895). *Theoretical from studies in hysteria* (pp. 183–252). London: Hogarth Press.

Bronstein, C. (2010). In psychosomatics: The role of unconscious fantasy. In M. Aisenstein, & E. Aisemberg (Eds.), *Psychosomatics today: A psychoanalytic approach*. London: Karnac Books Press.

Bronstein, C. (2015). Finding unconscious phantasy in the session: Recognizing form. *International Journal of Psychoanalysis, 96*, 925–944.

Davies, J. D., & Frawley, M. G. (1994). *Treating the adult survivor of childhood sexual abuse: A psychoanalytic perspective*. New York: Basic Books.

Ellman, P., & Goodman, N. (2012). Enactment: Opportunity for symbolizing trauma. In A. Frosch (Ed.), *Absolute truth and unbearable psychic pain: Psychoanalytic perspectives on concrete experience*. London: Karnac.

Faimberg, H. (2005). *The Telescoping of Generations: Listening to the Narcissistic Links Between Generations*. London: Routledge.

Felman, S., & Laub, D. (1992). *Testimony: Crisis of witnessing in literature, psychoanalysis, and history*. New York: Routledge.

Ferro, A. (2006). Trauma, reverie, and the field. *Psychoanalytic Quarterly, 75*, 1045–1056.

Freud, A. (1967). Comments on trauma. In S. Furst (Ed.), *Psychic trauma* (pp. 235–246). New York: Basic Books.

Freud, S. (1896). *The aetiology of hysteria*, S.E., 3 (pp. 189–221). London: Hogarth Press.

Freud, S. (1905). *Analysis of a case of hysteria*, S.E., 7 (pp. 1–122). London: Hogarth Press.

Freud, S. (1911). *Two principles of mental functioning*, S.E., 12 (pp. 213–226).

Frosch, A. (2012). *Absolute truth and unbearable psychic pain: Psychoanalytic perspectives on concrete experience*. New York: Karnac.

Goodman, N. R. (2012). The power of witnessing. In N. R. Goodman, & M. Meyers (Eds.), *The power of witnessing: Reflections, reverberations, and traces of the Holocaust – trauma, psychoanalysis, and the living mind* (pp. 3–26). New York: Routledge.

Goodman, N. R., & Meyers, M. B. (2012). *The power of witnessing: Reflections, reverberations, and traces of the Holocaust – trauma, psychoanalysis and the living mind*. New York: Routledge.

Hayman, A. (1989). What do we mean by "phantasy?" *International Journal of Psychoanalysis*, *70*, 105–114.

Isaacs, S. (1948). The nature and function of phantasy. *International Journal of Psychoanalysis*, *29*, 73–97.

Joseph, B. (1985). Transference: The total situation. *International Journal of Psychoanalysis*, *66*, 447–454.

Kogan, I. (1995). *The cry of the mute children: A psychoanalytic perspective of the second generation of the Holocaust*. London: Free Association Press.

Kogan, I. (2007). *The struggle against mourning*. Lanham, MD: Jason Aronson.

Krystal, H. (1978). Trauma and affects. *Psychoanalytic Study of the Child*, *33*, 81–116.

Laplanche, J., & Pontalis, J. B. (1973). *The language of psycho-analysis* (D. Nicolson-Smith, Trans.). London: The Hogarth Press and the Institute of Psycho-Analysis.

Laub, D. (1992a). Bearing witness or the vicissitudes of listening. In S. Felman, & D. Laub, *Testimony: Crises of witnessing in literature, psychoanalysis, and history* (pp. 57–74). New York: Routledge.

Laub, D. (1992b). An event without a witness: Truth, testimony, and survival. In S. Felman, & D. Laub, *Testimony: Crises of witnessing in literature, psychoanalysis, and history* (pp. 75–92). New York: Routledge.

Laub, D. (1998). The empty circle: Children of survivors and the limits of reconstruction. *Journal of the American Psychoanalytic Association*, *46*(2), 507–529.

Masson, J. (Ed.). (1985). *The complete letters of Sigmund Freud to Wilhelm Fliess, 1887–1904*. Cambridge, MA: Belknap Press of Harvard University Press.

McDougall, J. (1974). The psychosoma and the psychoanalytic process. *International Review of Psychoanalysis*, *1*, 437–459.

Perelberg, R. (in press). Maternal imago and bodily symptoms. In P. Ellman, & N. Goodman, (Eds.), *The courage to fight violence against women*. London: Karnac Books Press.

Poland, W. S. (2000). The analyst's witnessing and otherness. *Journal of the American Psychoanalytic Association*, *48*, 17–34.

Rosenfeld, D. (2014). *The body speaks: Body image delusions and hypochondria*. London: Karnac.

Shengold, L. (1989). *Soul murder: The effects of childhood abuse and deprivation*. New York: Ballantine Books.

Sloate, P. (Ed.). (2016). *From soma to symbol: Psychosomatic conditions and transformative experience*. London: Karnac Books Press.

Steiner, R. (Ed.). (2003). *Unconscious phantasy*. London: Karnac Books Press.

Stern, D. B. (2010). *Partners in thought: Working with unformulated experience, dissociation, and enactment*. New York: Routledge.

Chapter 2

The "Finding Theater"

A schema for finding unconscious fantasy

Nancy R. Goodman

In this chapter, I turn to imaginings about a theater, the "Finding Theater", to offer a schema for display of and locating of unconscious fantasy. I play with the construction of the "Finding Theater", grateful to Joyce McDougal for her writing on *Theaters of the Mind* (1991) and *Theaters of the Body* (1989). I see the unconscious mind as existing from infancy on, driven by instinctual life and death forces, multiply-layered with iterative scenes and fragments of scenes developing throughout life. Psychic reality makes itself known with efforts to discover and create metaphor. The metaphor that has story and becomes seen, known and felt is where patient and analyst live, in the theater that develops between them. I consider metaphor to be the intermediary frame from which the unconscious fantasy is inferred, from both narrative and enactment, and often imagined for the first time. Emerging metaphors bring scenes to the shared analytic space of analyst and analysand, enabling the finding of unconscious derivatives with their intense affects. Once the metaphor is active its connection to the repressed symbolized mind and the traumatic unsymbolized mind becomes available to feel in all of its passion and terror. Construction of the "Finding Theater" rests on belief in the existence of primal fantasies, a readiness in the mind for fantasy making, and flow of symbolic equivalences relating the most primitive to secondary revisions.

In the "Introduction" to his overview of psychoanalytic thinking about unconscious phantasy, Steiner (2003) describes Freud's creative development of the concept of unconscious fantasy. Theoretically and clinically, Freud struggled with location of unconscious dimensions – unconscious, pre-conscious, conscious, subliminal, dreams, and daydreams, etc. Steiner (p. 8) quotes from Laplanche and Pontalis (1973):

> Freud's principal concern, however, seems to have been less with establishing such a differentiation than with emphasizing the links between these different aspects.
>
> (p. 316)

Freud had insight about the link between layers of the mind ultimately connected to unconscious forces. The stage productions of the "Finding Theater" have links as well as the unconscious appears in various guises in different scenes.

The psyche, as the theater, is ready to make, receive, and enact unconscious fantasy. Visual scripts are ready for performance so the audience (analyst and patient) can find them and add their own imaginings to them. The patient and analyst are also in the wings ready for their entrance, or already on the stage interacting and communicating scripts from unconscious places in each of their minds. From the beginning, from infancy, the mind appears ready for pre-scenes, parts of scenes, and whole scenes fueled by body and object need. I see the mind, and now the theater, as a unitary whole, that is, where there can be full representation of internal experience, of trauma and narrative, objects and part objects, primary process and secondary process, conflict and the concrete, all co-existing, influencing, and building on each other. Trauma and narrative, the unsymbolized and symbolic representations, all appear, often simultaneously in one act, or one scene, or in the total performance. I also place the many major actors of psychoanalytic thought in the theater, each opening view to levels of depth of mind. These writers of psychoanalytic metathought can be visited as they sit in a special gallery observing and reflecting. All aspects of psychic life and all techniques for finding unconscious fantasy derivatives are elements of what I playfully propose to be in the "Finding Theater."

Importance of the scene

In explicating the workings of the "Finding Theater" (itself a metaphor) I describe the centrality of "the scene" in psychoanalytic thought, the appearance of the architecture I envision for the "Finding Theater", and stagings of clinical material, from Freud's (1899) "Screen Memories" and from the chapters in this book.

As this book, a clinical guide to the finding of unconscious fantasy, evolved and Paula Ellman and I received chapters from our contributors, the importance of the "scene" was evidenced. The clinical cases and reflections of the psychoanalysts/writers in this book speak of repetitive scenes inevitably appearing in the realm of transference and countertransference. Symbolic representations, dreams and narratives, and enacting processes bring about images often first to the analyst and later shared in the psychic realities of the analysis. Affects connected with wishes, fears, and trauma (hungers, arousals, terrors, helplessness) appear as soon as the curtain goes up. Music that sets a mood may already be connecting to the audience that forever more will be associated with what transpires on the stages of the "Finding Theater" (think of the distinctive music linked to the film *Jaws*). The audience receives and reverberates with sound effects and the actions and emotion of the theater pieces.

The audience receives and reverberates with sound effects and the actions and emotion of the theatre pieces. Humphries Mardirosian (2017) explains: "The famous theatre writer, philosopher, and actor, Constantin Stanislavsky, called this connection 'communion' – a type of spiritual connection that occurs between actors and then extends to the audience as they embody text (p. 233)."

A deep connection takes place as unconscious communications move from the staged scenes to the individual emotional experience of the members of the audience.

The unconscious pictures of the interactive object and part object world and the forces producing the scenes become palpable as the analysts/writers in this volume describe how they come closer and closer to the presence of unconscious fantasy derivatives and the affects belonging to them. In particular, the vibrancy of enactments (Ellman & Goodman, 2012) between analysand and analyst adds validity to the idea that it is in the dramas of action sequences and interactions of analyst, along with narrative, that offer ways to find unconscious fantasies. Instinct, as life and death forces, is not only a theoretical concept, but is felt as it finds its way into all participants, actors, and audience in the "Finding Theater".

"I feel it; I see it"

The idea that something in the mind appears through a visual presentation was primary for Freud as he told patients to imagine themselves on a train and they would tell what they saw. In his early work with hysteria he wanted to release capacity to see something. Freud's work with hysterics led him to the following:

> If hysterics refer their symptoms to imaginary trauma, then this new fact signifies that they create such scenes in their phantasies, and hence psychic reality deserves to be given a place next to actual reality.

(Freud, 1916, p. 414)

Freud went on to portray certain scenes as inherited, certain to be in the mind: the primal scene, castration (now expanded to female genital anxieties) the primitive horde, and annihilation (the death instinct). The feel of terror of castration/annihilation is severe and intense and is felt as true and can lead to compromises and despair. Melanie Klein posited further primary scenes in the infant such as sexual intercourse of parents and the internal body of the mother and early feelings of envy, depression, and reparation. Jacob Arlow (1969) follows Freud's ideas about linking in his depiction of films overlapping, conscious and unconscious streams of fantasy, and as Klein he thinks of the unconscious as always active and based in instinct and childhood experience.

Theater has a significant place in psychoanalysis. Sigmund Freud named major conflicts of the soul after Greek tragedies, Oedipus and Electra for example, referencing the dramas of love and conflict (being at war in oneself) and the tragic suffering individuals can feel. Anna O (Breuer, 1893) possessed insight in referring to her treatment as the "talking cure" in which she told about her internal world, "her private theater." For Hans Loewald (1975) psychoanalysis shares "important features with dramatic art ... viewed as a dramatic play, the transference neurosis is a fantasy creation woven from memories and imaginative elaborations" (p. 279). Joyce McDougal (1989, 1991) centered her thinking on the internal object relations and sexual longings scripted since infancy and played out in theaters of mind and body.

In psychoanalytic treatments scenes are created through macro patterns, the total transference situation, micro communications, unconscious to unconscious, associative processes, and through interaction sequences in analytic sessions. This is what is meant by psychic reality; and, psychic reality has depth and meaning in which one thing can lead to another. Ellman and Goodman (2012) refer to enactments, scenes created in interaction of analyst and patient, as the "royal road" to the unconscious along with other royal roads such as dreaming. As the da Rocha Barroses (see Chapter 6) articulate their idea of engram, a matrix of unconscious representations and scenes, they refer to Susan Isaacs (1952) who suggests that the attributions of meaning in unconscious phantasies "transform us into *agents* who *unconsciously* create internal and external scenes that have an enormous gravitational pull in molding our lives." Laplanche and Pontalis (1973) in *The Language of Psychoanalysis* state the following: "Even when they can be summed up in a single sentence, phantasies are still scripts (*scenarios*) of organized scenes which are capable of dramatization – usually in visual form" (p. 318).

Architecture of the stage sets

The architecture of the stage set is the schema for receptivity in the mind and entering the "Finding Theater" is how we "find" the psychic life of unconscious fantasy. I play here with how the architecture of the theater could appear. There are particular areas of the sets that would be universal, like the presence of a place for the playing of the orchestra, the burning and flare-ups of instincts, the music of Eros and Thanatos. This schema rests on the idea that core infantile fantasies with primary process are present in the later iterations of fantasies and their narratives throughout life. There is always energy or anti-energy driving the scenes in the "Finding Theater"; enlivening, sexual energy or devastating destruction, death, and traumatic helplessness. Oscillations between these domains of the mind enter the content and affects of unconscious fantasies.

However, each individual psyche and analytic experience has unique sets of stages and performances taking place accompanying the universal. There are multiple stages of all sizes, horizontally parallel to each other and with modern electronic capacities providing ease for projective mechanisms and melding together of multiple images. McLarnan (2016), a psychoanalyst and photographer, developed a display of photographs in which he attempts to show the "psychoanalytic third" by combining images. The "Finding Theater" has the ability to mingle these multiple influences of analyst and patient. While the main performance is taking place on center stage, the presence of actors preparing for other scenes (with their props and costumes) is glimpsed. Like free floating attention, there is movement between scenes. The structures of the stages themselves are invitations for the actors and scenes to develop their dramatic art. There is something in the psyche ready to receive the function of fantasying; the stages are ready for story and drama creating a register for psychic inner life. The stages of this "Finding Theater" facilitate the performance of and finding of unconscious fantasy.

Each level can have characters engaged in a theater piece. Layering is basic. Full depictions of theater pieces appear on each level and do so simultaneously. To demonstrate the interconnectedness of scenes and performances (of narratives, compromises, traumas, and the orchestra of affects) there are little ladders connecting the parallel stages. Schematically, we could think of one level as the infant theater; another, the toddler; another, the oedipal; another the adolescent; and then the adult. We could call each level by the affect or wish or fear most active, such as oral need or euphoria, or anal aggression and retention, genital excitement or fear of psychic castration, or fear of annihilation, or murderous oedipal jealousy and rage, or envy of the breast, or a darkened platform of dead space, trauma.

Lighting and sound are elements of the "Finding Theater" providing atmosphere and each level of these stages has its own intensities as if on a rheostat. As in psychoanalytic process what is being hidden behind a curtain or waiting behind the false back of the stage is sometimes the most urgent and fundamental. Producing the feel in the audience of "being there" in body and soul is essential in good theater. The audience (like the patient and analyst) is invited to be there and to suspend ordinary experience, to accept illusion. Some stages may be empty or blacked out as they have not yet been symbolized enough to present even fragments of theater action. It is on these stages where finding of unconscious fantasy develops so that darkness can give way to something that can be seen. There might be a flash of lightning or a slow dawning. At moments the stage is quiet and still and at other times the actors are chaotic, somersaulting over and under each other to land in new places.

"The play's the thing": examples of stagings in the "Finding Theater"

I develop staging of content of Freud's "Screen Memories" (1899) and of clinical cases written up by the analysts/writers in this book to demonstrate how finding unconscious fantasy takes place in the schema offered by the design of the theater. The phrase "the play's the thing" was said by Hamlet. In Shakespeare's *Hamlet*, the story proceeds with Hamlet being informed by the ghost of his father that he was killed by his brother who has now married his widow, Hamlet's mother. To awaken people to the truth of this he performs a play he calls *The Mousetrap*. He states: "the play's the thing" knowing that the "play within the play" will bring about the truth. On the stages of the "Finding Theater" the play, and all of the plays within the play, brings about finding of unconscious fantasy.

The staging of Freud's screen memory: finding through association

In Freud's chapter on "Screen Memories" (S.E., 1899), he reports a daydream of a patient. Freud is writing about his own self-analysis; he is both the patient and the analyst. There are characters, actions, and descriptions with vivid activity, bright color, and the smell of fresh bread. The memory easily turns into a drama script to be performed on the platforms of the stage. Freud is making the point that this screen memory relates to many conflicts in the mind (his mind) that are both current and rooted in childhood and instinct. In the "Finding Theater," many stages are ready for performances that will be connected. Freud chooses elements for association, demonstrating the utility of his technique to find deeper layers of the mind:

> We are picking the yellow flowers and each of us is holding a bunch of flowers we have already picked. The little girl has the best bunch; and, as though by mutual agreement, we – the two boys – fall on her and snatch away her flowers. She runs up the meadow in tears and as a consolation the peasant-woman gives her a big piece of black bread. Hardly have we seen this than we throw the flowers away, hurry to the cottage and ask to be given some bread too. And we are in fact given some; the peasant-woman cuts the loaf with a long knife. In my memory the bread tastes quite delicious – and at that point the scene breaks off.
>
> (p. 311)

It is easy to imagine bringing these characters and scenery to the "Finding Theater" for a performance. It is simple and direct. As Freud associates, other performances on parallel stages become filled in. He stresses two fantasies related to hungers and conflicts, one arising from an equivalence of money to bread and the other to erotic wishes to deflower, most likely active in him at the time and put back in time. At that time Freud was feeling his desire to conquer understanding of neurosis and the mind and to earn a living. The uncovering of derivatives of unconscious fantasy takes place as the mind of the patient (Freud) and the analyst (Freud) unravel series of associations. The complexity and beauty of the interconnectedness of the unconscious and conscious life is shown. On the stage of the "Finding Theater" there would also be scenes holding dramas more primary in nature, fueling the spoken associations. What about a knife image in response to deflowering, what about dropping everything for the bread, what about the color yellow? Freud writes:

> It can no longer be regarded as an innocent one (the memory) since, as we have discovered, it is calculated to illustrate the most momentous turning points in your life, the influence of the two most powerful motives forces – hunger and love.
>
> (p. 316)

These symbolic images could be projected throughout the staging of the manifest showing how depth of mind and internal dream-like wishes live in the psyche. Perhaps a knife could be hanging into the middle of the stage because of the meaning of castration central to the mind at the time. In 1899 Freud was demonstrating the power of associations, the power of moving between scenes to find unconscious fantasies.

Staging the full mind

The cases presented in this book are about analyses with individuals who have both a traumatized unconscious, often with body symptomatology, and a symbolized unconscious. Symbolized elements present as narrative, dreams, conflicts of wishes and fears, and verbal associations brought to the transference with words and enactment processes. The traumatic part of the mind enters the analysis mostly with enactments, action sequences that enter the transference/countertransference to create a symbol and a scene. A few of the cases have extreme trauma in the mind, the dead mind, the blacked out mind with little symbolic capacity until enacted in the room where the analyst is witness and receiver as the first to feel and know and decipher the roles and affects of the trauma.

The staging of Karen

The analysis with Karen (Janice Lieberman with discussants Carolyn Ellman and Ilany Kogan) presents scenes of trauma (a toddler tied to the crib and her mouth washed out with soap) and intensely felt envy, for brother's body, his penis, and for mother's body, her procreative and sexual body. These scenes of envy, of attack on the other, of self-punishment through attacks against her body via abortions, are repetitive and in a variety of forms.

In the narrative, Karen brings her symbolized dreaming mind:

> I was among a group of people and was pregnant. Eight out of the ten women were pregnant. We were in and around an empty swimming pool. The pool was deep and at the shallow end it gradually sloped up to meet the ground. The colors were soft pastel shades of blue and white. The dream had a warm soft quality to it. I was relaxed and happy (content) about being pregnant. It all seemed natural.

She says that in the dream she opens a white suitcase and it is empty. She is not upset in the dream and does what she needs to do. She then recounts how she felt when pregnant at the age of 20 she had an abortion.

The producer could arrange the dream imagery and its associative meanings on different stages all horizontally parallel to each other. For Karen, we can see the drama of three layers almost immediately, a stage for transference, a stage for traumatic scenes, and the stage for having and aborting (making the pool empty) in repetitive pattern. The actors enact the toddler tied to the crib, the various forms of envious attacks, and the turning against the self over and over. The scene of Karen as a tied down baby infuses the feel of the later iterations including the transference and most likely in scenes of sexual intercourse as well (feel, stop, be overwhelmed, internal aggression). The baby will protest, will cry, will become frightened, and will succumb or try to defeat the other with a fantasy of depersonalization – "I am not really here." The countertransference of the analyst will be the center stage as Lieberman finds the affects of envious attacks and trauma transmissions, her mind being tied down. This is an example of how trauma gets into narrative and unconscious fantasies, ready to be found in the "Finding Theater".

The staging of Miss A

Rogelio Sosnik's case of Miss A contains stories that are known and unknown and becoming known. Transgenerational hauntings of the Holocaust and unspoken deaths of grandparents would be vague impressions at first, perhaps like backlit puppet forms, and then with more and more lighting and articulation appearing as real people. In the case, the analyst often feels that the patient is not deeply in touch with her analyst. The staging of the transference/countertransference might be portrayed as foggy, a representation of the secrecy so important to the family and to Miss A. The past of the Holocaust and of death becomes known in tandem with knowing her own secret mind of desire and need. One parallel stage, under the main stage, holds images and actions and atrocity. The Holocaust is continuously there, sometimes with clarity and sometimes influencing the drama through a tone of silence or cataclysmic shutter of the stage. She has been overweight and Sosnik sees this as the implantation of anxieties: "The fragility and heaviness that A was feeling regarding her body … and her constant fear of falling apart were the result of that implantation." Multiple stages would be used and each level would depict ways of hiding from inner and historic psychic realities. Miss A brings metaphor to the ever-present disaster in her superego, and in her history:

> I saw that the sea was very calm, and I thought it was very nice, very pleasant, and I walked on a sort of sandbank, and suddenly, I made a turn and found myself in a rough sea, with a strong current, and I didn't know it was there.

The "Finding Theater" of the analytic exploration brings forth the rough sea, the internal mix of traumas and instinct. Once this scene plays out on the stage in narrative form, it brings along with it conflicts of feelings and closeness with her analyst.

The staging of Babette

Irene Cairo (with discussants Harriet Basseches and Catalina Bronstein) brings Babette to the "Finding Theater". The clinical work with Babette is an example of treating the unitary mind, the ever-present mix of trauma and fantasy and the way each influences the other. Babette comes and goes, gets rid of and returns, feels persecuted and repairs the ruptures. In the theater pieces there could be many props behind which she would hide. There are traumas to depict on the stages – her hospitalization for infection at 2 and a half where a new language was spoken and the terrifying hemorrhage from tonsillectomy at age 6 when she had to save herself. These scenes emotionally overwhelm; they might need to be half-curtained for a long time. She was afraid of the dark and taken into bed as a 3-year-old with her mother and father and "there were explosions." I think this scene with the parents would open the theater to her internal instinctual life of yearning, envy, and competition, always tinged with the affects of the traumas. Stammering may represent the need to stop such powerful wishes and fears interrupting body action and flow of memories and imaginings. It is particularly fruitful to see how the oedipal drama takes on the qualities of the traumas – "And something happens, and there is a great disaster, and I survive, perhaps I am the only one who survives … there is a young baby and I rescue this baby right?" She has seen her analyst outside of the office and likely imagines her as part of a couple. The scenes of terror for the young child are on the repeat performance stage and enter the analytic space with the analyst. Playing out of various forms of "rescue" could have a stage of their own: one moment the analyst rescuing; the next moment the patient rescuing. There are interruptions and the re-finding of her analyst, again and again. A stuttering in the analytic process is a drum beat revealing a rhythm of finding unconscious fantasy and trauma. The analyst who wants to know her inner language is a constant, replacing stammering with a flow of associations and metaphor making.

Stagings of extreme traumas with some mix of narrative

In the psychic theater of extreme trauma, it is all darkness, a night sky with no stars, planets, or moon. The sound effects could be the kind of silence when the only thing you hear is your heart beating or the deafening screeching of a crow or the clanking of a rusty moving train and its jarring whistle. It is difficult to know if the curtain is closed or open, leaving the audience confused. Dori Laub and Nanette Auerhahn (Chapter 16) use the term "traumatic blackout" to describe the impact of severe trauma – the lights have gone down, the performance scenes disappear until analyst and patient return to find fragments of scenes and full scripts:

> "Traumatic blackout" is the term we use for the moment or stretch of life (which can be long-lasting, even permanent) during which overwhelming

traumatic affect takes center stage and leads to a shutdown of thinking, self-reflection, reality testing, and conscious remembering. It is as though symbolization and dialogue with the internal other halt.

(p. 174)

I have used the term "dead places in the mind" (2012) to refer to a burned out unapproachable space. On the stages scourged earth occupies one of the parallel stages with areas of growth slowly developing around it as witnessing is felt. On the stage of trauma, there are strange sounds and inability to understand what is being perceived, creating intense anxieties. Laub and Auerhahn suggest that the story of Philomela, with the cutting out of the tongue and ingesting of a murdered child, is the "play within the play" of all severe trauma symbolizing silence and internalization of catastrophe. By placing a witness on the stage, there is establishment of a person who remains through the anxieties, overtime becoming as permanent as the scourged earth of trauma. The witness moves the audience from numbness to possibility of feeling terror, intense grief, and the finding of both recollections and unconscious annihilation fantasies enter the stage, enter the mind. Finding unconscious fragments, the traumatic unconscious and all attending fantasies is startling, overwhelming, and lonely until there are others to be with.

The staging of Margaret

In the case of Margaret (Paula Ellman with discussants Marilia Aisenstein and Batya Monder) all stages are designed to show stabbing pain, unrelenting sadistic attacking of the head and neck, of Margaret and her analyst. The actors play out sadistic acts in various guises – the pinning down of Margaret in the bathroom and the inserting of a hard enema nozzle. Over and over again, the audience sees body rape and psychic rape. The central stage could be set in a bathroom, the locale of the analytic sessions where almost every symbolic equivalent of enema nozzle forced inside the body takes place. There is force and emptying out. This is the scene that is immediately in the transference/countertransference. There is little protection for patient or for analyst. We see "soul murder" (Shengold, 1989) taking place. There are continuous enactments in the transference/countertransference, a psyche being reachable and unreachable, and the forcing of the analyst to feel and to contain the uncontainable. The analyst is steady, staying close as Margaret tries to deaden her. For the staging of this psychoanalysis, there is a special floating platform for Dr. Ellman who is always present, even after attempts to obliterate her. As the analyst feels the horror and Margaret's intelligence and hope, symbols enter the performances. Over time Margaret comes to feel moments of grief and her own assertiveness expressed in words, not only through repetitions of excruciating body pain. This stage of life forces emerges slowly, in view and out of view. Oscillations between deadly pain and enlivening work, including in the analysis, begin to turn on lights and bring more into the starkness of this theater performance.

The staging of Y and the patient who thought he was being "flushed"

In her descriptions of Y, Arlene Kramer Richards is immediately struck by multi-lingual and multicultural exchanges and translations. An English-speaking super-visor, a Chinese clinician, and most importantly the unconscious. In Y's worries there are scenes ready to occupy the center stage. Y is frightened and over and over again finds himself in a scene of haunting humiliations of the Cultural Revolution and his father's suicide. He cannot make eye contact when in the world away from his family. A stream of people may parade across his path on the stage and he will have his head down. His deepest underlying traumas and yearnings appear in his imaginings of his father being humiliated, shamed, and spit upon during the Cultural Revolution. Richards identifies a Hamlet drama as a central unconscious fantasy paralyzing Y's capacity to "act on his own behalf." Hamlet and his hesitation to murder his stepfather appear on the set of this theater in costumes of the Cultural Revolution. And Y enacts pieces of this intricate con-stellation over and over in grade school, with roommates, at work, and with his wife. He is afraid that a psychiatrist (his therapist?) will label him perhaps like the accusation of being "anti" the regime that led his father to commit suicide. Someone spitting (imagine the costume for the spitter and the spittee) and not being able to make eye contact would be enacted throughout the performance with varying objects of distain. With such death and trauma there seems to be little else motivating Y except to repeat and repeat shame and self-murder. Oedipal desire is too terrifying and always leads to the death of his father.

The patient who thought he was being "flushed" could be presented for the Theater of the Absurd until re-enactments of being a "turd" instead of a man with a phallus are diminished. The lights on the bathroom scene of this man/boy seeing his mother's bottom (the Medusa genital) as she produced a bowel move-ment will dim and turn into creative strivings. A projection machine could be used to play the shocking mother and fecal baby scene in all areas of the stage. The feeling of shock and trauma would ease as the analyst on the stage brings the elements of the central fantasy into focus. The audience becomes aware how controlling and powerful the presence of a scene can be when it occupies the psyche.

Stagings of Patty, age 5; Tyler, age 10; and Maxie, age 6

Robert Oelsner offers different ways of finding unconscious material, therefore requiring different types of stagings involving pre-unconscious fantasy forma-tion in Tyler and Maxie, who do not yet receive the fantasy function. Patty is a symbolizing child presenting narrative and then enactments with her analyst that have representation and lead to interpretation. Tyler and Maxie are pre-symbolizing, not yet capable of making fantasy, of receiving fantasy. It is simple and straightforward to stage the scenes Patty presents. Patty tells stories that can immediately be seen and heard and felt by an audience; for example, someone going away and a dog and cat getting sick and going nuts. A producer could have great fun with this, although it is a serious matter. We can have humans in costume as dog and cat chaotically running around, getting sick, being excited, and then exhausted.

The analyst is a secure presence and Patty can show with games her wish to go to sleep related to the wish to sleep with Mommy and Daddy and analyst. On this stage there can be multiple sleeping places with bright lights indicating various feels and conflict. Jealousy and anger can be acted out by the dog and cat and by Patty. This matches with what Oelsner says about Klein: "According to Klein unconscious dramas are ongoing with its *dramatis personae* and story-lines." The layers of the storylines of Patty are so visible. Tyler and Maxie need stages upon which disturbance is present, causing attention to be impossible. The audience must feel this. Each has come to the theater with "yet to be formed" unconscious fantasy, thus the dawn of unconscious phantasy has to appear with lighting that fades in and out and people who are at first like unsubstantial ghosts. For example, Tyler began a fantasy game in which he and his analyst are grandparents to stuffed animals, a whole inhabited feeling scene, which then became a repetitive ritualized happening. Maxie, over and over again, made pictures with stickies and drawings of robots/monsters. There is a stage with repetitive, attention avoiding, and slow making of unconscious fantasies. When Maxie clings to Dr. Oelsner, hope for birthing thinking appeared. This needs lighting to create a glowing scene, the dawning, in the Theater of Finding.

Conclusion

The dramas and the scenes appearing in the productions reach the audience, reach the analyst and the patient. There are feelings, semiotics, passions, identifications, and terrors. We see in this "Finding Theater," the workings of unconscious script writing, the world of psychic reality. Dramas can be created, experienced, and known. Performance with the analyst and analysand, with word and in action, make the "Finding Theater" the place it is – a place for discovery, imagination, pathos. The psychic theater brings forth scenes developing since infancy, bringing them into view for the "finding of unconscious fantasy."

References

Arlow, J. A. (1969). Unconscious fantasy and disturbances of conscious experience. *Psychoanalytic Quarterly*, *38*, 1–27.

Breuer, J. (1893). Case histories: Case I Fraulein Anna O. In S. Freud, *Studies on Hysteria*, *The Standard Edition of the Complete Psychological Works of Sigmund Freud Volume II (1893–1895)* (pp. 21–47).

Ellman, P. & Goodman, N. (2012). Enactment: Opportunity for symbolizing trauma. In A. Frosch (Ed.), *Absolute truth and unbearable psychic pain: Psychoanalytic perspectives on concrete experience*. London: Karnac.

Freud, S. (1899). Screen memories. In S. Freud, *The standard edition of the complete psychological works of Sigmund Freud, volume III (1893–1899): Early Psycho-Analytic Publications* (pp. 299–322).

Freud, S. (1916). The history of the psychoanalytic movement. *The standard edition of the complete psychological works of Sigmund Freud, volume XIV (1914–1916)* (pp. 1–66).

Goodman, N. R. (2012). The power of witnessing. In N. R. Goodman, & M. Meyers (Eds.), *The power of witnessing: Reflections, reverberations, and traces of the Holocaust – trauma, psychoanalysis, and the living mind* (pp. 3–26). New York: Routledge.

Humphries, Mardirosian (2017). A staged reading for remembrance, reminder and inspiration: Traces in the wind. In P. Ellman, & N. Goodman, (Eds.), *The courage to fight violence against women: A psychoanalytic and multi-disciplinary approach*. London: Karnac Books Press.

Isaacs, S. (1952). The nature and function of phantasy. In J. Riviere (Ed.), *Developments of psychoanalysis* (pp. 62–121). London: Hogarth Press.

Laplanche, J., & Pontalis, J. B. (1973). *The language of psycho-analysis* (D. Nicolson-Smith, Trans.). London: The Hogarth Press and the Institute of Psycho-Analysis.

Loewald, H. W. (1975). Psychoanalysis as an art and the fantasy character of the psychoanalytic situation. *Journal of the American Psychoanalytic Association, 23*, 277–299.

McDougall, J. (1989). *Theaters of the body: A psychoanalytic approach to psychosomatic illness*. New York: W.W. Norton & Company.

McDougall, J. (1991). *Theatres of the mind: Illusion and truth on the psychoanalytic Stage*. New York: Basic Books.

McLarnan, T. (2016). *The optical unconscious: Vignettes of images and texts*. Retrieved August 18, 2016, from www.virtualpsychoanalyticmuseum.org/. New York: IPBooks.

Shengold, L. (1989). *Soul murder: The effects of childhood abuse and deprivation*. New York: Ballantine Books.

Steiner, R. (Ed.). (2003). *Unconscious phantasy*. London: Karnac Books Press.

Chapter 3

Finding unconscious fantasy

Contact and therapeutic action

Paula L. Ellman

At the outset of this project, *Finding Unconscious Fantasy*, I was eager to gather a group of psychoanalysts, diverse in their theoretical perspectives, to reflect on what it means to find unconscious fantasy. We took as our focus the work of finding unconscious fantasy in treatments with traumatized patients, patients who are concrete and who lean toward experiencing affects and psychic meanings somatically. Finding unconscious fantasy includes working with metaphor and also with split off modes of expression. In many clinical instances unconscious fantasy appears inaccessible through metaphor, and actions and enactments contain the ways to find meaning (Ellman & Goodman, 2012). While working with patients whose mode of expression is more concrete and in a bodily form is most challenging, examining the process of finding unconscious fantasy has application to the broad range of our analytic work, both our working in metaphor and working with the non-symbolized.

We asked our case presenters to write of their work with patients with trauma, and our discussants to comment on the process of finding the unconscious fantasy that analyst and patient engage in when the body is paramount and trauma is rampant. The finding of unconscious fantasy is the way analysts work. Our discussants demonstrate this by writing about their process of finding unconscious fantasy as they considered the cases. That is, as the discussants become observers of the analyst/analysand dyadic finding process, they engage in a finding process. In reviewing the "finding processes" of analyst, analysand and observer, both the contact in the dyad between analyst and patient, and the realm of therapeutic action occupy pivotal foci of the book contributions. I want to visit "How is contact between analyst and analysand central to the process of finding unconscious fantasy?" and "What can we learn about the therapeutic action of psychoanalysis as we assume the observer position of receptivity to the analyst/analysand's finding process?"

In reviewing the four case presentations and eight discussions of the four cases, "the finding process" appears to be embedded in the mind of the analyst as that mind is IN the experience of analysand/analyst dyad in the moment. The discussant, when tasked with "finding unconscious fantasy," becomes the mind of the analyst engaged in the work of "finding." The finding process is in the visceral, in the physicality, in the smell, in the associations. As outsider to the process, the third tries to understand the "in the moment" process of finding unconscious fantasy. The "finding" is in the texture of the treatment, in the pressures to speak, to withhold, to remain silent, to dread, to yearn. The "finding" is embedded within the contact, the exchange, between analyst and analysand, and is where therapeutic action happens. Bohleber, Jiminez, Scarfone, Varvin, and Zysman (2015), the IPA Committee on Conceptual Integration Study, when considering the concept of unconscious fantasy, write:

> The description of the process whereby the analyst's mind embraces the idea that an emerging phenomenon in the relationship with the patient can be defined as unconscious fantasy is important. Monitoring countertransference has become a key tool in this process.... The unconscious fantasies we "find" during the process of "discovering" the patient's inner world constitute a way of describing the experience of the unconscious as it emerges at the interface of the analyst's and patient's interpersonal/intersubjective contact.
>
> (p. 711)

Therefore, the outsider to the analytic exchange must empathically imagine being in the place of the analyst and vicariously attempt to access the countertransference that can inform of the analysand's transference. Bronstein (2015) writes about her embodied experience that alerts her to the particular transference of her patient who wishes to push her at a distance. In times of trauma, the unconscious fantasy is often held in the body, and in this bodily way it is carried into the contact with the analyst. Through the exchange the unspoken, the unsymbolized, the nonverbal, the procedural, is taken in by the analyst often through the body. In the gradual subtle coming to awareness, frequently through enactment, the analyst with the patient begins to see the vague outlines of a form that develops further distinctiveness over time. "What the analyst calls unconscious fantasy is rather the verbal articulation of an unsymbolized affective experience.... The concept of unconscious fantasy can thus be understood as a metaphor that assists in understanding the patient's psychic material and behavior" (Bohleber et al., 2015, p. 711).

In exploring "finding unconscious fantasy," we are apt to think about the unconscious narrative as the substrate of psychic organization. Relevant to consider is that the structure of mental life carries unconscious fantasy. As trauma affects the development of personality structures, the place of the usually inaccessible traumatic unconscious fantasy is embedded in these structures. Gaining access to the nature of these structures is the process of analysis where the actual "holding" of the patient comes to carry the trauma. In his case presentation contribution to our book, Bohleber articulates that the knowing of the self occurs within the orbit of the self-other love relationship. He refers to the analysis with his patient as the "closed container" and himself as the plaster. Yet Bohlebor as the plaster can attempt to bring life, warmth, to where the edges of the plaster meet the skin of his patient. This is the point of contact and the place for therapeutic action. I think of the traumatized concrete patient psychically residing in an encapsulated frozen cylinder. Making authentic contact seems impossible perhaps even more so unbearable, as the actual contact carries the trauma and the potentiality for the unfolding and developing of the contours of the underlying horrific unconscious fantasy.

Psychoanalysis is the effort to create opportunities for contact. We listen to our patients seek contact, stave off contact, and find ways to both become known and remain unknown. Even when contact is ephemeral, fleeting, the nature of the communications contains aspects of unconscious fantasy and of the past. Efforts to avert contact become a form of contact that the analyst experiences in the countertransference. When there are descriptions of the body's aches and pains and burdens, these are communications of bodily and psychic memories, experiences, and fantasies. We must adjust how we listen and listen in a way that allows for our own free associative process even if painful. When the body is primary and trauma is in the body, we cannot expect our patients to consistently communicate in verbally symbolized ways. We must enter into their body language listening to our own bodies speak. Instead of enabling our patients to push us to a distance from them, we bring our attention to listen and attempt to understand their pain, the nature of their pain, and their associations to their pain, and to remain open to our own associations to the projections we experience.

It is in the process of making contact that the traumatic unconscious fantasy take form. Werner Bohleber's case of a patient with an early life trauma of being confined to a plaster bed at 18 months old, led to later development of a sense of timelessness and dissociation of his needy self. The patient struggles with bearing sustained contact as it carries separation trauma and contact with the encapsulated traumatized self. Elias and Elizabeth da Rocha Barros write of "kernels of meaning" in their discussion of Bohleber's case. Our analytic process builds on these "kernels of meaning" as they develop into "molds." In this way the unconscious fantasy becomes the unifier of the self. According to the da Rocha Barroses, Bohleber metabolizes the dyadic experiences thereby moving the patient from a place of being "paralyzed, congealed," to finding the self "which is the unconscious fantasy," the "organizer of psychic life." Nancy Goodman emphasizes the place of "opening up of space" in the treatment, "a wish to have space open, to have the cast removed, and to be reconnected to body and objects." She describes, "I highlight three ways that I see the opening of space taking place: through the analytic process of witnessing, through breaking the spell of timelessness with enactment processes, and with a capacity to feel grief." Embedded in the format of her discussion she includes letters that she addresses directly to the analyst/Bohleber in which she grants herself space to associate freely to the case material: her personal feeling reactions, associations to theater, her imaginings of the patient, her ideas about theory, and she recognizes the letter as a point of contact. The letters themselves capture the profound need for contact in the case, and serve as a metaphor for the contained space of the treatment's finding process where contact becomes possible.

In Janice Lieberman's case, images of sibling rivalry and penis envy bring meaning to the script of the envy, jealousy, and competition in the transference/countertransference. In Lieberman's movement from an "empathic" to a more "defense interpretation" mode, a script of rivalry opens and elements of trauma enter the analytic exchange in the form of an unconscious fantasy of sadomasochism and a withholding opposition. While it appears that contact is averted by the sadomasochistic resistance, the sadomasochism itself is the form of contact that carries the unconscious fantasy (Basseches, Ellman, & Goodman et al., 2013). The "finding" processes by the case's two discussants, Ilany Kogan and Carolyn Ellman, address aspects of an Arlowian drive/defense shaping of the perception (Kogan), and a Kleinian emphasis on the underlying envy of the mother and wish to attack the insides of the mother's body (C. Ellman). Contact between analyst and patient is averted yet the finding of the unconscious fantasy is in the averting process.

Irene Cairo's case captures the nature of "finding of the unconscious fantasy" in structure, in the structure of speech and in the analytic frame. Interruptions (in both speech and the analysis) convey the texture of early life relationships and the trauma suffered in the absence of contact. Breaks in the analysis bring both idealizing and resentful facets of relating, calling back to powerful historical absences and concomitant destructive fantasies. In her discussion, Harriet Basseches writes of her position as the "third," catching glimpses of the unconscious fantasy in the analytic dyad, in the manifest, the latent, in the progression and in the sequence. She writes of the patient's "doing" to the analyst in the form of interruptions of contact as revenge and payback, and emphasizes the powerful issues of separation and abandonment, and the fantasy of rescue. In her discussion of the unfolding of levels of unconscious phantasy Catalina Bronstein addresses the nature of the contact between Babette and Cairo in the permanent juggling between distance and separation from the object. Contact triggers early experiences of danger as internal conflicts between life and death drives yield perceptions of the safe object shifting to the unsafe object. She suggests that with the impact of early trauma and the phantasy associated with a rhythm of interruptions, there is the possibility of the shared phantasy of a contact where the treatment never ends.

In his treatment with two children Robert Oelsner emphasizes that,

> ... for unconscious phantasy to develop there has to be a baby with the innate expectation (Bion's preconception) of objects to meet him. Likewise, there needs to be a mother (and a father, as Maxie proved) to give the preconception its realization to create an idea and a script (phantasy). Exchanging with the world of objects that projections and introjections modify, serves to enrich and complexify its content and meaning.

His work with his cases involves the effort to "recuperate" or "enhance" an interest in the external world and enable a move out of an "autistic capsule" that would make possible the development of unconscious fantasy. This raises the question of the extent to which interest in the external world can be "recuperated or enhanced" and whether the connection with the object, with the external world, is necessary for the presence or discovery of unconscious fantasy. Prevalent in many of the case presentations and discussions is a focus on the contact between the self and object, and the articulation of the nature of the connection as it unfolds in the transference/countertransference arena.

Dori Laub and Nanette Auerhahn write about traumatic unconscious fantasy in their presentation and discussion of three clinical vignettes of trauma. They describe the way unconscious traumatic fantasy determines what transpires between patient and therapist, driving and giving shape to transference/countertransference enactments. They bring apt description to the analytic process and the contact that becomes possible. "Patient and therapist make room internally for the other, each inserting and projecting himself into the other, imbibing the other's representational world, and allowing each to chew over, taste and know what the other has experienced and transmitted." In their exploration of the place of enactment in the process of discovering unconscious fantasy, they offer that traumatic fantasy is a co-construction of patient and analyst after the fact of the enactment, and that then "exists as a representation once it is formulated and 'given back' to the patient." Therefore, the traumatic unconscious fantasy takes form as the dyad lives through experience that was previously incomprehensible. Paradoxically unconscious fantasy both determines the exchange of the analytic dyad AND is developed within the analytic dyad. The unfolding and discovery of unconscious fantasy is an interweaving of processes that demand authentic contact between analysand and analyst, and create therapeutic action.

Arlene Kramer Richards explores the original historical split between the theory of the impact of actual trauma of sexual seduction and that of unconscious fantasy. She distinguishes between "an event, a reaction to the event and a lasting outcome of the event" in her discussions of the "Case of a Hamlet Fantasy" and a case showing the impact of an elaboration of fantasy. Richards' focus is on "how important the elaboration of a fantasy can be in changing a person's life" and that "therapy may serve to reawaken old traumas and, in the presence of benign attentiveness, may enable the person to create a new fantasy that allows modification of the crippling effects of severe or repeated trauma." She reminds us of the painstaking and long process of psychoanalysis, speaking to the willingness to "endure pain and boredom" and the tedium of listening. Enduring pain and boredom is the commitment of analytic dyad to sustaining contact in the analytic process so that what is unknown and unbearable can become known and bearable, the therapeutic action that changes life.

In Rogelio Sosnik's clinical presentation, he shows the profound difficulty his patient suffered in terms of prohibited contact both in her life and with him: Sosnik realizes that the persecutory anxiety and terror of proximity and connection with him during the analytic hour is too strong, making that connection impossible for the patient. He writes that the analyst offers a space within which the analyst becomes the other actor of the scene while assuming the role of the warrantor of the truthfulness of the experience that is taking place. Sosnik describes the analytic process opening to explore the formation of the unconscious phantasy with his patient's changing connection to him as material moves from more primitive with the quality of part-object relationship to a closer transference-based connection. Herein the prohibited contact is actually a form of contact that Sosnik discovers in his countertransference – a contact involving the patient leaving him (the analyst) out. The unconscious phantasies play a central role in the defensive maneuvers that protect mental equilibrium AND that unconscious phantasies unfold with the deepening of the capacity for a transference relationship.

In my work with Margaret and her body pain, I often experience Margaret's physical pain, and metaphor seems far away. As the orbit of the earliest relationship gives the context for the development of the experience of the self, Margaret's early orbit held few opportunities for authentic contact. In fact Margaret does not know or understand authentic contact. Her bodily complaints, her reports of bodily discomfort and pain, are her effort to make sense of what her body and self are, and what her earliest self was in her primary relationship. Her painful image of her mother lives inside her. Viewed differently, Margaret actually repeats with me the nature of her contact from her early mother–child orbit. I work with her to make contact, to understand her variant of contact. Here is the possibility for containment for her, for her body and for her mind. Just as contact may bring containment, it may also bring the potential for destruction. It is in the tension between the life force, her (and my) wish to create, and the destructive internalized torture, that I work to find my moment to moment countertransference. My two discussants, Marilia Aisenstein and Batya Monder, bring further clarity to my work with Margaret. Monder raises the question of how to work with the internalized destructive object. She speaks to the projection of the destructive object,

> ... that Margaret desperately wants relief from distress; and her way to seek relief is to project into Ellman the violence, the terror and torture that she experiences but cannot understand, a way for a patient to "both communicate ... distress and temporarily rid [herself] of it and therefore of [her] understanding." (Joseph, 1983, p. 292).

Monder addresses the mind's chief function of splitting and evacuating bad fragments and the efforts to work in the transference, "to think disturbing experiences with the analyst that had previously been unthinkable." She says: "Ellman stays with her ... allowing her to feel heard and understood" and also writes about contact involving the sadomasochistic connection, the only one that the patient knows, and with contact comes destruction. Aisenstein, in her discussion, suggests that there is a way of "holding" the sadomasochism in the analytic dyad. She remarks on how the pain is transferred to the analyst who suffers in this sadomasochistic exchange. Hurting and suffering has been and is Margaret's way of loving. Aisenstein writes that Margaret needed to be taken into mother's arms and was not. Her pain is anachronistic pain. It is only pain (not depression or anxiety) that is available to her, and pain is her way of expressing affect and conflict. For Aisenstein, the unconscious phantasy is about maintaining pain as the pain is the attack on the intrusive mother, and, at the same time, is also Margaret's attempt at keeping her mother alive within her. There is the omnipotent fantasy of keeping the torturer alive, but without the torturer, there is too much emptiness which is more frightening. The pain is Margaret's attempt to not lose the intrusive sadistic grappling with the mother. The trauma is body and mind invaded by mother where there is no internal space. This paralyzes the analyst's mind also, so there is no space to think as the patient keeps mother alive inside her. The "finding process" occurs as the analyst receives these projections and digests them to attempt to find space. With the creation of mental space comes the opportunity for contact bringing a synthesizing of the parts of Margaret's dissociated self.

The emphasis of this book on "finding unconscious fantasy," while involving work with both metaphor and the unsymbolized, is implicitly also about how we transform pain into psychic suffering and bring the unsymbolized into a symbolizing process. The realm of "finding unconscious fantasy" therefore bridges to an understanding of therapeutic action (Strachey, 1969). As book contributors consider the finding of unconscious fantasy in their case presentations and discussions, frequently discussion of the therapeutic action of the treatment emerges. We might consider that the finding of unconscious fantasy actually constitutes as therapeutic action. Basseches states, "I see the underlying fantasy as the motor for the action within ... the analysis itself." Similarly, as the da Rocha Barroses speak to the finding process in their discussion, they write about the analyst's function as an agent of psychic change:

> Through his interpretations, the analyst renders visible (in the sense of imagery) and meaningful the unconscious mental representations of emotional situations. By these means, the patient re-articulates meanings from distinct symbolic fields, opening up new possibilities of experience and creating new meanings left in an incomplete state, which expand the possibilities for emotional development.

They suggest that the analytic work of revealing meanings that are inaccessible because of repression or other split off concretizing effects is texturally the work of the therapeutic action of psychoanalysis. "By interpreting the internal tension produced by an absence of meaning, which, by its very nature, can never be rendered explicit, the analyst creates new meanings." Richards, in her contribution, addresses the therapeutic action of finding unconscious fantasy in occasions of trauma. She writes that discovering unconscious fantasy brings an amelioration of trauma through the creation of new fantasy "that supports adaptation and promotes self-esteem." This way there is an "expanding [of] the web of associations so as to form a coherent story that enables him to actively master the trauma." In her following the movement of the phantasies in the session, Bronstein develops the conviction that Babette is "both reliving the conflict between mother and baby, but at the same time she is also able to create a metaphor, one that is a condensation of the conflicts she is experiencing in relation to her analyst." In noting that Babette's stammering symptom disappeared in the course of the analysis, Bronstein asserts that the analysis reached different levels of phantasy thereby enabling "a more coherent and integrated ego, ... [helping] Babette to find her own language." Babette's new ego strength is the outgrowth of her treatment's therapeutic action.

The centrality of finding unconscious fantasy in psychoanalysis is closely linked with our understanding of the workings of therapeutic action. It is in our living through with our patients the nature of their contact that brings associations in both the minds of the patient and the analyst thereby opening pathways to finding unconscious fantasy. It is in the discovery of the particular nature of our patient's contact through the transference-countertransference that allows for the knowing of unconscious fantasy and for the catalyzing of the therapeutic action of psychoanalysis.

The process of finding unconscious fantasy is embedded in the analytic dyad and occurs at its interface. Connectivity, having contact, coming to know the nature of the contact, becomes the means of discovery and creation. The finding of unconscious fantasy is closely linked to the creation of therapeutic action in instances of trauma and somatic expression when the metaphorical process is frozen in a concrete state of immobility. The finding of unconscious fantasy allows for a depth of meaning that brings an enlivening to internal processes.

References

Basseches, H. B., Ellman, P. L., & Goodman, N. R. (2013). *Battling the life and death forces of sadomasochism: Clinical perspectives.* London: Karnac.

Bohleber, W., Jimenez, J. P., Scarfone, D., Varvin, S., & Zysman, S. (2015). Unconscious phantasy and its conceptualizations: An attempt at conceptual integration. *International Journal of Psychoanalysis, 96,* 705–730.

Bronstein, C. (2015). Finding unconscious phantasy in the session: Recognizing form. *International Journal of Psychoanalysis, 96,* 925–944.

Ellman, P. & Goodman, N. (2012). Enactment: An opportunity for symbolizing trauma. In: A. Frosch (Ed), *Absolute truth and unbearable psychic pain: Psychoanalytic perspectives on concrete experience* (pp. 57–72). London: Karnac.

Joseph, B. (1983). On understanding and not understanding: Some technical issues. *International Journal of Psycho-Analysis, 64,* 291–298.

Strachey, J. (1969). The nature of the therapeutic action of psychoanalysis. *International Journal of Psychoanalysis, 50,* 275–292.

Chapter 4

The psychoanalytic treatment of an adult patient traumatized in early childhood[1]

Werner Bohleber

Among the research issues which have increasingly occupied me over the years are the long-term effects of traumatization occurring in early childhood. I asked myself, in what ways do traumatic experiences express themselves in the later development of the child? How has the child adapted to these and in what ways has the trauma influenced the development of the personality structure in adolescence and adulthood? I have several such patients in long-term analytic treatment and I hope to find answers to these questions using this clinical material.

Mr. A., a 55-year-old patient, came to me for treatment of depressive mood swings and a persisting sense of meaninglessness. He experienced his life as insipid, took no real interest in anything and nothing moved him; and yet this all seemed to fall short of how he envisaged his life. He characterized his primary feeling about life as being one of a perpetual mood of melancholy, which, around the beginning of the week, would grow into strong depressive states and feelings of meaningless. He would experience panic during the night resulting from a sense of being unable to move. He complained of a lack of vitality and experienced an almost complete lack of sexual desire. He has been married for ten years, prior to which he had several fleeting affairs with women. He experienced a frequently recurring dream in which he clung on to something, or he found himself in very small rooms that he was unable to leave. He was unable to remain seated in one place for a long period of time, and when visiting the theatre and cinema he would invariably select a seat at the end of a row.

He is a lawyer by profession, but today works in a social institution. He successfully took up a number of professional careers, but would resign each position for a new one. He explained his inability to pursue his career opportunities by feeling himself, after a certain amount of time had elapsed, to be caged in, pinned down and chained up. For this reason, he has until now been unable to establish continuity in his life.

He wanted to undergo analysis when he was 20 because of his sexual problems. He was finally able to orgasm several years later. But the analyst at the time advised against high-frequency analysis since this would reactualize a considerable amount of his early trauma. The analyst in question was referring to a traumatic event in Mr. A.'s life. At the age of 18 months, he was admitted to a clinic for hip luxation treatment. At the time, this defective position was treated by lying in a plaster bed. The patient remained stationary in a plaster bed at the clinic for a period of nine months. The clinic was located at a fair distance to his hometown. The parents were not permitted to visit him for the first six weeks after which period they seldom paid him visits. The mother was expecting another baby, and when the patient returned home the sister had already been born. The mother pampered this second child who was frequently ill.

He was in psychotherapy in his late twenties and in a psychoanalytic treatment that he concluded five years ago. The psychoanalytic treatment with me lasted seven years with a frequency of three sessions per week. During the sessions, Mr. A. always felt himself under pressure. Though what he told me was vivid, I was unable to gain access to his feelings. My impression was that he was closed within himself, as if he were a closed cylinder from which I would slide off.

He was unable to freely associate, and no childhood memories emerged.

I gradually formed the impression that we were constantly revolving around the same problems and that the analysis was being exhausted therein. To me it seemed as if nothing could touch him. However, his often illusory attitude to life, according to which everything should be easy, did improve. This change enabled him to develop his piano playing in a sustained and systematic way, and his block with respect to writing songs and chansons was significantly dissolved. However, the severe irruptions of bad moods he experienced in the morning along with his sense of meaninglessness did not recede. And there were only minimal changes in his relationship to his wife. She was dominating, and he felt an inner compulsion to fulfil her expectations.

During the sessions, it gradually became clearer to me that his discourse was marked by a very subtle superego attitude. His statements were, in essence, reproaches towards himself. This insight opened up for the first time a deeper emotional access to him. I no longer had the impression of slipping on his reserve, even if his own sense of self, of being withdrawn and frozen, persisted. With this insight into the superego attitude of Mr. A. towards himself, I began to feel that what he said did not come from him, was not the expression of an ego that suffered. He rather tended to complain about himself. The suffering self apparently had no voice.

At the same time, I noticed that he seemed to be dominated by a sense of timelessness. He had no feeling for the course of his life. In the moments he became conscious of it, this sense of timelessness would assume a threatening character, namely, that his condition would forever remain the way it was. It was in such moments that I would begin to feel a diffuse, concealed sense of anxiety that he would sooner or later discover he had done nothing with his life and would commit suicide. I interpreted this sense of timelessness and the dissociation of his suffering self as the long-term consequences of his traumatization.

At the end of the Easter holidays in the third year of analysis, he wrote me a letter in which he terminated the treatment. He saw no sense in continuing since he was unable to see any change in what were for him the essential areas. I was stunned and could not understand it at all. I invariably had the impression that an emotionally responsive contact had existed. Had this simply been a figment of my own imagination? I wrote a letter to him that led to his return, and for which he was very grateful. As our analysis indicated, it was the sense of timelessness that had triggered anxiety in him during the holiday period. Doubts about the analysis had amalgamated into an anxiety-driven notion that he would be in permanent analysis; that it would continue indefinitely with no success, and hence his note of termination. The analysis itself had become the plaster bed that constrained him, and he was unable to imagine ever bringing it to conclusion. My mentioning that unpleasure is something that can be given a space and which can be talked about seems to have been a real aha-experience for him. He explained to me that, for him, unpleasure is not something that comes and goes, but is total and that he has the feeling that it will never pass. I responded by remarking that the connection between his present difficulties and his early experience of being confined to a plaster bed was clear, but that it had occurred to me that this had found no echo within him, and that he simply wished to cast off his difficulties like a plaster bed from which he could walk away. This interpretation struck him to the core. His attitude had indeed been that he could simply cast off his suffering and rid himself of it in this manner. The fact that the suffering concerns himself, and that his innermost self is manifested therein, is something to which he could not relate. This traumatized part of his self had been dissociated or split off. For me it was quite evident that his sense of timelessness and feeling of never being able to finish analysis were repetitions of the traumatic pattern of his childhood, which I then interpreted for him. However, I had overlooked at the time something that was far more immediate, namely, the permanent pressure he felt of having to achieve something in the analysis in order to please me.

Shortly afterwards, his dog, to which he was much attached, died. I was astonished by the severity of his sorrow. A feeling of deep abandonment gripped him together with a sense of total dependency on his wife. Two months later, his wife also left him, suddenly, and without any forewarning. The patient fell into a serious crisis; he felt completely alone, desperate and depressive, and filled with a complete sense of desolation. Feelings of guilt alternated with homicidal rage directed towards his wife. His feelings now began to overwhelm him during the sessions and he began to weep for the first time. His sense of self-worth left him and he felt himself to be a helpless heap, needy and alone in the world. He felt packed off like a castaway by his wife, but still waited for her to return and redeem him. On the other hand, his experience of her was that she resembled an ice-cold goddess. Feelings of guilt for having destroyed everything alternated with a sense of longing and suicidal states of anger. He became suicidal. Antidepressants did not help. What made the sense of desolation and desperation so unendurable for him was his sense of timelessness coupled with the conviction that the condition in which he now found himself would never end. Although he felt himself utterly alone in the world, he upheld the inner relationship to me. In case of emergency, I gave him my telephone number.

He was now acutely aware of his feelings of abandonment, feelings to which he was unable to put a name to for a long time. After talking about this, and providing reconstructive interpretations that brought the feeling of abandonment into relation with his early trauma in a plaster bed in the clinic, he once again found that although this anxiety of being abandoned was something he repeatedly experienced in the past, for a long time he was unable to grasp it and put a name to it.

Above all, he was now in a better position to understand his behaviour towards his wife. The fact that in conflicts he would always back down and end up doing what she wanted was something he was now able to connect with his anxiety of being abandoned. By way of this concretization and clarification of his condition as a nameable feeling, and through the reconstructive connection with his earlier trauma a diffuse inner condition was psychically represented. However, this was not a unique process, but in the period that followed it had to be repeatedly worked through.

This crisis relaxed his hitherto inflexible characterological defence structures, rendered him less restricted and dissolved his 'shock-induced frozen state'. His dissociated needy self, pervaded by anxieties and panic about being left alone became accessible to him: it was as if he felt 'what a self is' for the first time. He did wish not to lose this perception again. And yet this is what happened. His sense of self was to elude him a further time, and he fell into a depressive state accompanied by unbearable feelings of abandonment. He frequently took Ritalin as an antidote, which returned to him a certain sense of self and something like a 'core experience', which was for him an extremely valuable achievement.

In contrast to earlier stages, our relationship now took on greater emotional significance. Thus, he once said that he would check whether my comments contained a criticism or judgment of his person. In one session he recounted a dispute with a telephone company during which he became increasingly furious with himself because he was unable to find the relevant documents. Initially, the dispute centred on his refusal to pay three euro. The value of the payment had meanwhile increased to 66 euro due to the default and collection fees. I first focused my interpretation on his sense of justice, but then also asked whether he felt the dispute really worth the effort. The following morning I found a message he had left on my answering machine to the effect that he would not be coming to the session today, and in fact it made no sense to continue. I was not prepared for this; the abruptness of this message struck me like a mini-trauma, and I felt numbed. What had I done wrong? However, I then had the feeling that he was doing something to me that he had himself experienced, namely, being abandoned. At noon the same day, he called again to say that he would be coming to the session. During the session he said that through my intervention in the dispute with the telephone company he had the sense of having done everything wrong. In the night, this sense, namely, that he always did things wrong, had intensified and become generalized. Unable to sleep, he had then become desperate. Mr. A. began to weep heavily on the couch. Behind his rigid superego attitude a suffering self that had constantly striven to do everything correctly so as not to be dismissed or abandoned then became visible.

Unlike the first break, it immediately became clear to me that my intervention had been a countertransference enactment. In the previous session I had in fact considered whether I really ought to have posed the question, namely, whether carrying on a dispute about such an insignificant sum was really worth it. I then thought, "why not", decided to waive this consideration, and so went ahead and posed the question. Reflecting on it afterwards, I realized that my spontaneous reaction of 'why not' was a counter-reaction against Mr. A.'s obsessive sense of justice.

Through my countertransference enactment, his ego-syntonic attitude of wanting to do everything right then became interpretable. I said to him that with this attitude he sought to avoid angering me or his wife, which would actualize the threat to be sent away. If he sought to do everything right he would then, for the most part, have control over the situation. Abandoning this attitude would make him vulnerable and place him at risk of being rejected by others. The patient replied, although these kinds of fears have disappeared, behind his will to be self-sufficient and autarchic, he has not, in fact, really been as confident as it would appear from the outside. The mother-transference was suddenly accessible. The patient began to develop hate towards his mother: "that damned woman, what a hell of harm she has done". She had always found occasion to criticize him for something, in spite of all his efforts.

This crisis in the treatment has made the dissociation of his traumatized self more permeable. I suddenly became aware that his desire to please everyone was not solely motivated towards gaining greater recognition, but also by his wish to be loved. When this occurred to me, I then referred to it without any further reflection, using the word "love" and noticing at once how this resulted in a change in the entire situation. For the first time his need to be loved was represented in the relationship, after which his neediness became palpably obvious to him. I asked myself why this had not been clearer to me at an earlier stage, since it should have been perfectly obvious. This clear designation of his desire to be loved had a surprising effect. He had had the feeling that this desire of wanting to be loved was something infantile, something which he was unable to accept on account of his desire to be independent and autarchic. A heavy burden had been lifted from him.

Through this countertransference enactment, his sensitive, anxious and traumatized self, fraught with panic of being abandoned which was dissociated and split off for such a long time, was now increasingly accessible. It had been safeguarded by his narcissistic defensive position by way of which he had demanded of himself that he remain sovereign and autarchic, but which had given him the impression of being untouchable. This defensive position concealed his efforts to attempt to do everything to please in relationships, to not be the bad party who could be packed off or abandoned, all of which would have been a repetition of his trauma of separation. Through my countertransference enactment a superego that would attack him whenever failing to conform to its demands also became recognizable. The obedience towards his superego protected him against being abandoned which had then evolved into an ego-syntonic attitude. It was also in this way that he felt he must be a good analytic patient. He presented his problems, but at the same time very subtly accused himself – an attitude which initially assumed the appearance of self-reflection. It was through this self-accusation that he would obviate his traumatic anxiety about being attacked, judged and dismissed by me. He actively anticipated that which was passively feared, and thus had it under control in this way.

About nine months after separating from his wife, Mr. A. met another woman who was very different to his dominant wife since she placed no expectations on him as to how he should behave towards her. She wanted to comply with his wishes. It then became clear that he was unable to do this, namely, to express his wishes, because he has no real idea what his desires actually are. He felt ill at ease and his girlfriend began to bore him. He would have also felt ridiculous had he expressed his feelings. His mother used to repeatedly shame him whenever he felt proud and expressed this. As if suspecting he had entered into another relationship, his wife contacted him again, and wanted to resume the relationship. She withdrew her official application for divorce. He then committed himself again to his wife. He felt attracted to the familiarity he shared with her. But he retained his own apartment as a place of refuge.

In the subsequent part of the treatment, the connection between his anxiety of being abandoned and the pressure to perform as an inner compulsion to orient himself according to the expectations of the object of his love became clear and possible to work through. He now sought to not simply comply with the expectations of others. However, whenever attempting not to comply with the expectations, he would experience a massive sense of guilt resulting in a fear of abandonment. I repeatedly interpreted his unconscious conviction that everything he does is in an attempt to avoid being the bad guy; that he fulfils the expectations directed at him, since he would otherwise run the risk of being abandoned; that he had been unaware of this anxiety for a long time because it was concealed behind his attitude of compliance and the search for harmony with his object of love. I connected this interpretation with a genetic interpretation, namely, that back then, when returning home from the clinic, he would have probably done anything to gain the love and attention of his mother, and that he was anxious about being sent away again.

However, working through these things in analysis hardly altered anything in his inner attitude and his behaviour. Because of his reactions to this kind of interpretation, it repeatedly occurred to me that he had no empathy for himself as a child. I raised this issue and said: as a 2- to 3-year-old boy traumatized in such a way, he would have probably done everything to gain recognition and to be liked. I continued that it seemed to me that he actually had no sense of sympathy with himself as the boy he once was. This interpretation triggered in him an inner movement; he repeated my interpretation to himself several times during the session. It was the last session before the long summer holiday. When returning from the holiday he told me that what had helped him endure the separation was thinking about what I had said about boyhood. He had planned to visit the clinic in which he resided for nine months as a child. However, on the night before the planned visit he experienced painful stomach cramps and decided not to follow through with the plan.

During this long phase of the treatment a symptom reappeared which he had suffered years ago: at night, he would frequently suffer from urinary retention and a catheter had to be inserted at the clinic. Urinary retention seemed to have a dual function: first, it appeared like a final bastion for asserting himself against the demands of others, while, second, it was like a defence against letting himself go, "to let it run".

There was another insight: when, in fact, he did not comply with what others wanted, a feeling of emptiness would arise which he found unbearable. Now he was in a position to perceive that he actually has little clue as to what he himself wanted, what he wished for and how he could give his life meaning. A pervasive, threatening sense of the meaningless of his life began to make itself felt. The far-reaching identification with the expectations of his object of love became perceptible: he spoke about his deep identification with others, and that he was unable to liberate himself from this. Another image which he used for this situation is that it felt like his wife was seated on his shoulders and that he was unable to throw her off. In several steps, I interpreted this as a form of projective identification: That he protected himself from being judged and rejected by identifying himself with others so as to perceive their expectations, or to project them into others as a means of controlling others from within. Were he to abandon this identification, he would then be clearly differentiated from the other; he would stand on one side and the other on the other side; and to feel this distinction and separation was the cause of his anxiety.

It was through this that something began to move psychically. He would repeatedly attempt to behave differently and occasionally begin freely associating during the sessions; but this would lead to silence until the session came to an end. Whenever I sought to intervene during this silence, he would again have the feeling that he was not doing it correctly. His apparently very fixed attitude towards his wife also began to relax: he would express to her everything he didn't like. She was hurt, and withdrew, but now he was more able to bear it. On another occasion, while actively resisting his wife's expectations and thinking how he would prefer separation than complying, he noticed how his inner state changed, and a sexual desire began resurfacing. However, resisting only became possible when saying to himself, "I don't care if she wants to separate, then I'll simply be alone". The sense of abandonment began to lose its massive threatening character.

He tried to make peace with himself such that he must accept his difficulties in dealing with the expectations of others, above all, those of his wife, to which he would conform. Now, however, whenever it became too much for him, he would withdraw to his apartment. The compulsive power that expectations exerted over him was apparently not so strong, and neither was his sense of abandonment. On the whole, he felt himself more stable. After reducing the frequency of the sessions from three to two, and then down to one session, we concluded the treatment after seven years.

Discussion

While psychoanalysis has always addressed the consequences of early traumatization, there are only a small handful of psychoanalytic studies – based on our contemporary understanding of early traumatization – which have thematized the specific consequences for the development of personality. Allow me to give a brief outline of what I gleaned from the treatment data of Mr. A. with respect to the effects of severe separation traumas. I am, however, aware that searching for a unilinear, point by point correspondence between the early trauma and later behaviour in adulthood proves fruitless; we are rather concerned here with a complex interplay of the various mechanisms and factors in further development. Today, we know that the physical sentiments deriving from the traumatic experience persist for a long time. Mr. A.'s prolonged sexual anorgasmy, as well as his urinary retention, can doubtlessly, at least in part, be traced back to his laying in a plaster bed. Coates and Moore (1997) assume that the persistence of the traumatic memory and its reactualization is connected to this persisting sensation. Thus, in Mr. A.'s case, the anxiety about being hemmed in or trapped persisted throughout his life, and not only in auditoriums or in the cinema, but by extension, also symbolically in his professional career, whereby he repeatedly felt hemmed in, a circumstance which, in turn, compelled him to resign from his respective jobs.

Over the course of the treatment, the intimate connection between the separation trauma, the development of autonomy and the identification with the primary object became manifest. The traumatically determined anxiety of being abandoned proved itself to be a central motive for further development. The traumatized self became dissociatively encapsulated, and was thus deprived of further development. A self that had adapted itself to the assumed expectations of the mother took its place instead. Mr. A. was a conspicuously well-behaved child. The identification with the mother served as a means of controlling the object such that it could not possibly be angry with him, since this would have resulted in his traumatic anxieties of loss erupting once again. Mr. A. was unable to use the oedipal conflicts in a sustained identification with the father, which might have enabled him to establish a certain distance to his mother. There had also been no opportunity during adolescence to moderate this frozen development. A character-neurotically anchored superego-attitude increasingly developed in which he sought to do everything properly and in compliance with the expectations of his object of love. By way of the virtually fusion-like connection with the primary object, the post-traumatic development of an independent self with its own needs and desires was massively impaired. And yet it functioned as protection against once again being exposed to the traumatic feelings of abandonment. This pattern of consciously and unconsciously orienting himself towards the expectations of his wife was possible to moderate therapeutically but was not possible to be completely dissolved, no more than was his attitude in analysis, namely, to comply with what he understood as analysis or what he imputed to be my expectations of him.

I found similar issues with other patients who had suffered from an early separation trauma. My thesis is that the early trauma led to a deficient development of autonomy. As a consequence, self and object representations were unable to establish themselves independently of one another, but were instead agglutinated due to abandonment anxieties. Hence, dreams of such patients show how aspects of the self are replaced with aspects of the object. Or you can find a self dreaming scenes which, in reality, are those of his object of love and vice versa. Through this agglutination the traumatized self is incapable of detaching itself from the expectations of its object of love. Thoughts where the ego assumes that his object of love would reject him threaten the sense of self and can induce a quasi-traumatic anxiety leading to a dissociated and alienated state of consciousness. One might, indeed, also describe these psychic processes by way of concepts of projective identification and introjective identification, but this would fail to get to the core of the issue, namely, the traumatically determined agglutination of self and object.

Note

1 Presented at the pre-congress working group "Trauma Study: Transmission, Enactment and Symbolization" IPAC Boston, 21–22 July 2015.

Reference

Coates, S. and Moore, M. (1997). The complexity of early trauma. *Psychoanalytic Inquiry*, 5: 163–189.

Chapter 5

The impossible and the possible

Finding unconscious fantasy dimensions in Werner Bohleber's case of Mr. A.

Nancy R. Goodman

The case of Mr. A. is about the analytic work with a man who suffered through extreme childhood trauma. He was hospitalized for a medical problem at the age of 18 months and put in a plaster cast for 9 months, having little contact with family. Often in my writing I have needed to start from a distance, in writing style and tone, before approaching the "toomuchness" of the months of trauma experienced by Baby A…. I also needed to continually reinstate the existence of someone with whom I could have contact when in touch with the trauma, someone to receive the story. I did this by writing letters to Dr. Bohleber and by allowing myself to circle around the unconscious fragments of trauma through repetitive revisiting. These oscillations, close and distant, essay and letter, helped titrate the shock and pain in finding unconscious derivatives in the analytic work with Mr. A. Unconscious fantasies concerning body, relationship, love, hate, and annihilation eventually came into view as I was able to "find" more and more of the unconscious fantasies appearing in the analytic work.

From the outset two remarkable events take place in this psychoanalysis – the presence of the traumatic plaster bed baby and an analytic treatment receiving Mr. A.'s pain. This makes the possible out of the impossible. The fabric of Mr. A.'s psychic reality is a mix of trauma reactions and affects and unconscious fantasies. We can imagine the 18-month-old baby alone and building whole fantasies and fragments of fantasies about body, disappearance, fear, destruction, persecution, and despair. Inner landscapes would be constructed and deconstructed, filled with objects of love and attachment and of horror and abandonment. All of this came with Mr. A. to Dr. Werner Bohleber who brings it to us to read and reflect upon.

There are multiple ways that Dr. Bohleber and Mr. A. "find" unconscious fantasies over the seven years of this treatment – fantasies connected to his stay in the hospital and his basic instinctual needs. Mr. A. comes to analysis with the psychic presence of enforced stillness alternating with impending explosions. In the psychic realities of the case there are unconscious beliefs about destruction and the unconscious presence of trauma and fantasies about what caused it. In Mr. A.'s psyche there are representations of dead internal objects who perpetrate betrayal and the constant feel of being disappeared and forgotten at any moment. There is a constellation of fantasies about being perfect in order to forestall future trauma. Body functions come to express unconscious dimensions of control concerning what can get in or get out. He has urinary retention and lack of sexual desire. There cannot be flow from the orifices of the body because movement portends disaster. Fantasies about sadomasochistic relations evolve from the idea that it is better to be hurt and deprived now than to wait for the inevitable. I believe that a particular fantasy about wished-for rebirth, to be released from a death sentence, was active in keeping Mr. A. in the analytic work. What is most striking about the analytic work of Mr. A. and Dr. Bohleber is that analysis was able to take place and to melt away rigid defenses and adaptations that Baby/Mr. A. had arranged in order to stay alive. Discovery of countertransference feelings and enactments between Dr. Bohleber and Mr. A. were primary vehicles for finding unconscious material related to the traumatic past, and the fantasies attached to it.

I have a deep resonance to the analytic work reported by Dr. Bohleber, making it difficult at times to think and write as trauma and annihilation fears were engendered in me. My solution to create the mix of commentary and letter writing opened the possibility to listen to the evolution of the treatment. Mr. A. arrived in Dr. Bohleber's office carrying with him an internal rupture. I wish there had been someone to write Baby A. a letter that would have been read to him so he would know someone was thinking about him. I wish he had been helped to color pictures and send them to someone eager to receive them. He must have been waiting for a long time to write and receive letters. Mr. A. found Dr. Bohleber who has thought and written innumerable articles about severe trauma along with his book (2010), *Destructiveness, Intersubjectivity, and Trauma: The Identity Crisis of Modern Psychoanalysis*. As a psychoanalyst he has worked with transmission of trauma across generations of Holocaust survivors and Perpetrator offspring. In the unfolding of the case, Dr. Bohleber is also someone who writes a letter to his patient.

Much of my writing, in essay form and in letters, is from a countertransference position; that is, from the affects, imagery, and terror conveyed to me through descriptions of the analytic work. My only chance to approach Mr. A.'s mind was to trust that the way to find unconscious fantasies and traumatic sequelae in all of their intertwined patterns was to become aware of and symbolize my own reactions. Simultaneously, I found an awakening in me of empathy for Mr. A.'s psychoanalyst, Werner Bohleber, for the terror he was willing to listen to in his patient as it appeared in narratives, dreams, actions, and interactions. He was unwavering and I wanted to follow his lead.

I experienced claustrophobic reactions, dread, and avoidance when I first heard Dr. Bohleber (2015) present the case of Mr. A. and again when reading it as a chapter for this volume. I read through the case again and again and felt that I had not read it. I would know and then not know the details of the analytic evolution. This is like the knowing and not knowing defined by Laub and Auerhahn (1993) who conceptualize the difficulties of holding on to rememberings and imaginings that emerge when catastrophic trauma, such as from the Holocaust, is experienced. My mind oscillated between seeing Mr. A. as real and unreal, as dead and as alive. His analysis showed movement and in the beginning I could only think of the trauma as if it were the only event, a timeless still dark presence, an eternal long night for an abandoned child. In *The Power of Witnessing* (Goodman, 2012), I develop the idea of "dead space" in the mind to reference catastrophic trauma and the idea of a "living space" that develops with witnessing – a space for symbolization, affect, and renewal. Overtime with innumerable readings of Dr. Bohleber's write-up, I could feel the solid witnessing presence of Dr. Bohleber and the new space created in the analytic work. I was then ready to write my associations to the case and my ideas about how Mr. A. and Dr. Bohleber were finding the unconscious fantasies and traumatic derivatives helping Mr. A. move out of his frozen state of terror to be alive.

> In the beginning
> Letter 1: Dear Dr. Werner Bohleber, I will write you notes throughout my reflections on your case as I show how "finding unconscious fantasy" developed, I found it so painful to enter Baby A.'s hospital room where I knew I had to go to understand his unconscious mind. There is overwhelming trauma behind the door and an 18-month-old trying to stay psychically alive. I want to bring him a toddler picture book with stories of fierce animals and sleeping babies and reunions with a menagerie of people offering care and feelings. I think this is what the two of you were able to do in the analysis. Somehow the analytic work transformed what you call a plaster bed, into a new bed, the pain about which you and he could eventually think and feel. I like your term plaster bed because that is what I see and feel in my mind – a psychic presence of total encasement. I imagine a fantasy of a womb from which birth can take place (my wish I think) – a nine-month timeless floating. You write about timelessness in the analysis as centrally important to unravel. A rigid unyielding plaster bed, and parents whose minds are not able to be in contact with him, is fragmenting and noncontaining. Your containing and meaning giving could bring about the fantasies and metaphors about encasement.
>
> Dr. Nancy Goodman

The traumatic story

In the fourth paragraph of Dr. Bohleber's case write-up, we learn the following:

> At the age of 18 months, he was admitted to a clinic for hip luxation treatment. At that time, this position was treated by lying in a plaster bed. The patient remained stationary in a plaster bed for a period of nine months.

Can you, the reader, picture this in your mind? Does it make you dizzy or numb or frightened, or angry? Or is it like a strobe light going on and off so you cannot really see the scene in front of you? Most likely, you are confused as I was and often still am. The actuality of the trauma entered my mind slowly and without clarity for many months. I persistently imagined a 9-year-old in a plaster cast. I kept forgetting Mr. A. was a baby in a plaster cast for nine months. An older child could read books or listen to the radio or watch television or tell people what he was thinking. An older child could speak to someone about his fears and have school friends visit. But the truth is that a very young child, a child who should have been walking, running, holding hands, talking, playing, forming internal pictures, living in a body, conquering wishes and fears, of being with Mom and Dad, of being in the world, was forced to become an immobile child. He went on living but with traumatic shock and a set of unconscious fantasies and beliefs cemented in place until dislodged in the analysis.

And, this may be the worst of all:

> The clinic was located at a fair distance to his hometown. The parents were not permitted to visit him for the first six weeks after which they seldom paid him visits. The mother was expecting another baby, and when the patient returned home the sister had already been born.

Now we have to think or not think, feel or not feel, even more. He was alone with no familiar Mom or Dad. First, they were not allowed to visit for six weeks, and then "they seldom paid him visits." As I write I want to create a "we." It is so important when trying to know trauma and the unconscious. We will together try to imagine the mind of Baby/Mr. A. and try to imagine Mr. A. and Dr. Bohleber in the consulting room. Together, we tiptoe to the door to the hospital room and the analytic consulting room. We find an 18-month-old forming impressions, developing attachment and detachment representations, splitting good and bad objects, perceiving the cast as friend (so present, unlike his parents) and foe, and creating shadowy parts of stories to explain and to keep contact, somehow, with himself. The little boy of 18 months must have wanted to run from room to room and enjoy "hide and seek." How was the plaster bed explained? Had he awakened from anesthetic to find himself encased and no familiar voice or face to make a "holding environment?" Were his baby struggles with love, hate, envy, and reparation shattered? There would have had to be fragments of fantasies about body, disappearance, fear, destruction, love and hate, persecution, and despair. Did he imagine that the internal world of his mother and father erased his existence? The act of disappearing a child, soul murder, arouses rage, horror, murderousness, and torture in our minds; this is the "too much" of trauma and annihilation. Somehow this little boy became a man both with psychic pain and with the ability to want help.

Capacity for dreaming

Early in the treatment, Mr. A. let Dr. Bohleber know that he had some psychic space in his mind. He spoke of a childhood recurrent dream. The dream was one in which "he clung on to something or he found himself in very small rooms which he was unable to leave." Reporting this to his analyst was a gift, even if a stilted report about the past, and evidence that even as a child Mr. A. could symbolize and dream/nightmare. It was also a predictor of how claustrophobia and clinging would enter the transference/countertransference. In the dream there is likely a wish to have space open, to have the cast removed, and to be reconnected to body and objects. As this case unfolded and some movement and dreaming together as analyst and patient appeared, Dr. Bohleber and Mr. A. were collectors hunting for and finding myriad buried impressions and affects that had separated from the traumatic events. As they were reconnected to the original trauma, sadomasochistic fusion (what Dr. Bohleber refers to as agglutination) and "small room" imagery expanded. The analysis at times was felt and thought to be the rigid surround, sometimes to seem as the plaster bed that was hated, merged into, and something to destroy. Later, a softening and peeling away of the cast took place and was replaced with space for affect and movement. The omnipresent plaster bed gave way to flexibility and empathy for the little boy, felt by Mr. A. and Dr. Bohleber.

Breaking through the plaster bed

I highlight three ways that I see the opening of space taking place: through the analytic process of witnessing, through breaking the spell of timelessness with enactment processes, and with a capacity to feel grief.

A letter about witnessing

Letter 2: Dear Dr. Werner Bohleber, I hope you realize that it is you, as a witnessing psychoanalyst, who provided a pathway for me and for the readers of the case to follow. Do you know the writing of Ariel Dorfman? He wrote a play/film called *Death and the Maiden* (1991) in which a woman is sure her torturer has appeared in her life. No one recognizes him; but, she does. Being from Chile during the terror, he knows about these horrors. He knows about survival and survivor guilt. But also, as a young child, newly arrived in New York City, he was hospitalized and his parents were not allowed to visit him. When he left the hospital, he no longer spoke his mother tongue, Spanish, but spoke only English. He again spoke Spanish many years later (Dorfman, 1999). Your treatment with Mr. A. shows how lost voice is discovered and rediscovered. This brings to mind the witnessing of Holocaust survivors by Dori Laub (1992) that had been considered impossible until the frame for receiving was created. The analytic work gave words, enactments, and unconscious fantasies a chance to come into being as Mr. A. found truths about his time in the plaster bed and his mind.

The transfer of feelings during witnessing

Witnessing of trauma in analysis inevitably means being a part of the traumatic scenes that are being found and clarified. Dr. Bohleber had to be the abandoner, the hardened, unmovable, ever-present cast, and the young traumatized child. He had to feel the affects of the baby including psychic helplessness, loneliness, rage, and grief. In other words, the analyst had to endure all parts of the trauma experience, to help find them, giving them symbolic presence. Dr. Bohleber demonstrates willingness to live with and witness the horrors of Mr. A.'s child trauma. This witnessing function brings about a sense of being known and having someone providing a "with," someone who is present. Transmission of believing in an object tie is brought to the patient to accompany the early transmission of being someone who is forgotten. Dr. Bohleber lives through the treatment and manages to write the chapter about the case. My own counter-feelings, distress, and fantasies of being in a plaster bed moved me between stillness (writer's block) and wishes to destroy the story itself.

In the analysis, Mr. A. enacted disappearance with threats to leave the analysis, almost bringing about a negative therapeutic reaction. This enactment of negativity represents the emptying of the parents' minds about their baby. Dr. Bohleber felt the immediacy of having the analysis vacated. However, Dr. Bohleber followed Mr. A., letting him know that in his self disappearing he still existed in his, the analyst's, mind. An expanding of the analytic room/space took place through this crucial hide-and-seek, bringing back play and a "new object" (Loewald, 1962) who did not empty out. It would have been so easy to become the thoughtless mother/hospital/cast that so unrelentingly wrapped the child in hopelessness, but Dr. Bohleber kept the connection.

Finding fantasies in timelessness, enactments, and awakening of affects

Throughout his case discussion, Dr. Bohleber mentions a problem of timelessness. Timelessness functioned for Mr. A. as a central unconscious fantasy related to wish, fear (the makings of compromise formations), and to the traumatic stillness induced by the plaster bed. Perhaps like the patient himself, the reader may also feel timelessness/floating/waiting as there is an attempt to take in Mr. A.'s development and analytic experience. There is also a wish that somehow waiting will make the parents come to save him from despair and make sure he is not alone. A baby will wait a long time for Mommy or Daddy to come back.

There are various ways that timelessness appears in Mr. A. and in the analysis. Dr. Bohleber notes boredom, harmony, lack of separateness from others, unawareness of feelings and urges, numbing repetitions, encapsulation, revolving around the same problems, inertia, agglutination with objects, a sense of meaninglessness, and no sense of a course to his life. Dr. Bohleber writes: "My impression was that he was closed within himself, as if he were a closed cylinder from which I would slide off." Mr. A.'s symptoms of lack of desire, retention of orgasm, of urine, and of associations and his need to make Dr. Bohleber feel like he is sliding off of Mr. A.'s psyche, represent the cataclysmic events in body and transference. The shocking disruption of Baby/Mr. A.'s infancy had induced feelings of timelessness and accompanying fantasies. Finding the traumatic experience and the traumatic and primal fantasies of Baby/Mr. A. in timelessness is like trying to see in a dense fog and being glad when some form is almost perceived. The traumatic dead space of timelessness holds the contours of fantasies about a womb and provides a protection against internal murderous rage against others and against self, marasmus. Dr. Bohleber helps Mr. A. recognize that what he feels now is connected to his traumatization. There are object relations, affects, and fantasies. This is a slow process of uncovering and discovering and through it unconscious fantasies about the need to be perfect and to "ride on the shoulder of others" appeared.

A letter about waiting

Letter 3: Dear Dr. Bohleber, It sometimes becomes difficult to type my comments when I am in touch with the cast, my arms get stiff and I want to cry or call out or scream at his mother and father. Did the wish for Mommy turn into a helpless fusion with the plaster bed? Did he give up imagining that Mommy even thought about him? Perhaps he imagined he had turned into a plaster cast/casket to her. Spitz's (1945) abandoned infants die. An abyss entered Baby A.'s mind as some timeless place in him where he waited for someone to return. Bowlby's babies (1969) would just wait too. In my countertransference to Mr. A. and you, I found it extremely difficult to finish this chapter – I could wait forever.

It occurs to me that the Plaster Bed itself is a core internal object competing for cathexis with you and all other whole and part objects. Fantasies were inscribed on the internal cast, including sensations of skin and muscle, much the way children's casts receive written messages and drawings. Bick's ideas (1968) about second skin and adhesive attachments seem apt; in this case, dead unbreathing second skin. Since the cast must have been present at all times, in the psyche and in the room, I want to ask you Dr. Bohleber: Did you become claustrophobic or ever find it hard to breathe? You said that Mr. A. "was unable to remain seated in one place for a long period of time and when visiting the theatre and cinema he would invariably select a seat on the end of the row." Did you sit particularly still or get sleepy or get agitated? Was there always a sense that an exit had to be available? Did Mr. A. ask a lot of questions, as I am – an activity to defy the power of the plaster bed and its timelessness?

Nancy

The enactment process

In this analysis (and likely in all analyses of severe trauma) it is the surprise of enactments that brings powerful affect into the analysis – both for the analysand and the analyst. I suggest that it is enactments that cause a pause in the sense of timelessness as they highlight the "here and now" marking distinction between past and future. Thus, enactments mark time interrupting timelessness. The enactments in this treatment awakened deep feelings and grief in Mr. A. and in Dr. Bohleber. The fog of trauma, present in timelessness, and its multiple meanings was able to lift fostering discovery of unconscious derivatives that had been overwhelmed by the traumatic terror.

Enactments break apart timelessness, bringing about punctuated focus. The cocoon of forever is intruded on. Enactments pierce the timeless web bringing about "here and now" experience inviting emergence. From the beginning of psychoanalysis, the unconscious has been considered to be timeless. In other words, then can be now and in the future, now can be what is imagined for the future or what was previously fantasized in the past. Deep, primitive primal fantasies and trauma gain access through enactments, allowing fantasy scripts to emerge. Arlow (1969) describes how wishes and fears, the building blocks of compromise formations and symptoms, can alter perceptions and feelings of time such as in déjà vu. In the article "Dream Space: A Story of Transformation" (a gallery display in *The Virtual Psychoanalytic Museum*, Goodman, 2015) I link fantasies about timelessness and space in exploring wishes by some female patients to negate their painful oedipal longings. Psychoanalysts relate time, space, sexuality, and phantasy and their interconnections (Birksted-Breen, 2016; Fiorini & Canestri, 2009; Perelberg, 2008). For Mr. A. it was as if timelessness were the plaster bed he carried around as a surround and as an internal presence, simultaneously protection and inability to live. Dr. Bohleber writes: "The analysis itself had become the plaster bed which constrained him and he was unable to imagine ever bringing it to conclusion."

I find it enormously interesting that it is in the enactments that new time awareness takes place, deepening the possibility to know new fantasies, powerfully felt grief, empathy, sexual desire, and murderous rage. Enactments arise to "speak" the unspeakable of terrifying psychic realities. I describe here in two sequences of action how enactments awoke Mr. A.'s internal life, his mix of trauma and unconscious fantasy.

The piercing of timelessness and awakenings

Mr. A. decides to leave treatment twice. Each time Dr. Bohleber is stunned at the turn of events. Perhaps this links to the feelings of Baby A. awakening from anesthesia in an altered world, after the placement of the body cast. Timelessness is broken by the sudden feel of rupture directly bringing the little boy's disaster into the room through Dr. Bohleber's psyche. Recollections, fantasy fragments, and capacity for grief are found in the wake of a wave of affect.

Enactment 1

Mr. A. wrote a letter to Dr. Bohleber soon after the Easter holidays (death and resurrection) in the third year of analysis announcing the end of the analysis. Dr. Bohleber describes his reaction:

> He saw no sense in continuing since he was unable to see any change in what were for him the essential areas. I was stunned and could not understand it at all. I invariably had the impression that an emotionally responsive contact had existed. Had this simply been a figment of my own imagination? I wrote a letter to him that led to his return, and for which he was very grateful.

This enactment contains elements of a fantasy that could not be spoken until the analyst felt it – that human contact might be a figment of imagination. Does this tell us that the baby became an inhuman presence in the parents' minds? Baby/Mr. A.'s psychic reality must have revolved around this basic sense that nothing about relationship could be believed. Dr. Bohleber sees Mr. A. as experiencing tremendous anxiety that he will be in "permanent" analysis, like in the cast. He tells us:

> My mentioning that unpleasure is something that can be given a space and which can be talked about seems to have been a real aha-experience for him. He explained to me that, for him, unpleasure is not something that comes and goes, but is total, and that he has the feeling that it will never pass.

Connections are made with the unthinkable traumatic feel of the past. Through this enactment affect is felt: the analyst feels stunned; the analysand feels gratitude.

When Mr. A.'s dog dies shortly after these analytic events, Dr. Bohleber is astounded by "the severity of his sorrow." It is a great advance that deep grief is felt and expressed. Soon after this, his wife leaves him and Mr. A. feels alone, desperate, and depressed. With his capacity to grieve, Mr. A. also discovers his suicidal rage. Dr. Bohleber gives him his telephone number. Again, reconstructive interpretations and the phone number provide something to hold on to that is not a rigid dead cast thus modulating the unconscious fantasy of the interminable cast and analysis.

Enactment 2

The second enactment begins with Mr. A.'s persistence in arguing with the phone company about a bill. Mr. A. is obsessed with locating the correct documents to present his case to the phone company. He cannot let go of his determination to correct the bill. In my thinking this is possibly related to repetitive contractions of anal mucosa when he could not move his legs in the cast. In a countertransference enactment, Dr. Bohleber first interprets Mr. A.'s desire for justice. I see this as a type of dream-wish that his parents be aware of their crime and his wish to prove it, accompanied by immobilizing guilt at the punishments he wanted to invoke. Dr. Bohleber then wonders out loud "whether he felt the dispute really worth the effort." Mr. A. leaves a message on the answering machine that "it made no sense to continue." Dr. Bohleber writes:

> I was not prepared for this; the abruptness of this message struck me like a mini-trauma, and I felt numbed. What had I done wrong? However, I then had the feeling that he was doing something to me that he had himself experienced, namely, being abandoned.

Mr. A. does come for his session able to speak of his feeling of having done "everything wrong." He had not been able to sleep and felt desperate. "Mr. A. began to weep heavily on the couch. Behind his rigid superego attitude a suffering self that had constantly striven to do everything correctly so as not to be dismissed or abandoned then became visible." This enactment too brought forth the combination of trauma and the intense feel of grief. The analysis continues.

There is so much in this enactment about affect, having something unjust and traumatic done to oneself and doing something to someone else, being numbed and numbing another and the solid unconscious belief that it is all one's fault. The threat to be sent away (or its reverse, the power to send away) connects to a core constellation of unconscious fantasies embedded in superego threats of disaster. More is felt and known as the "self-sufficiency and autarchic structures" (Dr. Bohleber's concept) could be released. His fantasy of being one with the cast diminished as the forced second skin gave way to his skin – what Dr. Bohleber calls being "more permeable." Dr. Bohleber tells us that the patient began to have hate towards his mother. This is a breakthrough. Soon after, Dr. Bohleber used the term "love" with his patient – that he, Mr. A., wished to be loved. This recognition awakened yearnings and desire in Mr. A.

A letter about the enactments
Letter 4: Dear Dr. Bohleber, As I read and re-read your case, I feel timelessness. It is so catchy. Perhaps the wish to find the unconscious induces timelessness, a quality Freud said we would locate there. There also can be a type of self-hypnosis around severe trauma. Henry Krystal (1978) considers this a major defense mechanism in his writing on trauma and affects. Timelessness can also be a compromise formation, an intense wish to paralyze and numb and a fear of retaliation. Mr. A. and you had a particular element in your shared psychic realities, the desire to keep him, Baby A. remembered. This may have helped to titrate Mr. A.'s attempts to almost bring about a type of suicide, the negative therapeutic reaction. It seems that he had to stay encapsulated until he could be sure there was a new container, a new object he could not murder; i.e., murder the representation of him within you. You sent him a letter meaning you were not killing the internal representation that lived in you. You became a different type of object

through constant work to bring his feelings back to the traumatic events, to the experience of his body and his fantasies, and to his excruciating certainty of abandonment and need for perfection.

After the first enactment of leaving and being found he developed renewed symptoms of urinary retention. He could not let out (nor in) with this blockage. Retention in a cement cast was necessary and provided control, no matter how frustrating. He needed to be catheterized – what a metaphor for what he wanted from his analyst. The only pleasure would be one of insertion into his body as he floated in timelessness. Oral, anal, urethral, and genital desire were off limits and when about to be felt, he sent himself away. He penetrated you to feel concern, anxiety, fear, shock, and guilt without destroying you; and, invited your penetration. Perhaps the fantasy of re-birth was more fully present – a melting into a container to then be born in a new way. Could a sense of sexual intercourse be felt around this birth? It seems to me that the ruptures of enactments made intercourse between the two of you possible – what Grotstein (2013) calls psychoanalytic sex. And, the patient began to feel sexual when he could say he did not care if his wife left him again, he would "just be alone."

The special place of metaphor formation

The plaster bed became an abiding presence and eventually metaphor in Baby/ Mr. A.'s mind, influencing the feel of self, time, relationship, and body. Over and over again the experience and fantasies about life itself could be related to the plaster cast. A true casting of a shadow onto the psyche had taken place. It is a relief to find and use metaphor and symbolic representations when confronted with the psychic helplessness of devastating trauma. For Mr. A., and for so many who experience trauma, there is the absence of an active witness, a bystander who sees and knows and acknowledges what is happening. Creation of a witness for the event brings about contact and metaphoric meaning at a distance from the trauma itself. I could see this happening in the description of this treatment. For example, Mr. A. presented the picture of his wife sitting on his shoulders and Dr. Bohleber could see this image as a monument to projective identification and a way to make known the new idea of agglutination of the object. If merged in some way, even a sadomasochistic way, abandonment and death were imagined to be averted. Creating metaphor is such a relief from the excruciating terror of trauma and in touch with and arising from unconscious forces. Dr. Bohleber (2010) has written that often metaphor is the only way to approach mass trauma. Enactment processes often provide building blocks for metaphor (Ellman & Goodman, 2012) which in turn is a pathway to unconscious fantasy. *The fantasy of* timelessness appears to have been at the center of Mr. A. and like an undefined fume was poisoning all until unconscious fantasies emerged to be interpreted and connected. Eventually the timelessness of the treatment became more like shimmering dandelion seeds floating through the air carrying the analysis to fertile places by landing in transference and countertransference and in the desire to be loved.

Last letter and love

Letter 5: Dear Dr. Bohleber, I have some thoughts to share with you about writing my letters as I tried to face the trauma and terrifying unconscious fantasies and beliefs that took root in Baby/Mr. A.'s psyche. Thank you for being the receiver of Mr. A. so I could see you receiving my letters. How Mr. A. must have longed to hear from his parents, to metaphorically receive letters. Writing letters is like analytic love. When you mentioned love to your patient, it brought about transformation. He had not recognized how much he wanted love. The plaster cast barrier had been erected to prevent pain and preserve some form and substance. Nothing could get in and nothing could leak out. In this way a wished for time bomb that could destroy, in a conflagration of self and all others, could be contained. You never gave up – holding your patient in mind even when he wanted to destroy in order to break the anxiety of timelessness, nothingness, and engulfment. Mr. A. became a man who could feel and empathize with his own suffering. Revelations broke through the plaster cast.

I also want to mention something about the primitive universal unconscious fantasies that were nascent in Baby/Mr. A.'s mind. I imagine that any wish, to get inside Mommy, to compete with Daddy, to be touched and fed and stimulated, to play and dance, to attack and wrestle, to feel sexual with another were thwarted and went underground but were not forgotten. The real trauma makes persecution, castration, annihilation too imminent, too real. Perhaps there were aspects of the primitive unconscious in the enactments and in the symbolic narratives especially when the barriers softened and empathy for suffering took place.

Conclusion

This case shows psychoanalytic process in a case of childhood trauma. Fragments of unconscious traumata and fantasy beliefs and stories were able to become known. The finding of the traumatic experience and the fantasies related to it and arising from it were developed into metaphor through transference and countertransference awareness and major enactments discovering landscapes in the fog of timelessness. In his write-up of the case, Dr. Bohleber was attentive to "the long-term effects of traumatization occurring in early childhood." He wondered about the impact of early trauma on later development and adaptation. I am interested in how the traumatic intersects with development of fantasy life, particularly unconscious fantasy. How does the deadness of severe trauma, the unrepresented, work into unconscious, even primal fantasy life, and how do developing oedipal and pre-oedipal fantasy constructions incorporate elements of the traumatic to augment unconscious scenes already taking shape? I have a fantasy that the instinctually exciting and terrifying internal and the traumatic external produce chemical reactions and interactions creating new substances, new psychic realities. Or perhaps it is like physics, like some form of unseen but explosive energy that is ignited when internal traumatic fantasy and external traumatic catastrophe meet.

References

Arlow, J. A. (1969). Unconscious fantasy and disturbances of conscious experience. *Psychoanalytic Quarterly, 38*, 1–27.

Bick, E. (1968). The experience of the skin in early object relations. *International Journal of Psychoanalysis, 49*, 484–486.

Birksted-Breen, D. (2016). *The work of psychoanalysis: sexuality, time, and the psychoanalytic mind*. London: Routledge.

Bohleber, W. (2010). *Destructiveness, intersubjectivity, and trauma: The identity crisis of modern psychoanalysis*. London: Karnac.

Bohleber, W. (2015). The psychoanalytic treatment of an adult traumatized in early childhood. IPA Pre-Congress Trauma Group, Boston, July 21–12.

Bowlby, J. (1969). *Attachment and loss: Volume I: Attachment*. New York: Basic Books.

Dorfman, A. (1991). *Death and the maiden*. London: Nick Hern Books.

Dorfman, A. (1999). *Heading south, looking north: A bilingual journey*. New York: Penguin.

Ellman, P. L., & Goodman, N. R. (2012). Enactment: Opportunity for symbolizing trauma. In A. Frosch (Ed.), *Absolute truth and unbearable psychic pain: Psychoanalytic perspectives on concrete experience*. London: Karnac.

Fiorini, L. C., & Canestri, J. (2009). *The experience of time: Psychoanalytic perspectives*. London: Karnac.

Goodman, N. R. (2012). The power of witnessing. In N. R. Goodman, & M. Meyers (Eds.), *The power of witnessing: Reflections, reverberations, and traces of the Holocaust – trauma, psychoanalysis, and the living mind* (pp. 3–26). New York: Routledge.

Goodman, N. R. (2015). *Dream space: A story of transformation*. Retrieved August 18, 2016, from The Virtual Psychoanalytic Museum, www.virtualpsychoanalyticmuseum.org/. New York: IPBooks.

Grotstein, J. S. (2013). Discussion of the case of Mr. B. In H. I. Basseches, P. L. Ellman, & N. R. Goodman (Eds.), *Battling the life and death forces of sadomasochism*. London: Karnac.

Krystal, H. (1978). Trauma and affects. *Psychoanalytic Study of the Child, 33*, 81–116.

Laub, D. (1992). Bearing witness or the vicissitudes of listening. In S. Felman, & D. Laub, *Testimony: Crises of witnessing in literature, psychoanalysis, and history* (pp. 57–74). New York: Routledge.

Laub, D., & Auerhahn, N. C. (1993). Knowing and not knowing massive psychic trauma: Forms of traumatic memory. *International Journal of Psychoanalysis, 74*, 287–302.

Loewald, H. W. (1962). Internalization, separation, mourning, and the superego. *Psychoanalytic Quarterly, 38*, 483–504.

Perelberg, J. P. (2008). *Time, space and phantasy*. London: Routledge.

Spitz, R. A. (1945). Hospitalism – An inquiry into the genesis of psychiatric conditions in early childhood. *Psychoanalytic Study of the Child, 1*, 153–174.

Chapter 6

Unconscious phantasy

Discussion of Werner Bohleber's case

*Elias M. da Rocha Barros and
Elizabeth L. da Rocha Barros*

Werner Bohleber presents us with striking and moving clinical material about a patient traumatized due to a forced immobilization, for medical reasons, when the patient was an 18-month-old baby. Bohleber then expounds his thoughts and reflections on the relations that hold between past traumas and their repercussions on the current life of patients, a theme that he has been carefully pursuing in the last years. Bohleber's work is challenging both in its clinical descriptions and in its impact on trauma theory.

In Bohleber's paper, we are introduced to a patient – a Mr. A. – who has been living his life, in our view, permanently enacting an unconscious phantasy that probably originated in a real life situation that caused him great suffering and anxiety. We will be discussing the nature of this phantasy in the following pages.

When Mr. A. was an 18-month-old baby, he had to be immobilized in a plaster bed, an experience that lasted for nine months. During this period, he was abruptly separated from his parents, who were not allowed to visit him for the first six weeks, by medical prescription, but who, even after the lifting of the visiting ban, failed to do so in a regular way. As an adult, Mr. A. suffers from panic attacks in his sleep, which manifest themselves as a sensation of not being able to move his body, even after insistent attempts. Furthermore, Mr. A. frequently feels imprisoned in a desperately small space. These feelings and sensations seem to repeat themselves and reappear in a number of different ways throughout a vast number of Mr. A.'s life experiences: e.g., Mr. A. has been repeatedly abandoning different employments after brief periods due to feelings of claustrophobia. A recurrent dream, mentioned by Bohleber in his description of this clinical material, goes in a similar direction. All in all, Mr. A.'s anxieties suggest an amazing analogy with the situation he lived through as a baby.

Before we move on in our commentary, we would like to take a step back in order to characterize what we understand as being "unconscious phantasy." For us, *unconscious phantasy* is, prior to anything else, *an unconscious way of thinking* that acquires certain stability by generating a *kernel of meaning(s)* that operates as an organizer of psychic life by creating links with other emotional experiences. *Traumatic unconscious phantasies give form* to lived-through experiences that were initially incomprehensible or unbearable. Yet, when becoming *kernels of meaning(s)*, these traumatic unconscious phantasies also *deform* other emotional experiences associated with them, resulting in a congealed and deforming way of attributing meaning to emotional experiences. Susan Isaacs (1952) suggests that one of the roles of unconscious phantasy is to transform sensory/bodily experiences into elements of "mental life." She also considers all mental processes and mental mechanisms as forms of unconscious phantasy when observed from the perspective of inner mental life. These ways and forms of thinking embodied in unconscious phantasies do not merely attribute meanings to our lives, but transform us into *agents* who *unconsciously* create internal and external scenes that have an enormous gravitational pull in molding our lives.

In our perspective, the reading of Susan Isaacs suggested by Thomas Ogden (2012) led us to a renewed understanding of the concept of unconscious phantasy, more attuned to our clinical experience of 30 years.

Ogden (2012) writes:

> A good deal of the importance of Isaacs' (1952) contribution lies in her groundbreaking conception of the work of phantasy, which she clearly and systematically presents. And yet, I find that much of what makes Isaacs' contribution pivotal to the development of psychoanalytic theory in the twentieth and twenty-first centuries resides in what is only implicit in her paper. Specifically, it seems to me that Isaacs does not fully recognize that her paper is not a paper about the nature and function of phantasy, but a paper about the nature and the function of phantasying, i.e. it is a paper primarily about thinking as opposed to a paper about thoughts.
>
> (pp. 34–35)

It is the work of phantasy that shapes psychic life and allows for its great plasticity throughout all stages of our development. Its role is very *active* in the shaping and organizing of mental life, and in generating meaning.

This conception of the work of phantasy implies the existence of an internal world in which the meaning of emotional experience is something *gradually construed and open to shape shifting*. In other words, meaning generated by the work of phantasy is not a static thing, but a constant outpour of ways of organizing emotional experiences throughout life. It is these outflows generated by unconscious phantasies that we have given the name "kernels of meaning."

These kernels are constituted of unconscious phantasies formed around internal objects, which, as structures of the ego, function as complex magnetic poles that organize emotional experiences. These phantasies operate as internal unconscious molds that attribute meaning to affective experiences as if they were structures. It is through these kernels of meaning that unconscious phantasies continue to exert organizational power over emotional life and, as such, generate lasting mental states.

In this chapter we are using the terms "affect" and "emotional experience" as synonymous. Freud himself (*apud* Green, 1999, p. 17) justified this equivalence of the terms when referring to his own translation of the word *Affekt* as "emotive state" in his article "Obsession and Phobia," originally written in French.

We find in the work of Marcelo Viñar (2004) a useful and insightful definition of trauma:

> Yo llamaría hoy trauma o situación traumática al hecho de que este metabolismo perpetuo de autoconstrucción se vea invadido, inundado o excedido por una situación que el psiquismo no puede significar, o no puede modificar y se rompe o *interrumpe la producción simbólica que funda la existencia psíquica* y transitoria o definitivamente se crea un agujero o un desgarro que se requiere remendar.

> (Based on my clinical experience and reflections on the matter I will call trauma or traumatic situation to the fact that this perpetual metabolic activity of self building is invaded, flooded, or exceeded by an amount of pulsional excitement that the psyche cannot signify and therefore cannot change that which breaks or interrupts the symbolic production that is foundational to the psychic existence and produces temporarily or definitely a hole or a tear that keeps requiring to be mended.)

Given this theoretical interlude, we would now like to return to the paper and the clinical material by Bohleber. It seems to us that Mr. A.'s traumatic experience of being suddenly immobilized in a strange place and away from his parents, at a very young age when he still did not have the means to cope and understand what was happening to him, led to the production of one or more unconscious phantasies that still hold him "captive," limiting his range of mental and emotional "movements" (his thoughts and phantasies).

It is important to underline that Mr. A.'s experience happened at an age when his ability to comprehend and to come to terms with what was happening to him was very limited. Our hypothesis is that initially the activity of phantasyzing had the function of offering to "Baby A." both an "explanation" and an expression of the horror he was living through; a means for comprehending, metabolizing, and defending himself against the insufferable anxieties he must have been experiencing. Could we venture to imagine that, at this point in his life, Baby A. might have construed an unconscious phantasy where his hip dislocation neurological illness (luxation) was responsible for his "abandonment" maybe felt as a "punishment?"

It is never easy to put into words the contents of an unconscious phantasy. These encompass a wide range of things – unconscious desires, wishful thinking, etc. – that are organized in a scene, or in scene-like fragments, that, even though they are mental representations, cannot be exclusively described and understood through the concept of unconscious representation. We would like to suggest that a potentially useful way of looking at them might be through an analogy with the neurological notion of an *engram*. An engram is not a mold, but a sophisticated *matrix* that functions as a kind of template for the organization of emotional experience in the unconscious around kernels of meaning.

Lear (2011, p. 47) suggests that an unconscious phantasy is *a unifier of the self, or part selves*. Mr. A.'s traumatic experience seems to have resulted in an unconscious phantasy that then became a generator of meaning to a large number of experiences throughout his life, including his affective relationships, his professional life, and the ways in which he dealt with all experiences of loss.

We are not told many details about the day-to-day experience of being immobilized in the clinic. We are not told, for example, how Mr. A. was fed, how he bathed, how the nurses and caregivers dealt with his bowel movements, nor are we told whether there were people talking with him, explaining what was taking place, stimulating him, nor if there were things for him to play with. In other words, we know next to nothing about how his bodily and mental needs were met. We know nothing of his linguistic skills at the time, and we can also only have a very crude idea of how his physical development responded to this plaster bed. Was the plaster remade from time to time in order to accommodate for growth? Was there any wiggle room within the plaster? Surely Baby A. must have experienced muscular pains due to his immobility and have suffered from harrowing skin sensations (such as itching)? Perhaps we are afforded a glimpse of how his caregivers dealt with his urination needs due to an episode in his later life, retold by Bohleber. During an episode of urinary retention that happened while Mr. A. was enjoying a summer holiday, a catheter had to be inserted in him in order to treat it. Bohleber's understanding of this episode is very smart and keenly sensitive:

> Urinary retention seemed to have a dual function: first, it appeared like a final bastion for asserting himself against the demands of others, while, second, it was like a defence against letting himself go.

Even lacking the aforementioned details and information, it is not hard to imagine the anxiety experienced by Baby A., who had very limited resources to fashion modes of expression or ways of projecting them so that these formless anxieties could be metabolized by a container. Baby A. was only rarely visited by his parents and was looked after by multiple caregivers, so that he had meager opportunities to establish firm bonding with specific individuals. When we use the term "metabolize" we wish to suggest that the mind in producing symbolic forms obeys a need to interpret or understand one's self, in a continual mental work process and, as such, of *working through* psychic suffering. In the case of Baby A., his chances of metabolizing his experiences were severely hindered by his traumatic experience.

We know today that phantasies associated with misunderstood or poorly metabolized projective identifications return to the ego, they take the shape of nameless dread or misdirected horror. For example, Baby A. might have misinterpreted his imprisonment in his plaster bed as resulting from some awful wrongdoing and, therefore, as deserved punishment for his evil actions. This could explain the reason why Mr. A., during his whole analysis, always felt the need to prove and show that he was not "a bad guy," as Bohleber points out on several occasions: due to the thwarted metabolization of a traumatic experience, Mr. A. was unable to develop much empathy for himself. In his unconscious phantasies he could have identified with a suffering maternal object and devoid of love and sense of care.

This pattern of deep mental organization led to an obstruction of Mr. A.'s capacity to constitute himself as a proper person, and even arrested his capacity of symbolization, which could have led to the possibility of living his suffering as a fully functioning human being, with the capacity to ponder over what happened to him. Therein lies the *traumatic* nature of his childhood experiences. Due to an "arrested" capacity for symbolic metabolism, Mr. A. was *lived by* (Ogden, 2001) the feelings that overtook Baby A. Without being able to develop into a "thinking self" (in the Thomas Ogden sense of the expression), the patient was unable to reflect on his sufferings and thereby metabolize them. A traumatic situation is created that pervades the patient's entire life and that reasserts itself indefinitely while being inaccessible to consciousness, although its features remain traceable on the horizon.

Under these conditions, the patient is incapable of developing an adult self and remains imprisoned in the precarious ways and phantasies of his childhood self. The probable result of this is an impossibility of developing empathy with his suffering self. We have the conditions for the fostering of what Luiz Meyer (2013) has called a "nefarious dynamic" described as a:

> conflict between knowledge and crudeness, between the transparent and the opaque, between the struggles of the infantile to co-opt the adult and the efforts of the adult to understand the infantile. Each one of these parts will try to impose its vision upon the other, in an attempt to give the experience a univocal meaning, if not a totalitarian one.
>
> (p. 4)

We believe that such a nefarious dynamic must have taken over Mr. A.'s internal world, with the infantile aspects of his mind imposing a totalitarian dominion, never allowing his mind to metabolize and work through his suffering and pain, therefore never allowing his adult self to truly and fully develop, rendering Mr. A. paralyzed and congealed even in adulthood. In a sense, he never left the plaster bed.

This totalitarian dominion of the infantile probably took shape as an unconscious phantasy that then became the organizer of his psychic life, with special powers over situations that might cause anxiety. At this point, not being the patient's analysts, we can only surmise what the nature and contents of these unconscious phantasies could be. Our hypothesis would be that Mr. A. construed himself as the cause of all his sufferings, misinterpreted as the rightful retribution/punishment for being a naughty baby, a bad person. Of course this phantasy does not manifest itself verbally in the patient's mind, but operates as an engram that immobilizes and restrains the adult, making him feel as always on the verge of being "caught" and perceived as that bad boy who deserved all that he got.

Given the traumatic nature of the event, i.e., given that we have an excess or overflow of multiple and diverse feelings of anxiety that neither Mr. A.'s baby-self nor his adult-self can fully elaborate, we end up with a paralyzed and congealed situation. This situation of mental immobility or paralysis expresses itself in Mr. A.'s life in many variations or transmutations of the unconscious phantasy of the traumatic immobilization as legitimate and due punishment. Among the expressions of this unconscious phantasy we would like to call attention to a few.

An interesting first impression we get from Mr. A. is that he seems to project his paralysis onto his interlocutor by evoking in his interlocutor an equivalent sentiment of immobility that manifests itself as a feeling of hopelessness in being able to help him in any way.

Devoid of the inner capacity to construe symbols that would allow him to think over his life and experiences in a more adult way, Mr. A. becomes incapable of conceiving and living life as a gradual, sometimes naturally painful or pleasurable complex process of living through and acquiring experiences that would help him construe a feeling of self-respect that could lead to self-esteem. As a result of this, Mr. A. lives his life as an experience of timelessness, as something that does not move, progress, or flow. He is congealed and paralyzed in time.

Devoid also of a shifting and ever-evolving perception of himself, Mr. A. is stuck with Baby A.'s unconscious phantasy about himself. Mr. A. is haunted by a feeling that he is a bad person and from this, perhaps, stems his imperious need to be liked and appreciated by others, a need that becomes a famished compulsion that expresses itself as a submission to others, especially in intimate relationships: Mr. A.'s relationship to his first wife might be a case in point. He feels a domineering need to always please, to never be a bad boy, and therefore has no room to explore who he really might be. After all, he lives in constant fear of being unmasked and exposed as a fraud. The patient feels he is essentially a bad person and does not believe that he can be seen otherwise.

The paralyzing and frozen state of mind we are talking about seems to have two levels. On a first lever, it refers to a stagnation in the patient's capacity to produce adequate symbols to represent and think in an adult way about his traumatic experience and the phantasies that ensued. On a second level, the patient's paralysis expresses itself as a corporeal sensation of being stuck or imprisoned.

Perhaps Mr. A.'s necessity to abandon his job after a brief period stems from his frozen vision of life and the many implications of this view of life as a kind of paralysis. When will his naughtiness and meanness be found out? How long can he get away with it? His unconscious line of thought could be "perhaps I should quit now before anyone discovers what a bad boy I've been and they lock me up in plaster once again." Mr. A. is driven by a compulsive need to abandon his work, or his analyst, in order not to be abandoned himself. Life for him becomes black and white, pervaded by a twisted logic of totalitarian absolutes: he either abandons or is abandoned. This is all a result of his unifying unconscious phantasy.

It is probable that his original trauma (being abandoned by his parents and imprisoned in a plaster bed) has gradually become associated with other traumas or has colored a number of his life experiences so as to produce a situation of incapacitated mental functioning, giving Mr. A. the constant sense of being invaded and attacked by a number of uncontrollable forces and objects. This could have led to his predominant sense of constant vulnerability.

Britton (1998) uses the term "psychophobia" to refer to a traumatic state in which the patient's ego loses its capacity to think and to dream. With this restraint, the patient loses his or her ability to transform experience into rich symbolic representations. In these comments we are suggesting that traumatic experiences affect above all else the patient's capacity to express emotions in a more plastic or flexible way, an essential and basic component to the capacity to construe and deal with symbols.

Bohleber does not tell us a great deal about his countertransference, but when he mentions his own feelings, these are very vivid and informative. Right at the beginning of his description of his patient, Bohleber writes:

> Though what he told me was vivid, I was unable to gain access to his feelings. My impression was that he was closed within himself, as if he were a closed cylinder from which I would slide off.

Our impression is that, despite the vivacity of the facts that happened to him, Mr. A.'s expressive abilities were very limited. And it is our patient's expressive capabilities that give us access to them. It was Mr. A.'s ability to symbolically represent his feelings of imprisonment and immobility that led to what Bohleber calls a "shock-induced frozen state." For example, in the recurrent dream in which Mr. A. "clung on to something, or he found himself in very small rooms that he was unable to leave." Nevertheless, Mr. A. was unable to understand the deeper meaning of these symbols in such a way as to transform this situation of pure nameless suffering, thereby being able to elaborate it through thought and through an understanding of its multiple and complex meanings. The symbolic forms that represent the situation of being immobilized, and the anxieties associated with it, will constitute the core of his unconscious phantasy. In our opinion, Mr. A. lacks the resources to access the expressive aspects of these symbols that would allow him to recapture his feelings as a child and reflect on them side-by-side with his experiences and emotions as an adult. He simply feels immobilized in a perpetual state of melancholy. Here we have an elegant illustration of what Melanie Klein (1975, p. 136) called "*memories in feelings*": in his unconscious phantasy, Mr. A. possibly blamed his mother for all his sufferings while stuck to his plaster bed, but also felt himself the deserving party to this suffering, as one guilty of causing great suffering to his mother due to his bad deeds. But these phantasies have remained frozen in a mental childhood and split from all his other experiences. It is our belief that in order to work through an unconscious phantasy, one needs to revive this phantasy in a richly expressive way so as to access what we have called its kernels of meaning.

In a previous paper (Rocha Barros & Rocha Barros, 2011) we have developed the idea that a harmonious personality keeps in touch with its kernels of meaning in an integrated manner, and thus maintains a live contact with its emotional history. We hypothesize that the capacity for expressiveness and therefore the contact with more expanded connotative aspects of the experiences depends on this live contact, above all with more infantile kernels.

This emphasis on the importance of remaining in touch with the infantile kernels of the psychic apparatus requires some reflection. In the child the unconscious world is less distant from consciousness than in the adult. The border between them is more fluid. Because the unconscious mode of functioning is not discursive and is more closely based on intuitive contact with internal emotional reality based on presentational connotative symbolism which is the more proper form to carry mental states and feelings, it is more subject to the anxieties and expressive forms of representation of experience. Hence the greater dramatic and evocative power in the world of emotions also results in greater freedom of imagination from the conscious and unconscious point of view. Riccardo Steiner (2009, personal communication) considers Bion's alpha-function as a semiotic function essential to feed unconscious imagination. The relative loss of this contact with emotion does not completely prevent dreams from being generated, but may render it difficult to grasp the emotions transmitted by the symbols, making them more difficult to understand.

Past experiences on being transformed into memories become "embedded or embodied in a virtual dimension mediating between the real objects and us" (Innis, 2009, p. 63). These memories become accessible through visual images (presentational symbolism) that appear in dreams and that virtually have a tendency to turn metaphorical. "*Metaphorical seeing*" as Langer understands it, involves a semantic displacement from the primary object meaning, which a symbolic image, or symbolic functioning image, has, *to its transferred sense, a displacement based*, she claims, *on a "logical analogy*" (Innis, 2009, p. 64 and Langer, 1942). It is this semantic displacement that facilitates the elaboration of an unconscious phantasy generated by a traumatic experience or situation.

We believe that the normal superego is construed from a person's earliest relationships, while the abnormal superego arises from the earliest and:

> its dangerous aims is to dissociate the patient to attack the link with the object, the features both Freud and Abraham emphasized as crucial, since it is upon the link with the object that the safety of the ego depends.
>
> (O'Shaughnessy, 2015, p. 179)

We believe it was under similar conditions that Baby A. was led to form an internal figure functioning as an exactor of punishment and a pointer of failure: an abnormal state of mind in the mother condemning the baby for most likely not matching her "anticipated ideal" like the patient described by O'Shaughnessy. Perhaps we find here another source for Mr. A.'s sense of meaninglessness, which led to his perpetual melancholic mood.

Finally we would like to add a few words on how we perceive the analyst's function as an agent of psychic change. Through his interpretations, the analyst renders visible (in the sense of imagery) and meaningful the unconscious mental representations of emotional situations. By these means, the patient re-articulates meanings from distinct symbolic fields, opening up new possibilities of experience and creating new meanings left in an incomplete state, which expand the possibilities for emotional development.

The analyst's work, therefore, goes beyond the unveiling, or the revelation, of meanings that have been hidden by repression. By interpreting the internal tension produced by an absence of meaning, which, by its very nature, can never be rendered explicit, the analyst creates new meanings.

References

Britton, R. (1998). *Belief and imagination*. London and New York: Routledge.

Green, A. (1999). On discriminating and not discriminating between affect and representation. *International Journal of Psychoanalysis, 80,* 277.

Innis, R. E. (2009). *Susanne Langer in focus: The symbolic mind*. Bloomington, IN, and Indianapolis: Indiana University Press.

Isaacs, S. (1952). The nature and function of phantasy. In J. Riviere (Ed.), *Developments of psychoanalysis* (pp. 62–121). London: Hogarth Press.

Klein, M. (1975). *Narratives of a child analysis*. London: The Hogarth Press.

Langer, S. (1942). *Philosophy in a new key*. Cambridge, MA: Harvard University Press.

Lear, J. (2011). A case for irony in *The Tanner Lectures on Human Values*. Cambridge, MA: Harvard University Press.

Meyer, L. (2013). Forum Teórico-Clínico: Sonhos. Lecture presented at the Brazilian Psychoanalytic Society of São Paulo on March 13, 2013.

Ogden, T. (1994). *Subjects of analysis*. Northvale, NJ: Jason Aronson/London Karnac.

Ogden, T. (2001). *Conversations at the frontier of dreaming*. Northvale, NJ, and London: Jason Aronson.

Ogden, T. (2012). Reading Susan Isaacs: Toward a radical revised theory of thinking in *Creative Readings*. London and New York: Routledge.

O'Shaughnessy, E. (2015). Relating to the superego. In C. Mawson (Ed.), *Bion Today* (pp. 173–187). London: Routledge.

Rocha Barros, E., & Rocha Barros, E. (2011). Reflections on the clinical implications of symbolism. *International Journal of Psychoanalysis, 92*(4), 879–901.

Viñar, M. (2004). Noción de trauma en psicoanálisis y campos afines. *Boletín de la Asociación Psicoanalítica Argentina, 72,* 89.

Chapter 7

A Soma case of pain

Paula L. Ellman

She walks in, sits down on the edge of her chair, and looks at me.

She is stiff and erect and her face is red.

She speaks about muscles and bones wrapping around her face. She pulls her face to the left, saying it is always the left side. She chuckles with embarrassment, self-consciousness. She pulls her face to the left, pulls her lips and mouth to the left and tells me "I need to do this … it's the only way … the bones are breaking inside." Each time she pulls her face she speaks about the trauma, the nights of sleep and being hit in the head. I feel as if I am throwing the punch that causes her face to twist to the left. The pain, she says is unbearable – her face, her mouth squeezes to the left. She has to keep moving it (what is it?). This is how she relieves the pain.

A 50-year-old biochemist, (Margaret) recently married, was raised in a small town in the North Carolina mountains. Her family lineage is rooted in the town where her family has owned local businesses. After a number of years of psychotherapy, the patient entered psychoanalysis looking for further relief from her disabling somatic symptoms: severe pains throughout her body and sharp pain in her scalp, neck, and jaw. She also complained of ongoing stomach pain that she had endured since early childhood. While she believed to have found a solution by identifying a food allergy, she also clings to a belief in the post-traumatic effects from a head injury at 5 years old.

Early on, Margaret was fascinated with the biology of animals and plants. Frequently, her grandfather engaged her with a high-powered microscope. Also, she remembers long hours with her father as he established and maintained a mountain-top campground. In comparison with her fascination with the world beyond, the world within her family walls was suffocating and empty. Margaret's familial culture put a premium on physical appearance and with a precise prescription. Women had to be thin and hair coifed in a particular "poofy" way. From the time Margaret was a young girl, her mother regularly put permanent curls into her "much too limp hair." Makeup was always heavily applied, even while at home. Margaret's mother, aunts, and grandparents focused on maintaining their homes and selves, sleeping with hair curlers and hairnets, and fixing makeup fastidiously every morning and throughout the day. Margaret's mother's hobby was collecting dolls, perfectly dressed and coifed, and on display throughout the house, seeming to provide her with the pleasure that real life, with her alive and human daughters, could not bring her. She had complete control over the presentation of her dolls – immobile and "beautiful." Margaret's mother concerned herself with appearance and her preoccupation with Margaret's appearance brought criticisms of her hair, poking at her protruding stomach and a forced regulation of her diet and bowel function. She administered enemas while Margaret was positioned on all fours, wedged into the bathroom corner "to give my mother leverage." Margaret remembers her childhood fantasy play: she was a dog on all fours barking and running freely inside and out. She wonders if the nature of her fantasy play was evoked by the enema positioning where she felt more dog than human. Family control was central. Margaret has the memory of being fed cookie after cookie while moving down the supermarket aisles in order to keep her quiet. Her mother took over what went in her and what came out.

Frequent extended family celebrations were often the staging ground for the sadism of older male relatives. They held her underwater or tickled her for far too long. At one holiday season event Margaret remembers her hopeful expectations opening a gift from an older adolescent male cousin, only to find dog feces inside. The peals of laughter from her family left her feeling painfully degraded. Summer trips to Florida in the family recreational vehicle necessitated excessive, at times, unbearably tortuous bowel and bladder control as Margaret's father limited the stops. Family hugs were absent, even greetings were rare, with Margaret expecting not more than a nod of a head.

Margaret's schooling in this mountain town, as well as living with her family, continued through college. Her academic efforts and capacities established her as a top student. Also, Margaret was driven and excelled at music and drama. Her drivenness extended into many areas. For example, while in high school she decided that since her school had never had a homecoming parade, she would single-handedly organize one. She became the marching band leading majorette early on in college, and took leads in many musical productions. As with all of her involvements, she did not expect recognition. Margaret believes that her many successes set her up as a scapegoat. She remembers working on the musical scenery set in her middle school art class and being dragged behind the set and covered with paint. Also, as lead majorette in high school and exempt from rainy day practices of marching in the mud, the band players lifted her up and threw her in a mud pit. Margaret is puzzled by what incited such sadistic acts of contempt by her classmates and family as she describes her ambitious efforts at every project or activity. She gave unending hours to art and theater projects. She perfected her abilities in band and music endeavors through long practices. She ingratiated herself to her teachers, unaware of the enraging envy-arousing impact this likely had on her peers. Within her family it was only her grandfather who took an interest in Margaret's intellect, ambition, and accomplishments.

As a peerless female college student pursuing a science track, Margaret faced challenges. The male faculty demeaned Margaret often relegating her to providing the coffee for the group. Her science professor's discouraging words when he witnessed her engagement ring did not deter her from moving from her mountain town to a major university to pursue her postgraduate education and a career in the biochemical sciences. Margaret was able to reach into the world beyond to free herself for her further development, educationally, professionally, and psychologically. However, her move away brought the onset of a multitude of somatic symptoms: swollen hands, painful scalp, unbearable intestinal distress, the pain frequently traveling from place to place in her body. Margaret repeatedly returns in her associations to the years of her post-doc when she became dangerously anorexic, her weight falling under 100 pounds. This was set in motion by excruciating abdominal pain occurring whenever she ate. Her anorexia was reinforced by the praise and compliments she received from the women in her family for how fabulous she looked and, in fact, it seemed to them that she looked the best she ever had. Only with the serious concern expressed by her roommate at the time did she get medical attention to determine a diagnosis of an allergy, then bringing the needed adjustments in her diet. She also availed herself, for the first time, of psychotherapy. She entered psychoanalysis 15 years ago.

The early part of her analysis was like a performance and I was her invisible audience behind the couch. Each hour was (and is) a performance-like presentation of her emotional state where I serve as "container" for her outpourings. Margaret kept me in my place behind the couch, perhaps even wedged there, so that I was not the mother who wedges her into a corner to insert into her or take out of her what I want. Margaret showed interest in bringing me into more contact with her with her request to move from the analytic couch to sitting up face to face. She was attentive to my appearance and self-conscious of her own, and also expressed her feeling of safety that I could be more "with her" with her seeing me. There is a pressure to looking and being looked at – a demand to keep my focus on her as she did not avert her gaze from my eyes. Her "overworked" manner had a dramatic dissociative quality reminiscent of her years of theater performances – controlled and purposeful. Margaret's descriptions are as if she is a shell, a *cylinder* of motivation, competence, and interest, but without an authentic connection and ownership. She rigorously pursues her interests but in a way that suggests that she has not internalized them. What appears internalized is Margaret's way of bending to the forces of the object to mitigate any distress, both internally and externally. She consistently overworks at science, theater, and music, often seeming used, taken advantage of, by others. Never could she consider standing up to or disagreeing with others, yielding to whatever she came up against. She describes staying up all night to complete, on her own, the design and construction of a theater set. Unselfconsciously she describes her oppression at work at the hands of supervisors and her readiness to overwork to compensate for her graduate students' shortcomings. Since being in her analysis she refuses assignments, as well as sets limits with her supervisors and graduate students who fall short on their responsibilities. Margaret's description of herself early on in her studies and throughout her professional development and career is as if she is a shell, a container of motivation, competence, and interest, but without the connection to and ownership of it. This is her compromise: she pursues her interests but in a way that suggests that she has not internalized them. Both in the displacement and transference of her psychoanalysis, she is gradually and painfully becoming aware of what she does as a reflection of her having little sense of self-ownership. Dissociation is rampant. The search for unconscious fantasy when trauma, dissociation, and somatic expression fill the analytic space is particularly challenging. Margaret's psychoanalysis fills out the picture of her early world. This rural home was one where little remained private, bringing a hyper-vigilance about one's impact on surrounding others. Margaret's mother was forever concerned about disturbing others and believed that Margaret's achievements were an imposition, a burden. Everything had to be equal; no one could excel and stand out, averting the risk of arousing envy. Even in the context of family relationships, Margaret's successes went unrecognized. The paradox between hyper-visibility publicly and invisibility privately is stunning. Intimacy is severely curtailed. Margaret's parents lived parallel lives, infrequently coming together as a family. Her father retreated from the family, launching a campground business in the remote mountains where he situated himself three seasons a year, seldom sleeping at home. Her mother was immersed in caring for her younger sister, ill with childhood diabetes. The two parents did not share the marital bedroom. Margaret recalls experiencing her father's move to a greater distance from her as she entered puberty, describing a memory of her father's disgust at discovering evidence of her menses. Margaret's invisibility is starkly apparent in her description of her visits home when the television remains the center of family life and acknowledgment of her entering the home is absent. There are never expressions of affection, even at times of greeting or parting.

While my countertransference includes my identification with Margaret's invisibility, I also have some experience of being taken in by Margaret. Her brittle self-presentation developed into a kind of softening to her spoken word and a naturalizing of her appearance. Margaret shifted from permed sprayed hair, to naturally styled hair; from heavy makeup, to barely any. This change in her external appearance suggests a comparable internal shift of greater accessibility and openness to a relationship with me. The challenges of her marriage capture her struggle with relatedness. Frequently Margaret insists on keeping separate bedrooms, stating that her husband's snoring is disruptive and she needs her time apart. Closeness seems impossible, though she identifies a longing to feel close to her husband: "I follow him around everywhere, like a puppy dog." Her husband desperately wants children. Yet with Margaret not giving birth to her own psychological self, or even imagining her own birth, she is unable to understand the wish for procreativity and generativity.

A recent dream illustrative of Margaret's sense of fragmentation carries aspects of an unconscious fantasy.

> My body is in pieces in compartments in a box. It is not bloodied and still alive, but in pieces, with my head, my limbs and all my body parts in separate compartments. There is another person also in pieces just next to me. Then I had another dream where I am large and am holding the box with all the body parts and tending to them. I am going to help put these pieces together.

I consider that I must be "the other person in pieces just next to her" and with our mutual effort, we will assemble the parts. Margaret works hard, often overworks, to bring me her ideas, not allowing room to hear from me, not seeming to take me in. On the surface, she values the treatment: she comes on time, pays on time, and appears committed to our work. However, the curtailing of a deepening of the transference relationship along with her profound psychosomatic expression is communicative of a dissociative process that holds her trauma and makes so very crucial the finding the unconscious fantasy.

Recent process material focuses in on the body pain as an expression of unconscious fantasy in the psyche: clinical material from three consecutive hours, emails, and a last session.

Unconscious fantasy/the body-mind

Session I: in the room

MARGARET: I never had a normal sleep cycle. There is physical damage. Depression is the side effect of trauma. I am inflamed when I wake up. My face is red – like someone comes into my bedroom at night and smashes me in the face and smashes my body and smashes me down. Red, bruised, a rash…. Like there are tiny white pieces popping out of my face. Like sand. Little tiny bones. Remnants of the bones that have been broken up that my body is pushing out.

ANALYST: You're telling me of the assault on your body. When you sleep your face is not red and inflamed, but during the night something absolutely awful happens.

MARGARET: My body is processing something – something horrific.

ANALYST: You want me to see that when your mind is at rest, is when the horror begins. (*I am thinking that this is an association to thoughts about the couch and feeling at rest with me in the hour brings the danger of contact.*)

MARGARET: There is a gash, an internal one. It is moving to my nose from my left eye. It feels like I had a brick in my face. My skull is broken. It comes down out of my nose cavity, through the left of my head and palate. It lines up with the lower part of my jaw. When they were manipulating my jaw (*referring to a physical therapist a year earlier*) it compacted me. I want to sue my doctor – the guy that I went to for my jaw.

ANALYST: They were manipulating you – there is such danger that comes with contact. (*Something about the mouth, speaking, eating, at the mercy of the assaulting object. Margaret believes she is vulnerable to my manipulation, as if it is a psychic rape.*)

MARGARET: They pinched my nerve and my jaw. It was abusive. (*Margaret is tearful*) – I was there for help. He said you don't need physical therapy; you need an appliance. He made me wear an appliance and made me bite down on stuff. If I felt better I would go after him, but I can't. Now when I have to dialogue, I can't hold back my anger. I found out how Nick left (*past work supervisor who failed her*). The staff knew only 48 hours before he left.

ANALYST: Nick was damaging, and he's gone. There never seems to be a moment of safety.

MARGARET: Nobody knew. Now I can be with people again. Nick is not over-head. I am putting up pictures on the walls in my office. Saturday morning there was not one single person there. I was the only person in the building. Every time I breathe, it brings about a broken neck. Now is when I can have an honest conversation. I have the right to say I'm in pain and you're an insensitive person. (*She is speaking about "the third" when she says "you're an insensitive person," but is also a reference to me in the transference.*)

ANALYST: You are so very uncertain when you can honestly be yourself – since that brings the pain from neglect. You have doubt that I, or anyone, can take you in and you show me the awfulness of the pain, the assault.

The unconscious shows itself in the dream-state and there is massive destruction. The associations to lying prone, an association to the couch, brings the danger of destructive contact with me. Contact brings vulnerability to manipulation, and what's left is a ravaging of life. Margaret communicates her torture to me and I am tortured and painfully guilty that I bear witness to the assault on her body. I believe that our contact must involve torture and destruction. The only alternative seems to be annihilation and being the only alone person which may be preferable to an assault...

Session 2: next day telephone

MARGARET: I want to change from 9:00 Tuesdays. In the mornings I want to be in my office. I would like afternoon appointments. It's a better time for me.

ANALYST: You need a change right away. Something is wrong with our morning time. (*Something is wrong with me I am thinking.*)

MARGARET: Yes, the afternoon will work. I made a fire at home and am now sitting in front of it. (*I wonder if she wants me there next to her or wants to set me aflame.*) I never made a fire in my home in 12 years. (*The same length as her analysis – fire as the expression of her rage followed by feeling of conquest – her sense of mastery with me or conquest over me.*) It's fun to watch the cat. I gave Rose catnip and she loses her mind. She loves it. She is on her back, feet up in the air. When I ordered it the woman said, "I saw you on TV, talking about biology." (*Her concerns about losing her mind accompany her longing for the admiring object.*) When screening that, I was much too aware of what was around me.

ANALYST: You absorb too much, but then when you need, your need can take you, like Rose and the catnip. But being the expert and being seen, known, and admired can save you and protect you.

MARGARET: I don't know how I was able to produce that TV programming. How could I have that kind of output when I struggled with so much input? This pain stuff – my jaw is starting to open in the back. The twists are underneath my neck and going to the back, it's twisted in a knot. My jaw is inside out. (*Conquest brings bodily suffering.*)

ANALYST: You recognize your success then your body turns against you and attacks you.

MARGARET: The twist is so twisted, wrapped inside. My brain doesn't like how tight it is. Waxing and waning. I think it's starting to unwrap. I don't know how tight it was before. Someone should have noticed the bulge on my neck. It showed up sometime after 1992 when I began to notice it. It was not until I started performing theater that I had a photo that could show it. (*She believes that she is a victim of negligence.*)

ANALYST: You could see it ... they could see it, but no one noticed and you want me to notice. To notice your pain, to notice you.

MARGARET: There is a bulge there – it feels like my entire jaw muscle. I don't know where it goes or what it is attached to. My jaw feels yucky. It's no longer a cutting searing pain in my eyeballs. When I wake up, I crack my neck and then it's OK. It's not fighting me, but it's working with me now. (*I am thinking that she and I are in a battle and there is assault everywhere.... Also she is destroying herself right in front of me which is a form of attack on me.*)

I finally was able to run a meeting yesterday. I collected input from all the labs. I said I wouldn't beat up people, but I was sending out requests. I emailed a woman just once so she cannot claim that I beat her up, since last year she complained about my bullying emails.

ANALYST: (*I am thinking about her bullying me to change the appointment time.*) There do seem to be times to force, to bully.

MARGARET: The meeting was brief and we came out with a list of actions. The problem is that the employees don't trust. In management, there is the law of sadism, it's vicious. There are layers of angry opportunists in all the agencies. Mob bosses, who use fear to control.

ANALYST: You want me to know that there are painful reasons to not trust when you feel subject to the vicious use of control.

MARGARET: I am enlisted to prevent disasters from happening. People who are sending information up the chain were completely ignored. Such explicit harm is rare. (*Margaret's insistence that explicit harm is rare is a disavowal of her history of trauma.*)

ANALYST: Perhaps not as rare as we would want.

Margaret is wracked with her pain and shows it to me, filling me with the assault and bodily destruction. She fears losing her mind to her grandiose wishes or her assaulting longings to control. I feel controlled by her pain, her assaulting words. Every hour is a beating up.

Session 3: next day telephone

MARGARET: The entire left side of inside of my face is coming out. It's coming off. The whole layer. (*Margaret chuckles.*)

ANALYST: And you laugh with such disaster going on.

MARGARET: Otherwise it is tragic. It would be funny but it's preposterous. How do I exist on this planet? I don't get it. I shouldn't be alive right now. I drove into work; my meeting was at 4:00.

ANALYST: Shouldn't you be alive? Yet you are at the meeting. (*I become concerned about suicidality, yet Margaret seems to subscribe to life, to meetings at work. Margaret feels herself falling apart, perhaps longing to be held by me, but is dismissive of herself and me.*)

MARGARET: Clearly what I have going on is not going into anything vital. I went to the eye doctor and he could detect muscle imbalance in my eyes. The movement, it's not balanced. He asked "how do you do that?" He could see my pain. No one who had a brain trauma can accurately communicate it to the outside world. It is not possible for another person to believe it. He could see it. It is so helpful to have a medical doctor concerned about it. He was saying that there are clinics for pain management. But this pain is not pain like other people's pain. This is hard tissue pain.

I looked up child broken bones. A child's broken collar bone. Nowhere does it say that a child is screaming in pain. It says that if a child falls down, and has trouble lifting an arm, and there is a bulge in neck, and bulging in the body. The child has restrictions, the child has headaches.

ANALYST: A child with restrictions and headaches. Your body trauma of the past lives on today.

You show me your search for soothing from your pain but doubt that I can understand. (*Margaret calls out in pain, attacks me with her pain, but at the same time again is dismissive of herself and me so that authentic contact is impossible.*)

MARGARET: I have talked of my arm hung by my side, forever. (*She is forever dissociated.*)

ANALYST: For many many years your body is not yours, doesn't belong to you.

MARGARET: Forever. I have balanced something in the right arm. If I feel with it, it's irrelevant. The neuropsychologist says if you feel, then everything is OK. That it's not indicative, not a break.

NPR (*National Public Radio*) talked about brain injury; TBI, traumatic brain injury. A person lost their memory. He was physically disabled and not able to communicate.

ANALYST: Shut off from the world. Completely and thoroughly. (*I am thinking about Margaret feeling dissociated from me.*)

MARGARET: No one can understand it. People are living in it, in hell. Nothing can be seen from the outside. Just because it looks good, does not mean they are well. Just because you don't see it, does not mean you do not have it. It takes years of struggling to speak my voice.

ANALYST: Struggling again and again; when will you truly know your voice is heard.

MARGARET: How much struggle have I had on my own, with no one around giving me their thoughtfulness. It took a massive crisis to turn Bob (*husband*) around. It is sad. Some days I feel so alone. I am not flexible; at 49, I can't take the bone out. (*I think is this about a birth of some sort.*)

ANALYST: Because the bone was not seen or heard ever before.

MARGARET: So it grew wrong. My head's in the wrong position. My jaw is growing bigger. I know it's the way it should be. I have complete faith. What do I do? Where do I go? I need to go to a doctor now. It's hard for me to talk. The pain is telling me. (*This is Margaret's expression of a dissociated state. She loses contact with me and herself. Alternatively, might there be a wished-for dissociation from the trauma of an enema displaced upwards to her face.*)

ANALYST: The pain has become a signal … an awful terrible signal of something that has gone wrong. For so long you lost the signal, where there should have been pain and there was nothing, and now pain is all there is. Nothing is right. All is wrong in you and with me.

MARGARET: A signal, now to be dealt with. There was restriction before – restriction was allowed to be part of me by my mother.

ANALYST: The restriction, coercion, the immobilizing, all took the place of pain. There was restriction – but no pain and no signal. You are telling me that I cannot hear your signal.

MARGARET: This is what I can feel where things are dulled, paralyzed. It's coming out of it. Ripping out, the scar tissue.

Margaret is falling apart. There is the potential for annihilation of herself or me. Margaret feels outside of the world – removed – and her pain is the manner by which she eliminates herself from the world. She does not know if she feels, and believes she is broken off from herself. She is wrong and I am wrong. She assaults me for my wrongness and her assault causes paralysis.

A series of emails last fall

Now that I have had my third spinal injection, things have loosened up enough that it's clear I have something very wrong in my throat.

It crunches and it's hard; it chokes me. I was at an event on Friday evening and as I was talking, I felt like I was a little kid again, panicked, trying to breathe and talk at the same time. Awful. (*A memory of her little kid traumas.*)

I suspect that the cartilage in my throat is broken. In order not to choke when I eat and talk, I have to lean forward. I guess I've been doing that for a long time. (*Margaret's body does not belong to her. She shows me her torture and tortures me with her words.*)

Next day:

I feel really sick today and am in just too much pain to travel.

So, I'll be calling.

I have finished my book review and am attaching it here. If you have a chance to read it over, we can talk about it before I submit it to the editors this afternoon. (*Margaret longs for my affirmation and admiration. Also sees me as her degraded self-object.*)

Next day:

I feel too bad to drive today and my headache is bad.

I did go into the office last Friday and I was able to do the TV interview.

But, then after driving home, I was really sick and actually dizzy.

I have not driven since. I'm in a horrible place with this mess right now and I just don't know where to turn. I'll be calling at 3:00. (*The sadomasochistic attack on the self is subsequent to her success, and then she degrades me as useless, inconsequential.*)

One month later:

I can't do today (*meaning our consultation*). Not only can I not get into a car, I simply cannot talk, or even eat. This hard/broken stuff is now winding its way through my esophagus/trachea. I am in agony. (*Listening to the torture is likewise torture. I think that her cancellation is annihilating me or saving me.*)

Session 4: telephone session

MARGARET: I have my sticky with your name Paula in front of me.... I asked you last time if I could call you Paula – I want to "see" Paula written. (*First time she asked to call me by my first name. Is her sticky her way to have me, own me, control me?*)

ANALYST: You have many feelings about calling me Paula, and wanting to see me in front of you. (*Referencing the sticky as her way to have me close but in her control.*)

MARGARET: I have called you Dr. Ellman for so many years. I needed you as my doctor. Now I have so many doctors examining me, assessing me, – I don't need you as a doctor anymore. I want you as Paula. (*I am thinking is this her wish for greater contact or to degrade me?*)

ANALYST: You are speaking about a kind of contact that a name might bring. The contact we used to have with being in the room together has changed with the telephone and email.

MARGARET: I think back to four and a half years ago when I could not get out of bed. Your voice was my lifeline; talking with you every day. I would not have made it if it were not for your voice. Your voice kept me going. Now I don't need that in the same way. I want to be getting places in person, but how can I when I feel the pain like an axe going through my head. (*Her masochism averts her efforts at contact = her words sear me, deter me from wanting contact.*)

ANALYST: The axe through your head is unbearable. Might your concerns about bringing the axe with you into the room with me, keep you away from being with me in person?

MARGARET: But I want to figure this out. I believe I have internalized my parents around the traumas – the axe fell on me, like when I fell while performing acrobatics on the stairs. I used to have an idealized image of my mother who was in control. She could do no wrong; she had every right, until recently. (*The unconscious fantasy is about the destructive power of the axe that may fall on her or on me. But there must be an object that is wielding the axe – is it Margaret, is it me? Who wants to destroy whom?*)

ANALYST: You stay away because you believe that I have too much of a right.

MARGARET: Yes and I am at fault. John tells me "put it down" when I pick up his cell phone so he won't text while driving – I feel in danger, he's in the right and insists. I think he is in denial – even when I was crashing four years ago. Then I hear him today talking with his father about me. I told him I don't want him to talk with his parents about me anymore. I actually told him that. (*Margaret shows her beginning belief in her right but does the fantasy of having the right to exist necessitate wielding an axe?*)

ANALYST: It's like there is a crash going on right now, between us … with the question of whether you can be the one in control. Driving here to be in the room with me brings on the crash, the axe in the head. Yet you also have the recognition of your right.

MARGARET: I can too easily back myself into John's passive aggression.

ANALYST: Where you cannot freely think. Being back here in the room together with me again means there are no rights, and wielding an axe is the only way out.

MARGARET: (*insisting*) It will be good. I need to be seeing you. It hasn't been my choice. I need to be around people again; it is changing. (*Margaret insists on the presence of the good object, yet battles the belief in the destructiveness of the self and the other.*)

(*Margaret searches for ways to control the sadistic object, and her words have the effect of controlling and torturing me. She keeps me out of authentic contact with her, and degrades me as a nothing who cannot touch her. Contact brings annihilation and must be averted. The only contact is one of sadistic control.*)

The "widening scope" of communication by telephone and email in an ongoing analysis brings to the fore the dissociative process as it removes the effects of corporeality, of physically being together. Yet even through the hard wires of technology, Margaret's words enter me, carrying the threat of destroying me as her inner objects tear away at her. Herein lies an entry to the unconscious fantasy. Margaret lives her unconscious fantasy in her body. Her bodily existence fills her mind. Pain is everywhere and nothing exists other than pain. Margaret's use of technology, email and telephone, removes the human, the gaze, the softness of the body, the ongoing potentiality for touch. Finding the unconscious fantasy in working with Margaret as I enter her painful body is about incorporating the inhumane, the axe-wielding self and other. The stark frozenness of the written, the spoken word sears, scorches, rips, tears, and eventually destroys. Her objects/herself carry the unconscious fantasy of a sadomasochistic engagement.

Engaging in the task of this book on "finding," I reflect even further on the transference/countertransference where the "finding" is most possible. I see my tentativeness with interpretations that are direct. My speaking to her bodily pain as an attack on me and our process feels too close to an assault. The attack and counterattack carry traces of unconscious fantasy embedded in the therapeutic relationship. Our process of "finding" brings me to see that she and I exist only in her bodily pain. I remind my patients that I am away the week after the following week, but I notice that I forget to remind Margaret. My oversight belies my conviction that I do not exist for her, therefore it does not really matter whether I am with her or not. Margaret chuckles as she says that her mother never wanted a relationship with her – if her mother calls, it is to seek some needed information – not to speak with Margaret – and her husband can provide what's needed. Margaret's pain, and the pain in our process becomes a form of existence. It is all she knows, and can know with me. The challenge is on how to "find" the unconscious fantasy with Margaret who lives in her body where people do not exist.

Session 5: a recent session (in the room) before I am away

MARGARET: My mouth is opening up, unknotting, releasing.

ANALYST: There's space...

MARGARET: I feel there's space, an opening up.... I need to take breaks.

ANALYST: Do you mean breaks from body pain? Or break from me and others to attend to your body?

MARGARET: No, I mean taking a break from work, from what I am doing ... to focus and have a break for my body.

ANALYST: You want a break from the onslaught, the impingements.

MARGARET: Yes, I want a break from all that.

ANALYST: Your body pain takes you from the impingements; the pain is because of the impingements, and also a way to retreat.

MARGARET: I used to never feel my body and never know it.

ANALYST: You were subject to many impingements from the world around you.

MARGARET: My mother never attended to me. After the accident, nothing was done.

ANALYST: Nothing, no attention to your pain. You were completely fully overlooked.

MARGARET: Now, even now, I am feeling a sore throat. I can actually feel my throat. I never used to feel it.

ANALYST: It is because of my impingements, that your throat is sore.

MARGARET: No – I can feel it. I remember a long time ago I was calling you from my car and I felt a sore throat. I could feel my throat.

ANALYST: So there is contact and then there is pain. Pain becomes a way to manage the contact. Also the contact brings the pain.

MARGARET: Right now I feel my mouth spasming again. It was not in spasm and now it is.

ANALYST: Because of my invasion, you have spasms.

MARGARET: No, it's just the normal cycle of how it goes.

ANALYST: There is no meaning to it then.

MARGARET: No, there is no meaning. It just happens.

ANALYST: And yet there are the invasions that your body pain fends off and you take your break and your body pain is your shield.

MARGARET: See you next Monday.

The somatic expresses the trauma, and also creates a brittle shield that prevents contact, because contact means repeated trauma. The trauma for Margaret is about the body and mind invaded by the mother. There was no internal space. And internal space must be foreclosed now, because what comes with internal space is the fantasy of invasion and destruction.

Chapter 8

Painful transference and pains of transference

Discussion of Paula Ellman's case[*]

Marilia Aisenstein

> Quiet down, my Pain, keep still.
> You cried out for Evening: it's falling, here it is.
> (Charles Baudelaire, "Contemplation," in *The Flowers of Evil*)

This rich and complex clinical material calls to mind the expression, "pains of transference." What I mean is that the patient's pain is transferred onto the analyst, who suffers. I have firsthand experience of analyses in which the analyst feels pain even in her body.

I would even say that in the case of sado-masochistic exchanges, the patient's sadism is revealed in the clinical material. For Margaret hurting and suffering seem to be a less dangerous way of loving than others or, rather, her only way of loving. Margaret is a disconcerting and enigmatic woman. She is at once a successful, professional high-level scientist, a married woman, and a rich and gifted person but likewise a lost child suffering terribly. She is victim and tormentor. She tortures herself with sadism and pleasure. She speaks of physical pain and never of anxiety or depression. Pain seems to be the only means of expression available to her.

Her infantile history makes me think of a very beautiful opera melody, Olympia's (soprano) aria in Act One of *The Tales of Hoffmann* by Jacques Offenbach. Beautiful Olympia is a speaking doll created by the mad scientist, Spalanzani.

Margaret's mother loved dolls and I imagine that she would have wanted a marionette-daughter, an automaton doll like the one in the opera her creator brings to life as he pleases, before she falls to pieces.

Being manipulated and falling to pieces are recurrent themes in the clinical material.

I would not define Margaret in terms of a "somatic" patient according to the criteria of the Paris Psychosomatic School. In fact, if I have understood it correctly, strictly speaking she is not ill; there is no evolving morbid process even if she is "in pain." She suffers in her body. She undoubtedly also suffers from the sequela of under-nutrition of a deficient body stricken by serious anorexia when her adolescence drew to a close.

Her pain is real and poses a theoretical question. It is her way of expressing affect and conflict and yet I would not speak here of a "language of the body," as in conversion hysteria. I wonder however if one might not imagine some elements of conversion hysteria without it being a matter of true hysteria. There exists in any case a "magnification [that] is hypochondriacal in character" like the hypochondriac magnifying capacity of the dream Freud described in 1917 in "A Metapsychological Supplement to the Theory of Dreams" (S.E., 14, p. 223).

My spontaneous and entirely personal hypothesis of the unconscious fantasy animating Margaret resembles the one put forward by her analyst, even if it is a little different: By maintaining her pain Margaret is attacking the intrusive mother but also keeping her alive within herself. It seems to me to indicate an omnipotent fantasy of keeping "her torturer" alive since without this the patient would run the risk of contending with an emptiness which frightens her more than the excitation caused by her pain.

When Freud speaks of unconscious fantasy, he often mentions conscious diurnal reveries which have their roots in the unconscious. In section six of "The Unconscious" (S.E., 14, pp. 190–195), he writes:

> Thus *qualitatively* they belong to the system *Pcs.* but *factually* to the *Unc.* Their origin is what decides their fate. We may compare them with individuals of mixed race who, taken all around, resemble with white men, but who betray their colored descent by some striking feature or other, and on that account are excluded from society and enjoy none of the privileges of white people.

I believe that the patient's painful somatic expressions should be understood as the negative version of a conscious script whose occulted side would be not to lose the "intrusive and sadistic grappling" with the mother. As the analyst says, "The somatic expresses the trauma, and also serves as a brittle shield that prevents contact, as contact means repeated trauma. The trauma for Margaret is about the body and mind invaded by the mother. There was no internal space."

This is what Margaret tirelessly repeats by not granting the analyst any internal space for thinking. She unconsciously seeks to paralyze the analyst's mental functioning. Her complaints aim at overwhelming the other's psyche at once in order to make her experience what she herself has suffered but also, at a more unconscious level, in order to maintain the sadistic and living mother inside her.

What is important here is that the analyst survives, all the while showing step by step how much her pain protects from that emptiness that, above all else, she fears.

I would now like to return to my association on Offenbach's famous opera in which the automaton doll, Olympia, sings and dances while being manipulated by her creator. Olympia is a marvelous piece of machinery lacking in soul and affect but who unifies all and gives everything meaning. This meaning is what

Margaret has been seeking for years with her analyst. I am very admiring of the quality of the analyst, who remains reliable and calm, showing thereby that she has survived Margaret's attacks and continues to function psychically.

I will limit my associations here to three consecutive sessions, the first in person and the two others over the telephone. During the first session, Margaret immediately takes to complaining, I would even say that she is "recriminatory." No sooner on the couch she says:

> I never had a normal sleep cycle. There's physical damage. Depression is the side effect of trauma. I'm inflamed when I wake up. My face is red. Like someone who comes into my bedroom at night and smashes me in the face and smashes my body and smashes me down. Red, bruised, a rash.... Like there are tiny white pieces popping out of my face. Like sand. Little tiny bones. Remnants of the bones that have been broken up that my body is pushing out.

The analyst suggests to her that something awful happens at night. I myself imagine that she is thinking of dreams, of perhaps forgotten dreams? Margaret avoids the psychic path by replying that her body "is processing something horrific." In a very subtle way, the analyst suggests that sleep equals a lowering of watchfulness stimulating the return of the horror ("when your mind is at rest the horror begins").

Margaret does nothing with the suggested interpretation and returns to a description, which I find very aggressive, of her physical pain. She accuses one of her former medical doctors of "manipulating" her badly, which her analyst hears in the transference. The patient goes on and continues complaining, and finishes by mentioning "an insensitive person." The analyst concludes:

> Margaret communicates her torture to me, and I am tortured and painfully guilty that I bear witness to the assault on her body. Our contact must involve torture and destruction. The alternative seems to be annihilation, or being the alone person, which may be preferable.

Dr. Ellman is correct, Margaret tortures her psychoanalyst. She gets as far as making her take on the guilt of the tormentor. Margaret is triumphant; she refuses all the offered interpretative leads. And in fact the day after, during the phone session (I asked myself, why over the phone?), she reveals herself clearly and begins the session as she usually does, associating on her fireplace, her cat, her notoriety.... She behaves like a patient in a typical analysis but when the analyst emphasizes the positive movement, pain returns to the material.

At this point there comes to mind a patient from long ago whom I treated for many years. She only spoke to me about her (psychic) suffering, her misfortune, and my lack of understanding of the hell she was going through. Nothing seemed to change. I myself was in despair and felt incompetent.

She was a sculptress. One day at an art opening, I completely met by chance an artist who, when he had heard my name, spoke to me about her telling him that she was delighted with her analytic work, she was doing very well.... I was stunned to learn that she had made friends, was joyful, confident, and full of humor... I will skip over my countertransferential fury that happily I had the time "to unpack" during an entire weekend before I understood that due to the paternal transference onto me my patient only allowed herself to change at a safe distance from my peering eyes.

Margaret seems to have greatly evolved due to the analysis. She has met a man; she is quite successful. There exists however an area in which she does not appear to change, that of her pain. I asked myself if the painful complaints are not intended for her analyst. Isn't this a mode of exchange with Dr. Ellman, which she does not (or cannot) give up in connection with an intense maternal transference? Can't we consider that her somatic complaints, which cause the analyst suffering, are addressed to her mother but above all they help Margaret live daily life better?

A passage from the third session is impressive:

MARGARET: Clearly what I have going on is not anything vital. I went to the eye doctor and he detected muscle imbalance in my eyes. The movement, it's not balanced. He asked "how do you do that?" He could see my pain. No one who had a brain trauma can accurately communicate it to the outside world. It's not possible for another person to believe it. He could see it. It's so helpful to have a medical doctor concerned about it. He was saying that there are clinics for pain management. But this pain is not like other people's pain. This is hard tissue pain.

I think I hear in this material how much Margaret is attached to her pain. She wants nothing to do with a pain clinic, hers is unlike the others, it is irreplaceable. Her pain helps her to live, as if it were giving meaning to her life.

There comes to mind an article we published in 1999 in the *Revue française de psychosomatique* (No. 15) on the theme of pain, "Pain: A Therapeutics of Survival?" by Patrick Miller. Building on the narrative of the film, *Sick*, by Bob Flanagan, the author takes up a reflection on physical pain as a surfeit of excitation counter-cathecting the excitation of trauma. Pain in this instance is at the service of survival.

I would willingly say that Margaret is battling her painful traumatic reminiscences with a surfeit of pain. This is what it costs to feel alive and through which she conserves within herself the object, even if it is cruel. Thanks to the transference onto Dr. Ellman, she survives and manages to bypass melancholic breakdown or psychic death.

These few notes are associative. As a conclusion, I would now like to share my fantasies, or divagations, with my colleagues.

In my mind I see Margaret as an intelligent baby but in the hands of two incompetent parents, taken in by their own difficulties and incapable of facing the sufferings of a newborn. The child has a stomachache, she cries, is cold or hungry or too warm, she needs arms to take her in and a voice to put her mind to rest. Trusting in the object requires a bath of tenderness and language.

With regards to Margaret, I imagine that these auspicious conditions were insufficient. As a child, she probably presented "ego prematurity" which made possible a byway through sublimating. Since she was a good student, she should have obtained the narcissistic benefits of her success at school; yet, this too was withheld from her.

At 50 years old, she suffers from "anachronistic" pain, a phenomenon about which Freud spoke in the *Project for a Scientific Psychology* (1887–1902, pp. 281–391) in which he writes that pain leaves a facilitation between the tendency to discharge and the representation of the hostile object: "Moreover, there is no question but that pain has a peculiar *quality*, which makes itself felt along with the unpleasure." "It only remains to assume, therefore, that owing to the cathexis of memories unpleasure is *released* from the interior of the body and freshly conveyed up" (Freud, 1887–1902, p. 320). But for Freud, apart from pain and discharge, there exists another way, that of the affect.

We may ask ourselves why Margaret could not transform these reminiscences of pain into affective suffering. I suggest the hypothesis of an insufficiency of drive fusion through primary erotogenic masochism described by Freud in 1924 in "The Economic Problem of Masochism" (pp. 159–170). For him, this primary masochism is very early and permits the binding of contradictory impulses in the infant's ego. To put it simply, through the binding of the libido (the force which pushes) and the death drive (a movement which unbinds and immobilizes), primary masochism allows the capacity for painful waiting to be integrated. It is the mother's psychic work that makes this possible. A "good enough" mother is one who is able, by means of her words, to help the baby wait, "wait my little one, I'm going to take you in my arms but not right now … you'll eat soon, just keep calm and wait a little." The mother envelops the infant with words; she gives him word- and thing-presentations. She thus helps him to wait, which implies trusting in the object.

If pain is to be tolerated, it must be "cathected masochistically." The infant has to learn gradually that *there is also pleasure in this painful waiting due to the psychic work that it implies.*

Analysis is a long road. If Margaret has had any luck in her life, it was in meeting Dr. Ellman, a competent and committed psychoanalyst who tolerated her attacks and patiently helped her express herself in words and transform her pain into psychic suffering.

Note

* Paris, April 2016. Translated from the French by Steven Jaron.

References

Baudelaire, C. (1857) "Contemplation". In *Flowers of Evil*. Auguste Poulet-Malassis.

Freud, S. (1887–1902). *Project for a scientific psychology*, S.E., 1 (pp. 281–391).

Freud, S. (1915). *The unconscious*, S.E., 14 (pp. 159–215).

Freud, S. (1917). *A metapsychological supplement to the theory of dreams*, S.E., 14 (pp. 219–235).

Freud, S. (1924). *The economic problem of masochism*, S.E., 19 (pp. 59–170).

Miller, P. (2014). Pain: A therapeutics of survival? Some elements for further thought. In P. Miller (Ed.), *Driving soma: A transformational process in the analytic encounter* (pp. 209–219) (D. Alcorn, Trans.). London, Karnac.

Chapter 9

Discussion of Dr. Paula Ellman's case

Batya R. Monder[1]

Ellman begins her presentation of Margaret with the start of a clinical hour. In so doing she brings us right into the consulting room with her and confronts us with Margaret's psychotic description of muscles and bones in her face.

> She walks in, sits down at the edge of her chair and looks at me.... She is stiff and erect, and her face is red. She speaks about the muscles and bones wrapping around her face. She pulls her face to the left ... pulls her lips and mouth to the left ... the bones are breaking inside. [And the analyst adds:] Each time she pulls her face ... speaks about the trauma, I feel as if I am throwing the punch that causes her face to twist to the left.

I can appreciate how assaulted the analyst feels by her patient's words. This patient is one who cannot experience another without experiencing pain, thus her analyst feels forced to cast herself as an inflictor of pain. I am struck by how alienated from empathy I feel hearing about this patient. Her suffering is so assaultive that I, perhaps, shield myself from feeling it. I am both put off and baffled by the portrait of this patient who has such a primitive underpinning and wonder how she can be as functional as described, be a middle-aged biochemist who maintains an academic position, interacts with students and colleagues, appears on TV. What is it about Margaret that makes it so hard to want to know her? Perhaps it is that she will only allow herself to be known in ways that repel closer involvement in the hurt she feels. I note my reaction and read on. I have to learn more about this woman and understand how her analyst is engaging with her.

Throughout the chapter Ellman provides many examples of her patient's vivid, fantastical portrayals of what is happening within her body. Are these descriptions an attempt "to communicate by proxy" (Williams, 2004), speak only of bodily distress, not emotions? Affects of sadness, anger, frustration, etc. seem foreign to her, but she finds brutal words to show her analyst what she believes is happening in her head, her jaw; the analyst, in turn, experiences the "interior wounds, the broken skull, the gash from nose to eye" as direct blows to her own body. As I read the back and forth, I feel I have entered a universe of psychotic metaphorizing and have lost my footing. But not so for Ellman who stays with the primitive body fantasy of her patient, containing the multiple projective experiences.

Elizabeth Bott Spillius points to the aspects of Klein's thinking that help us to comprehend how Margaret is communicating with her analyst and how Ellman, in understanding this, is able to tolerate the attacks on her:

> It was Klein's view that the most basic and primitive anxiety of the paranoid-schizoid position is a fear of annihilation from within the personality and that, in order to survive, the individual projects this fear into the external object as a defensive measure.
>
> (Spillius (2003) in Anderson, 2003, p. 60)

For Klein, "normal splitting and the projective identification associated with it were necessary parts of development, and ... without them the basic differentiation between good and bad and between self and other would not get firmly established" (ibid.). Further, "the concept gives an intellectual guideline for understanding and analyzing the way the patient perceives the analyst." And over time, "it has become part of the Kleinian focus on the analyst-patient relationship, particularly in understanding how the object relationships of the past, [now] part of the patient's internal world, are lived out in the analytic relationship" (p. 61).

We understand that Margaret desperately wants relief from distress; and her way to seek relief is to project into Ellman the violence, the terror, and torture that she experiences but cannot understand, a way for a patient to "both communicate ... distress and temporarily rid [herself] of it and therefore of [her] understanding" (Joseph, 1983, p. 292). The latter is key, since in her insistence on the catastrophic actions of her body, Margaret refuses to allow understanding to mitigate her experience of pain, or connect it to emotional trauma.

The task of locating unconscious fantasy shifts when that is the stated terrain of the treatment. With a more neurotic patient, one would be looking for the derivatives of unconscious fantasy in the process material – in dreams, metaphors, transference. But with a patient like Margaret, where one is confronted with fantasy in every somatic description, the task becomes to better understand what was happening between Ellman and her patient, how Ellman was able to engage her in a 15-year analysis and help her life progress. Margaret moves in and out of psychotic process; and much of the time, Ellman stays with her, responding directly to the patient's words, allowing her to feel heard and understood. She does not attempt to wean Margaret from her images of a destroyed and destroying face.

Susan Isaacs' foundational paper "The Nature and Function of Phantasy,"[2] written in 1943, and expanded in 1952, remains relevant here. Her paper was discussed and its implications elaborated upon by Ogden in his 2012 book *Creative Readings: Essays on Seminal Analytic Works*. The combined contributions of Isaacs and Ogden provide a very different window into understanding the interaction between analyst and patient. Building on Freud's profound understanding of the unconscious, Isaacs comments that

> the patient's relation to his analyst is almost entirely one of unconscious phantasy.... In his phantasy toward the analyst, the patient is back in his earliest days, and to follow these phantasies in their context and understand them in detail is to gain solid knowledge of what actually went on in his mind as an infant.
>
> (Isaacs in R. Steiner, 2003, p. 156)

"All mental processes originate in the unconscious and only under certain conditions become conscious" (p. 159). Ellman shows us that these conditions are not yet present for Margaret. Isaacs goes further, "the earliest phantasies ... spring from bodily impulses ... and external realities are progressively woven into the texture of phantasy." The source of phantasies is internal, "in the instinctual impulses" (p. 168).

Ogden (2012) positions Isaacs as a bridge between the Freud-Klein era, which focused on "*what we think*," and the Winnicott-Bion era, which focused on "*the ways we think*." And for Ellman's patient, it is the *way* she thinks, or rather is unable to think, that commands our attention, not the *what*. She thinks in bodily terms, showing us what she imagines is happening under her skin. Building on Isaacs' original ideas, Ogden (2012) enlarged their meaning:

> If transference is phantasying and phantasying is unconscious thinking then transference holds significance not simply as a symbolic expression of internal object relationships originating in infancy and childhood. In addition, transference ... constitutes *a way of thinking for the first time* (in relation to the analyst) an emotional situation that occurred in the past.
>
> (p. 40)

In other words "it comprises an effort to think disturbing experiences with the analyst that had previously been unthinkable" (ibid.). This is what Margaret seems to be doing with Ellman, thinking the unthinkable with her analyst, thinking the experiences of injury and attack that she could not conceive of as a child, let alone voice.

Before I discuss the process material that Ellman provided, I want to turn to the patient's history and the aspects of it that stood out for me. Ellman conveyed to us what she has learned about the traumas of her patient's early years: her mother's abusive treatment of her calls to mind Shengold's (1989) soul-murdering parents. I say this not because of the abuse per se, but more pertinently, because of the "brainwashing" Margaret seems to have been subjected to, leaving her with a belief that her mother's mind was the valid one, not hers, a belief she held on to well into her adulthood.

Mother administered enemas to her child, wedging her, on all fours, into a corner of a bathroom, unable to move. We are not told exactly how old she was or how long these enemas continued or for what reason they were deemed necessary. Enacting a caricature of femininity, her mother was equally excessive in criticizing Margaret's appearance, which she "repaired," poking at her protruding stomach, perming her too-limp hair from a young age. Mother and her female relatives would be coiffed and heavily made-up at all times; and mother seemed to expect the same from her daughter, wanting her to be as static and presentable as the collection of dolls that mother had accumulated and displayed throughout the house. In her pre-adolescent years, father sometimes provided a doorway out of the claustrophobic home environment and introduced Margaret to the outdoors, taking her to the campsites he maintained. But he treated her cruelly on family road trips when he ignored her agony and limited bathroom stops, and showed his disgust for what was inside Margaret by shunning her once she began to menstruate. Only her grandfather seems to have recognized and taken a genuine interest in Margaret. Letting her explore specimens under a microscope, he introduced her to the world of science that would become her career.

Always a good student, we learn that Margaret, somewhat surprisingly, excelled in the arts, even though standing out in anything earned the displeasure of her mother. Despite her successes, fellow students mistreated her and male relatives singled her out for humiliation at family parties. It is not apparent what part Margaret might have played in this hostile treatment of her, though from indications of an internal as well as external identification with the mother, we can imagine that she expressed enough of what inhabits her to cause her demeanor or behavior to elicit real antipathy in others. We surmise that no one protected Margaret, no one wanted to rescue her, so that observers came to collude in abuse perceived and experienced.

Abuse from a bad object permeated her childhood, and became an early principle in her internal world. When abuse is tyrannizing, as with Margaret's mother,

> the need for a loving and rescuing authority is so intense that the child must break with ... what he or she has suffered, and establish within the mind (delusionally) the existence of a loving parent who will care and who really must be right.
>
> (Shengold, 1989, p. 73)

Deprived of any idealizable provision of goodness, Margaret had to construct and protect a painful tie that would keep her from breaking away from home until graduate school. Separation proved difficult and led to a host of somatic symptoms. Her hands swelled; she experienced pains in her head and her abdomen; she found it agonizing to eat, and her weight dropped precipitously. This last, rather than alarming her relatives, won her praise from the women in the family for being so thin. It was her roommate's worry combined with her own physical distress that allowed Margaret to seek out medical help. It was then that she discovered she had a food allergy, which she could think about only concretely as a cause of weight loss and physical pain. Also at this time she began a psychotherapy treatment.

The roommate is perhaps the most caring relationship that Margaret knew, someone who noticed what was happening to her and expressed concern. From this point on, however, Ellman becomes the central figure who will "care" for the patient by accompanying her through the distorted channels of her body and psyche. Ellman comments that "intimacy is nonexistent," not only for Margaret but also for her parents who spend most of the year apart. Within the confines of the exclusive dyad now inhabited by patient and analyst, interactions with others appear as a backdrop, and we learn about her marriage primarily through a report of the dissension between her and her husband of a few years. Her yearning for more closeness only emerges as she tells us that she imagines following him around like a puppy. It is not clear if he belongs in the string of males with whom she has had at best experiences of diminishment. Beyond her father, they included the adolescent male cousins who held her underwater too long, tickled her too much, humiliated her with a "gift" of dog feces and the patriarchal graduate school professors who saw her as an intrusion into their male bastion of science, better suited to bringing tea than doing experiments. An undergraduate professor ridiculed her for wearing her engagement ring. We hear no more about that engagement or about any other romantic relationship until she marries in her late forties. Somehow with skin and, as she calls it, "hard tissue" so much a focus, the absence of her sexual body hovers.

Ellman makes no direct reference to Margaret's sexuality, contributing to our sense of her as not really flesh and blood, but rather a collection of bloodless body parts as presented in the surreal dream. Even with her analyst she sits stiffly at the edge of the chair, and Ellman tells us that her sessions were more like performances, at least at the start of treatment. Relationships with others remain difficult to navigate, and closeness is sensate as abuse. The relationship with Ellman, though tortured, bridges impossibility and necessity, and is lasting. Clearly it is the most significant relationship in Margaret's life.

From the process material, we are aware that there have been big changes in Margaret's life while seeing Ellman. She married; she is writing book reviews; she appears on TV as an expert in her field; and her appearance has softened, showing her identifying now more with her analyst than her heavily made-up mother. Despite these positive steps forward, the need to retreat to a psychotic process persists. It may be a measure of her trauma that she continues "to think disturbing experiences with the analyst that had previously been unthinkable," showing Ellman more about the mad world she lived in as a child when there were no words and no witness to see what she endured.

Something else is percolating as well. Ellman shows us Margaret's assertiveness with her, some of which is in the process material, some in the narrative. The various instances of standing up to Ellman seem to have multiple meanings.

We are told that outside the consulting room, Margaret bends "to the force of the object to mitigate any possible discord," unable to speak up or stand her ground. But with Ellman she pushes back. She wants to *see* the analyst, be treated face to face. Ellman explains the move away from the couch as Margaret's wanting "more contact with me," and feeling safer, but also describes the pressure that Margaret places on her to look and be looked at. Other complexities apply as well. Distrust is such a significant part of Margaret's background; one can imagine Margaret's positioning Ellman across from her in order to control the space. Margaret has here assumed her mother's domineering and perverse role. She can look and demand to be looked at, discomforting her analyst; she can be the voyeur, or dominatrix, in the face of Ellman's submission, and by so doing undo the passivity she felt as a child when submitting to her mother's sadism. In other words she is again thinking a "disturbing experience with the analyst that had previously been unthinkable" – the perverse, sadistic relationship with her mother. It is unclear how long Margaret needed to face her analyst, but we hear later that Margaret is again on the couch.

In the process material, Ellman provides many examples of Margaret's shifting to psychotic descriptions to communicate the fear and torture of her childhood. In the first session, Margaret describes the assaults during the night. Her words are frightening and violent:

> Someone comes into my bedroom at night and smashes me in the face and smashes my body and smashes me down.... Like there are tiny white pieces popping out of my face ... little tiny bones. Remnants of the bones that have been broken up that my body is pushing out.

Ellman stays with her in the present while I wonder what she is telling her analyst about the past. Is this a response to the forced enemas, a pushing out of the cruelty imposed on her as a child, an expelling of a harsh intrusion from her mind? Is that the disturbing experience she is now reworking with her analyst? She says her body is "processing something – something horrific." And she continues: "There is a gash, an internal one ... my skull is broken. It comes down out of my nose cavity, through the left of my head and palate." And then she shifts to resentment, less psychotic sounding but no less off, and tells her analyst about her jaw being manipulated by the physical therapist and how she wants to sue him for harming her, focusing her internal rage on the physical therapist, a more distant object. Ellman stays with the idea of danger with contact. The session is fragmented and hard to follow as Margaret shifts between psychotic and non-psychotic states. O'Shaughnessy, who has worked with patients like Margaret, credits Bion's conceptions as making that work possible:

> Bion's theory is that in psychotic states there is overall divergence from the normal due both to what the mind has lost – the power of thinking, the capacity for awareness, sense organs for perceptions, mental depth and

contrast – and to what the mind has become – fragmented, its elements concrete and without variety, its sense organs become apertures, its chief functions splitting and evacuating of bad fragments, an abnormal projective process which makes the world bizarre.

(O'Shaughnessy (2003) in Anderson, 2003, p. 101)

The shifts from psychotic to non-psychotic states continue, and Ellman as her analyst has to endure her patient's projections. "Under the load of anxiety and the barrage of splintered hostile projections, the therapist has to find a way of working, while meeting constantly the kind of ego-destructive internal object in the patient" (p. 97). If she can do that, the patient can tolerate movement in her internal world.

> Bion thinks that such shifting back and forth can gradually lead to the patient sustaining a more human contact with whole objects and an increased ability to think and use verbal thought in place of action and projective identification. He stresses that the foundation of any improvement is the patient's own recognition of his psychosis: once he gains insight into the fact that he is ill he may begin to get well.
>
> (p. 98)

The first hour ends with a more cohesive comment from Margaret and some mental space: "Now I can be with people again.... I am putting up pictures on the walls in my office." ... But the psychotic description creeps back in: "Every time I breathe, it brings about a broken neck." Ellman responds with an interpretation that acknowledges she knows how much despair the patient endures: "You are so uncertain ... you can ... be yourself, since that brings the pain from neglect. You have doubt that I, or anyone, can take you in and you show me the awfulness of the pain, the assault." It is the final comment of the hour so we do not hear if Margaret can for a moment feel less alone with what she carries.

Session 2 is on the phone, and Margaret again asserts herself and wants to change a morning hour. We cannot tell what the change in hour signifies for the patient. What we hear is how the request, or demand, affects Ellman who thinks, "something is wrong with me." The session moves away from the change of hour to Margaret's successes – being on TV and producing the TV program. Margaret wonders how "she could have done that kind of output when I struggled with so much input." But she moves quickly away from that musing to the psychotic description of her jaw opening in the back. John Steiner's ideas add another layer of understanding to Margaret's need to retreat from reality and Ellman's appreciation of this need. "Despite its delusional foundation, the [psychic] retreat offers a measure of stability as long as the psychotic organization is not challenged" (1993, p. 65). For much of this treatment, one sees that Ellman has kept in balance the stability of the analysis, and not challenged Margaret's psychotic organization.

In session 3, also on the phone, Margaret again shifts from psychotic imagery to non-psychotic thinking but with the latter, she is touching on how much pain she is in and how little thoughtfulness there is around her. If there is a kernel of mourning here, it is not what Ellman feels can be addressed at this point. She provides us with her inner monologue: "Margaret is falling apart" and Ellman recounts the destruction that she feels: "There is the potential for annihilation of herself or me.... She is wrong and I am wrong. She assaults me for my wrong-ness and her assault causes paralysis." The mournfulness of the patient and the thoughts of annihilation on the part of the analyst suggest the presence of an unconscious fantasy such that a destructive power is in the thoughts of each. Both analyst and patient appear to have created a pattern of veering off in dif-ferent directions, perhaps under the sway of an unconscious fantasy that contact may bring destruction. Possibly, this pattern of respite from connection functions to preserve the analysis. We glimpse that an acknowledgment of grief could destroy the sadomasochistic connection between analyst and patient, the only kind of connection that Margaret knows.

In this difficult treatment, Ellman shows us how understanding the patient's fantasy structures is central to the treatment. Further, thinking in terms of fantasy allows us to ask how and at what point, and to what extent, does the analyst mediate the patient's internalization of an unreceptive or negating external world? In the latter part of the process provided, that question resounds. Margaret's life has improved in significant ways, but in order for her to be more integrated, feel less of a need for the psychic retreats of psychotic organization, she has to undergo what Bion describes as "reversible projective identification" or a "return of the fragments previously got rid of" (J. Steiner, p. 67). This, says Bion, is

> necessary for the development of the capacity for thinking. Even when rudi-mentary, such thinking takes account of objects, and, with its help, the non-psychotic personality enhances its capacity to tolerate reality and in this way to modify rather than to evade it.
>
> (Bion (1962a) in J. Steiner, 1993, p. 67)

In between session 3 and session 4 are several emails. The first email lets Ellman know that her patient will be calling that day. Margaret has finished a book review and sends it to Ellman, hoping for her input: "If you have a chance to read it over, we can talk about it before I submit it to the editors this after-noon." Ellman recognizes Margaret's longing for "affirmation and admiration," but adds that "she [Margaret] sees me as her degraded self-object." Margaret appears to be demanding that Ellman cease to be her analyst and be, like herself, devalued in the world while at the same time imagining a less-degraded accept-ance of her competence. In that demand, one could imagine a disowned rage about never feeling valued that is projected onto Ellman. The unconscious fantasy is one where Margaret remains without the longed-for admiration, and the fantasy of being without builds to somatic intensity as we can see in the email that follows. Margaret tells Ellman that she can't drive and "my headache is bad," but says she will call. Importantly, there is only a headache, not a retreat to a psychotic state in this or the next email. Ellman sees the content of Margaret's email as a sadomasochistic attack on herself that "follows her success"; and in that attack, Ellman feels "useless, inconsequential." Margaret's bodily state is her way to experience unconscious rage at her mother/analyst as well as a "sadomasochistic attack following her success."

A month later, in session 4, Margaret again asserts herself and wants to call Ellman by her first name. Ellman acknowledges the wish but segues instead to the "contact we used to have ... in the room together" while now there are emails and phone sessions. And while Ellman pushes for more in-person contact, Margaret lets her know how much she has valued being able to be in touch with her analyst on the phone when unable to get to the office. She recalls with gratitude that Ellman's voice was her lifeline when she couldn't get out of bed four and a half years ago. "Your voice kept me going. Now I don't need that in the same way. I want to be getting places in person, but how can I when I feel the pain *like an axe* going through my head." In this session and the next, it is striking that Margaret does *not* retreat to a psychotic process. She uses a metaphor "like an axe" rather than her earlier formulations of being smashed, hit, etc. Ellman responds, "Might your concerns about bringing the axe ... into the room with me keep you ... from being with me in person." Margaret continues with her own thread: she wants to "figure out" things. She tells Ellman how she has "internalized [her] parents around the traumas," how she "used to have an idealized image of [her] mother who ... could do no wrong" and "had every right, until recently." She seems to be "seeing" her mother with more clarity, struggling to separate from the destructive internal object.

Until Margaret can find symbolic voice for her rage at her mother, it likely will continue to envelop the treatment, though less completely. Ellman does not minimize how unbearable it is for either to acknowledge the rage. She experiences Margaret's absence as a need to control the sadistic object (the mother/analyst) and tells us that Margaret's words have the effect of "controlling and torturing me. She keeps me out of contact ... contact brings annihilation." Maybe the analyst has come to feel that leaning on the rational risks missing what is more real, and therefore more grounding to the patient.

Before the last hour, session 5, Ellman tells us that she overlooks reminding Margaret that she will be away. Margaret "chuckles as she says that her mother never wanted a relationship with her." This seems to be as close as Margaret can come to showing her hurt and anger at not being remembered. In equating Ellman's forgetting with her mother's behavior, is Margaret retreating from reality and clinging to what Steiner calls a "melancholic solution," projecting the internal critical object "onto new objects who play the same role in the patient's equilibrium" (J. Steiner, 2011, p. 150)?

The last reported session is in person, and Margaret fights to be understood in this hour. She pushes back and clarifies her meaning. She revels in the awareness that she can now *feel* her body, something she didn't know in the past she couldn't feel. She can feel her sore throat, experience it, no longer have to numb herself as she did as a child nor slip into a psychic retreat to escape the pain and anxiety. She is distraught about not having been taken care of as a child, even "after the accident," presumably a reference to her head injury as a 5-year-old. Might this be the start of a mourning process, which could provide significant movement in her internal world and is so crucial for healing?

Ellman's treatment of Margaret has lasted for many years, and even more years will be needed for Margaret to experience herself as a more whole human being. It takes a very long time for patients to show us what they have endured, and Ellman has illustrated that in her paper. She has also illustrated how she has endured. She suffered her patient's need to evacuate dangerous feelings into her and the troubling realization of how at times Margaret's projections took possession of certain aspects of her mind (Rosenfeld (1971) cited in O'Shaughnessy, 2003, p. 62).

Margaret has been able to think the disturbing experiences of her childhood with Ellman, the very experiences that for her were unthinkable earlier. Having shown her analyst what she has suffered, and having had an analyst who could endure that suffering, she now seems to be struggling to tolerate allowing her mind to comprehend what her body knows, and to name and begin to contain what she can name. Her analysis continues to be the arena that allows her to mentalize her experience, not only suffer it.

Because of Ellman's resilience and patience and her ability to provide containment for this difficult and disturbed woman, there is now room for more acknowledgment of the trajectory of opposing emotional states in the treatment and perhaps love and rage can begin to co-exist. Ellman has given her a place to mourn without engulfing her, and with more time, possibly she will be able to reassemble the discontinuities that have defined her.

Notes

1 I would like to acknowledge my appreciation to Jane Kupersmidt for parsing earlier drafts of this chapter with her keen eye and intellect.
2 I am using the word "fantasy," more common in American analytic literature, throughout the chapter, while recognizing that it has a far less precise connotation than the usage of "phantasy," employed by British analysts.

References

Anderson, R. (Ed.). (2003). *Clinical lectures on Klein and Bion.* New York: Routledge.

Isaacs, S. (1943). The nature and function of phantasy. In R. Steiner (Ed.), *Unconscious phantasy.* New York: Karnac.

Joseph, B. (1983). On understanding and not understanding: Some technical issues. *International Journal of Psycho-Analysis, 64,* 291–298.

Ogden, T. (2012). *Creative readings: Essays on seminal analytic works.* New York: Routledge.

O'Shaughnessy, E. (2003). Psychosis: Not thinking in a bizarre world. In R. Anderson (Ed.), 2003. *Clinical lectures on Klein and Bion*. New York: Routledge.

Shengold, L. (1989). *Soul murder: The effects of childhood abuse and deprivation*. New York: Facett Columbine.

Spillius, E. B. (2003). Clinical experiences of projective identification. In R. Anderson (Ed.). *Clinical lectures on Klein and Bion*. New York: Routlege.

Steiner, J. (1993). *Psychic retreats*. New York: Routledge.

Steiner, J. (2011). *Seeing and being seen*. New York: Routledge.

Steiner, R. (Ed.). (2003). *Unconscious phantasy*. New York: Karnac.

Williams, P. (2004). Incorporation of an invasive object. *International Journal of Psycho-Analysis, 85*, 1333–1348.

Chapter 10

Babette, interrupted

Irene Cairo

The patient I will call Babette is a European woman of Jewish Moroccan ancestry whom I saw for the first time when she was 20 years old. The middle child and older daughter of a Jewish family where all five members had different countries of birth, she obtained "permission" from the family to consult me, because they worried about her stammering, a symptom present since early childhood. She regarded this concern of her parents with a mixture of resentment and humor, pointing out that since this was a "visible" symptom, they had agreed to therapy, while ignoring all she knew was emotionally wrong with her.

A bright, attractive, exotic-looking young woman, she engaged me from the first interview. She had lived in several countries because of her father's business and thus spoke, fluently, many languages. She believed her main problem was to find a man whom she would like enough to defy the parents' requirement that she should only date – and of course marry! – a Jewish man. We began twice a week psychotherapy in the spring of her junior year in college. She worked diligently and intelligently, was interested, vivacious, easily making connections and reflecting on many aspects of our sessions.

Three months into the therapy she announced with visible regret that she was going to travel for the summer, and was not sure if she would settle in Europe or come back to the States. Months passed.

One day, I received a call from her younger sister, 15 years old at the time, asking if I would consult with her. She said Babette had encouraged her to call me. I objected to seeing her, saying that I could both offer another name and that I believed given her age the parents should make the initial call to begin a consultation. I also said "in my mind, Babette is still my patient." One month later, Babette (who I learned had already been back in New York when the sister called me) called me. We resumed our twice a week psychotherapy.

In the next two years, Babette graduated from college, developed many different friendships, and began a passionate relationship with an appropriate, bright, successful young man ... who was not Jewish. At that time, her father interrupted the treatment by refusing to pay and found a "very" Jewish therapist, insisting that Babette be in therapy with him. She resisted, and, crying, asked me what solution I envisioned. I knew it would not be possible to have our work together be a clandestine therapy, and was as supportive as I could be during the transitioning to the new therapist.

I heard from Babette occasionally for the next year, and then nothing from her for 10 years. At that time, she called to say she would like to see me.

She had married a Jewish man, an accomplished artist, and had two children. She brought her 10-month-old daughter to the first session. We resumed a treatment that progressed from twice to three times per week and continued for four years at which time it was interrupted for financial reasons. Both she and her husband suffered at the hands of an exploitative art dealer, and experienced real financial hardship. Following that interruption, she gradually paid me the outstanding debt. Five years later she called again and we began a psychoanalysis, four sessions a week on the couch. Although we were beginning to talk about termination, this analysis was also interrupted after eight years for financial reasons.

I have been asked in my contribution to present a case with either a history of trauma, or a psychosomatic symptom, and to illustrate the way I worked to explore and discover unconscious fantasy.

In Babette's history, there are two highly traumatic events, both related to medical conditions. One, when at age 2 and a half she had to be hospitalized for an infection in a country where she did *not* speak the language, and where no family was allowed to stay with her at the hospital. The family tells the story that when mother returned to visit her, she stammered for the first time.

The second situation was at age 6, following a tonsillectomy. Babette came back from the surgery to a hotel room in the foreign city where the surgery had taken place. She and her brother were left alone and she began to hemorrhage. She could not wake up her brother and then called the hotel concierge, who then called an ambulance. The first time Babette used the couch, once lying down, she immediately talked about being face up – explaining she never sleeps in that position – and adding that she wondered if that was related to the memory of being left in the hospital.

My foreignness served as a vehicle of identification and also idealization. The idealizing transference often disguised resentment, a resentment emerging as a response to the frustration of my silences, the weekends, my relative anonymity, vacations, separations, all the differences. As will be seen, there is a redundancy of themes: against the background of the real interruptions, those in the treatment; there are many references to silence, the power of words and of language, both in the healing aspects, and in the destructive fantasies that emerged in reference to words, as will be seen later. The stammering itself is a concrete expression of something interrupted, an attempt that does not carry through to its end, an approach to and a withdrawal from the object.

Much of the manifest material was about words, the use of different languages, and the variations of speech and silence, both in the past and within the analysis. The specific destructive fantasies associated to the use of words, and connected to the symptom, were only uncovered quite late.

The probing into my willingness to see her, through "sending" the sister, related to what later emerged as a rescue fantasy. In retrospect, we may hypothesize there was perhaps a hint of the wish for being rescued in her bringing her baby daughter to the first session after the long interruption.

In the first sequence we can see both the idealization, and the struggle to cover her frustration and to disown the resentment. Her puzzlement about why I called her back I believe expresses her wish to see me as available and supportive. She refers to my voice as gentle and remembers Nisha, the maid who would spend the most time with the children, especially with her, being also the caretaker who toilet-trained her.

Clinical material

Her sessions were normally Monday through Thursday, but an art course on Thursday evenings occasionally made for the fourth appointment being on Friday. She called on Thursday to verify the time, if it is 10:00, she said, I do not have to call. I called anyway.

Friday

P: I was confused about the time – it's funny – when I called I said you didn't have to call but you did anyway ... and also thought about my not knowing. It's something my mother would do, she'd get things mixed up.

I got nervous that since I didn't have my session Thursday that I could also miss Friday, and make a mistake. It's interesting that you called anyway.

A: Interesting?

P: Yes, you probably sensed that I did want to talk to you, I needed to hear your voice, then I also needed you to hear mine. Maybe you were saying that silence is not a communication. In my family silence is a communication. When there were words it was terrible. That's when trouble started.... I also think your voice is different.

Remember that time when I couldn't sleep, and in the night I would hear my mother's voice? I think your voice is soothing, I mean serene. I do not know any voice like that. There was no voice like that in my childhood.

There's always that shrill voice, angry or crying. And maybe I thought "Dr. Cairo is too busy to call me" – my father was always too busy.

My mother would speak on the phone and I wouldn't hear all the words, and she spoke in her language. So I didn't understand a lot of what she said (*Chuckles*). I don't know for sure why you called. Yesterday, also, I was chatty. (*Smiles*) I wanted to have a conversation. I wanted to tell you about a movie. (*She tells me the name.*) Did you see it?

It's funny that I'm thinking of my mother's friends and that makes me think of the synagogue we'd go to in Europe. It's the Persian Jews synagogue. There were no Moroccan Jews. There was another synagogue where the aristocratic French Jews went.

A: So, in your mind, in part, I'm too busy like your father, but perhaps I'm also like those aristocratic French Jews ... (*She interrupts.*)

P: I know ... I have no access to you.

It's all so different to remember it now. Your voice, you know it does remind me of Nisha, she would talk to us, like one talks to children. She'd tell us stories (*She chokes up.*) Even if it wasn't so much time ... each time was precious. (*She cries.*)

Monday

P: Friday I took you on a little journey around my city, perhaps prompted by thinking of the movie. When I came out, I wanted to tell you, Nisha is such a precious memory, but she is bitter now. Of course you remind me of her ...

I am still thinking you saw the movie ...

(*Long silence*)

(*Seriously*) Must be frustrating for you this job.... You cannot answer.

A: It's a comfort to think *I* am the one frustrated.

P: In the movie it's the crazy woman who doesn't talk.

She tries to commit suicide. (*Silence*) I just ruined it for you. I can't believe you won't tell me a simple thing, like whether or not you saw it. (*Chuckling*)

I am sorry for you; you cannot have a normal conversation.

A: Your humor covers up how frustrating it really is.

P: It's a stammer in the session. How scary silence is.

A: All silences ...

P: In a way ... I remember my piano teacher, Anne ...

She'd wear perfect suits, always in black, and ... she wore pearls.

Nisha loves that style, but it's not quite hers ...

I don't know what I'm saying; you said it was all right.

A: What is "all right"?

P: You said I could talk about whatever.

A: But just now you were scared.

P: Yes, a bit. So different from my old city, which is not classy, full of noises....

The noises on the street are different.

So different from the silence. The silence is sad.

A: But you're frustrated with me when you can't get an answer. You're silent about those feelings, that sadness is because of my silence ...

P: Perhaps you are my French teacher, all elegant, always the same.

(*In the end I say I'll see you tomorrow at 1:30 p.m.*)

P: Oh I had forgotten.

One can see again in this session the flow from the idealization (Nisha) to the aggression and the violence (crazy woman, suicide, "ruining" the movie for me), followed by her humor, and again the fragile idealization with the image of Anne, the piano teacher. Her forgetting that I had changed the time is related to her wish not to think of me as having a life outside, in particular, as will be seen later, my being part of a couple. In between the times of treatment, she had once had a glimpse of me on the street (she was on a bus, I was walking carrying apples). Much later she related how disturbing that had been as she thought of my family, my children. Now the changed hour indicated a need of my own, an intrusion.

Tuesday

P: Yesterday I had completely forgotten about the change. You had told me two weeks ago. I did not register it, or I did, but I forgot. These days I am so self aware, meaning all my life, my memories. All of that is passing in front of my eyes. I was giving you a description of everything in my childhood, though you know many of those things already. It may be the movie then …
I can say you see, it is the way it was. I turn the tables on Dan (*husband*) who is always in some way demonstrating how he is the one who knows … this way I felt that I could be more assertive, he is not willing to risk a confrontation. But it is not fair … I shouldn't analyze him, it's not right.

A: But analyzing is a weapon, and you were, you are angry at me …

P: Well in a way, I said I saw you a bit like my French piano teacher I guess it is a sort of complaint about you. You are rigid, that is what I was saying.

A: But perhaps I'm not *so* rigid when I changed the time …

P: Well, it's a part of me. That's true. Actually I was thinking that when I left. And my mother of course, she fit so much with the rigid parts of my childhood.

Wednesday

(*Twenty minutes late*)

P: Neither the 4 or 5 or 6 trains are running. People are scrambling for the buses. It makes me think of German movies. All the Jews trying to get away – they can't.
… All things considered, I didn't do so badly.
(*Long silence*)
The most difficult thing to talk about is my marriage.
I don't want to leave because when I tried to do that, leave my parents' home, it was chaos.
Maybe it's the same. Or maybe I never left.
(*Long silence*)
In my marriage, I get complete loyalty…. Loving, like from a child…

A: When you said "I didn't do so badly," then you talked about what is difficult, the marriage, what does that mean?

P: Well, when I tell you about the center of town, all that, the past – it's easier. It all happened already, I can't fix it. But now I have to fix something and it's too hard. It's exhausting just to think about it. If there were no children it'd be easier. I'm afraid I had half of my life. If I give it up, I'll lose the other half.

And I can imagine that Dan feels the same way. He loves me in his way. But there are other feelings I never will know. We look to the world as if there is nothing wrong. We've come a long way, overcame great difficulties.

We are looking to buy an apartment.

It's so difficult to talk about my marriage … oh well …

  …

I think it is what you said at the beginning, that I'm afraid of the judgment. It's a failure. What I came here for was my career, my career is not such a bad thing, my marriage is.

In these sessions, the persecution, covered by idealization, is emerging more clearly.

It starts with the reference to Nazism. Then clearly her marriage is where she feels most vulnerable, especially with regard to me. It's where rivalry will appear. In her glimpse of me as part of a couple, the issue of her own marriage is most threatening to our connection. (The glimpse of me in a couple was in my having changed a session. I speculated she felt there was a third involved in her mind.)

Friday

P: I thought of some things after I left. But I thought particularly about being judged by you. And the other thing was that I don't have to act. I can talk and *think*. That was comforting.

(Silence)

Yes, I do feel judged by you. I don't know what I said at the moment but I do. When I was taking Lisa to school this morning I was thinking: I can *think* about all this.

Yesterday I was talking to my cousins. Their mother, my aunt, remembers my mother saying to me on *(she mentions some minor Jewish holiday)* "you can't go to the beach," and my aunt remembers thinking: "how can she do that to that girl?" So that was on my mind from last night…. Ah, that's it, that my parents, both of them, I never, we never, had a chance to find out what we wanted. What I mean is I always have to conform. I always did what others wanted. So what do you think?

(Silence)

(She chuckles.)

A: I think now it is me you have to conform to.
    (*Long silence*)
P: I see what you mean (*however, goes back to the beach story with mother*). Can you imagine? Not letting us go to the beach for something irrelevant that happened thousands of years ago? (*Silence*) (*Softly*) I see what you mean. You are saying you are my new religion.
A: It saddened you, what I said?
P: When I first came to see you, you said that I came to find the parts of the words I didn't have. (*Smiles, with tears in her eyes*) But I knew what to tell my father. To him I said, I have to understand why I stammer. That he would accept.

I noticed her emphasis on being now able to think. The frustration about my not answering her questions painfully evokes the lack of encouragement and support, her isolation as a child, the lack of a common language and the mother's strictness.

The following sequence is from a month later – Monday

P: (*Saunters in*)
    Well, I have been waiting since Thursday to tell you something I wanted to tell you but couldn't. It is about the last thing you said. You said that in a way I didn't want to have my own voice, that I wanted you to tell me, and to make the decision for me, about which school to choose.
    And besides that I couldn't think, I wanted so much to go to the toilet, and I couldn't really be in the last few minutes of the session.
    By the way, on Friday I went to my doctor and he said I had a urinary tract infection so that could have worsened the feeling...
    So, I was thinking if it is true. It is, but it is not because I really want you to make the decision for me. It is that I am convinced you have an opinion, and your opinion says you are different and may have completely the opposite opinion, and I am so afraid of your judgment. So, that's why. It seemed so difficult anyway to make the decision about Sonny's school and I would have to think about it and on my own make the decision.
    You have your own mind, you are a different person, separate from me, and of course you think differently.
    I am afraid that I will tell you my opinion and of course you will not tell me yours, you will just have contempt for mine (*I register the word contempt with some disbelief, annoyance, sadness?*) and then I will feel terrible.
    Ah, and there was something else, you said that there is always a choice, well you didn't say exactly that, but I understood that, there are other

choices, but I do feel that if there is only one choice if there is only one school that it is a lot easier. Does that make sense?

A: You feel if there is "no choice" you will escape my harsh judgment...

P: That's right! It is safer, a lot safer...

I have been thinking about this decision all weekend, and had bad dreams, I didn't remember the dreams but I know they were about that. Dan tried to wake me, said "You were having a bad dream." I tried to go back to sleep. I did but it was not restful.

It is *terrible* to make a choice...

... Oh, there is something else I have been wanting to tell you. It is funny, that I never told you. Since September 11 you know, I have been afraid of subways, and of course, I managed not to take them. But since I am in ana-lysis of course I have to take them. Taxis are so terribly expensive and the buses are too slow.

So, I take them, and once I am in the subway, there is nothing to do. What will happen will happen of course, but this time as I was coming here, – please Dr. Cairo do not laugh at this, I imagined, I had this fantasy that I am in the tunnel, yes? And something happens, and there is a great disaster, and I survive, perhaps I am the only one who survives. I survive for days, and not only that, but I, there is a young baby and I rescue this baby right? And, here is where you can't laugh: I ... I nurse this baby, and they find us ... I nurse this baby for days.

A: What is the part where I would laugh, in my contempt of you?

P: (*Smiles at my using "contempt"*) In ... that I am a hero, that I want to be a hero ... it is really pathetic, no? ... I am nowhere near a hero, I cannot even make a decision about my son's school...

(*Silence*)

A: I think you want to tell me that when you come here taking the subway you *are* a hero, but you think that would be "pathetic." I am the person whose judgment you fear. You know so little about me, I don't tell you about my weekend, and yet you are willing to make these efforts ... I am so high...

Also, ... I wonder if you are the baby...

(*She is reflective for a while.*)

P: Are you also saying that I make myself into you? Into what I want you to do for me? I want you to save me?

A: Perhaps...

P: Well, I don't know...

I felt very alone in a way with this decision, I wanted someone to help. I do not want to do the wrong thing; I do not want to go through what hap-pened with him in third grade. This woman was very insecure and she had her own issues with the school. Here I go, playing therapist, obviously another judgment here ... but I think I could say as much, that she felt very unsure of her position.

He had a terrible experience. You are right. I idealize all the time...

It is always something perfect on one side and terrible on the other, I guess. ... You, for instance, it is true I don't know about you. I imagine you as a mother, you are never unruffled, you are always soft spoken, the way you are here.... You never got mad at your children ... I think that is probably not right...

Again there is identification with me, the wish to know what I think, the idealization, but also the persecutory aspects ("contempt").

At the same time, there is the issue of her son's learning disability or her own disability? Is it her stammering, or even the "stammering" of her thinking?

There is poignancy in her idea that to have no choice about a decision is a better alternative to not knowing my judgment. There is danger both in not knowing my judgment, and in being in my hands, a doctor who cannot be trusted.

The daydream of the subway is the beginning of what soon emerges more clearly as her rescue fantasy.

In hearing this material I felt the tenderness that characterized a lot of my affective response to her. I always saw her struggle, when she tried to protect both of us from what she already glimpsed as her destructive feelings.

Tuesday

P: (*Silent for a moment on the couch, with her eyes closed, and she smiles.*) I am resting ... I am actually exhausted. I am also very puzzled. I went to the urologist today. She said I do not have a UTI. I am now confused. How can two doctors with the same information say two completely different things? (*She sounds worried through all this.*)

The urologist wants to do a renal sonogram.... Do I really need one? Is this part of the same thing to charge for another procedure?

Of course you know what that reminds me of...

...

The Hotel H, in X, and Kurt, (*the concierge*) you know I was so distraught recently that somebody told me they tore it down, or were going to.... How can they? I loved that building!

[I make some brief comment expressing surprise, since the story has always been so dramatic. She certainly could have died from the post tonsillectomy hemorrhage. It was her initiative and resourcefulness that saved her, when she found herself without the parents, and could not even succeed in waking up her older brother.]

P: We went there other times.... Father liked to celebrate the Jewish Holidays in X ... I remember so vividly, the Bible in the drawer, the little bidet, and the ... what do you call it, the little potty in the night table. It was very important for me, because, as you know, I used to wet the bed....

The "hand held potty" I think they call it ... I would arrive in X, in the hotel room and run to find them, the Bible and the potty.... It was exciting, it is not clear to me why, I do not know, because there were many stories connected with that place ...

I remember Kurt so well. (*She describes the night of the surgery, and the way she went to find him, how her brother slept so heavily and she knew that she had to find an adult ...*)

A: But you are also frightened, and would want me to be like Kurt and rescue you ...

P: (*She is silent a long time, then moved.*) Someone who would know all the answers. I think I am always looking for the voice of authority ...

These two doctors don't know anything ... I feel a bit helpless.

A: You don't have answers and I do not either, or I may have the wrong answer ...

P: I talked to my cousin. She wanted to know about my career.

She is very nice, she likes me, really, she says things like "you are so wise." She is a grandmother, she is beautiful and kind, then I think "Is it possible that *everybody* is nice but my own mother?"

How exhausting this all is. I see everything black or white.

She is more clearly afraid that beneath the ideal picture she has of me, she does not know if she can trust me. Doctors have contradictory opinions, and may be exploitative. Children are abandoned, exposed, and left in danger. The rescue fantasy emerges clearly here. In the daydream, she was the rescuer. But in the unconscious fantasy she wants me to nurse her, to save her like Kurt did.

Wednesday

P: I have been thinking a lot about boundaries ... and I realized what I actually like about them.... You remember I would tell you about Mme. M's apartment? The sewing room, every room had a function, it was orderly.... There was something pristine about it.... Imagine, my mother went there also to sew.

In our apartment things were messy, rather, you could have everything everywhere ...

Hers was different.... It is a bit like I feel about this room.... You are here. And that's it! (*She smiles.*) You never leave ... and I *never* imagine this room with someone else in it.... There is never another patient, person. (*She says it as a slip, tripping on the words.*) ... But my favorite place in the world actually was that of another woman who lived in the building, below Mme. M., her apartment and ours were similar, but this other apartment was vast.... She had two poodles, you see. Like you see in the movies from the sixties. I do not remember a husband, was she never married? I don't know.... She lived with luxury.... She seemed like an independent person.... We didn't have to put those slipper-like things on our feet, to protect the floors.... Her apartment was never messy.... Well, ours was not so messy. Part of that time Nisha was coming.

My mother also was more active, not depressed the way she was later. Later she was angry, angry at me, I think jealous, or perhaps I yearned for more, and then the memory is more complicated.... Or is that what is complicated about me? Those two images...

Maybe I do not remember the early years well.

(*As I wonder what role all these apartments have in all this, she says:*)

All the images have matching surroundings...

A: So, for me it is necessary that it be like Anne's apartment or a picture of me alone in this room, with nobody else...

P: You know, father is nowhere in these memories!

A: So, that's what "no patient/person" was about ... I am never with "father"...

P: Hmm ... I was alone with mother you see.... B (*brother*) is also not in these memories. (*Silence*)

So, you see, there is a lot of confusion in my mind...

Was there a sort of friendship with my mother? Then? Ever? Did we share anything?

I was soaking up these places.... My father is totally absent. Was he traveling? (*I am puzzled, and challenge this by reminding her of how she had told me many other times about her father's presence.*)

Yes, that's true, (*smiling*) we did go to Temple on Saturdays. Actually I would go with him, he would take me. And sometimes B and me.... You know, there were these transactions, these auctions, like ... to have the honor to put these things, these little ... crowns, what's the name, on the Torah, and of course it is completely forbidden ... (*She seems amused in the telling.*) There was no money. I'd wonder, when do they pay?

(*Excitedly*) I never saw a hand go in the pocket!

So then when my father would do this, he would lift us up, in turn, and we would do it!

That would be the biggest moment, when I was the tallest person in the place ... I could hear the jiggly sound these things made.

It is so different...

A: So you have these two very different pictures, your father is "never there" or you are in this great place with him.... And later it is totally different...

P: Yes, you see, it's true, there is an explosion later ... I am a voyeur, I am absorbing it all, never saying that much.... Most of those memories are silent.... When the volume gets turned on, later, you start to hear the chaos...

A: Why a voyeur? Such a bad word ... is it because you were seeing the men conduct business in the Sabbath?

(*Unusually long silence*)

P: You know, I was afraid of the dark, so ... my parents would make me sleep between them ... I feel so uncomfortable telling you.

It is funny that I said to you that I never saw them together.

I feel so uncomfortable...

(*Again silence*)

A: Do you know what about?

P: It's funny I don't really...

It is hard to think what a 3-year-old might feel or think ... but now, it is embarrassing in a sense, because I think that you are thinking, "poor little Babette ... no room to sleep in, no voice, no career..."

The boundaries are welcome if they protect her. Are they to keep parents apart?

What is the role of these pictures, these rooms, the spaces that were occupied by such different people? Calling herself a voyeur is an expression of her guilt, it led us to the conflict vis-à-vis the parental couple. Her self-mockery "poor little Babette" is a veiled protestation of innocence.

Further course of the analysis and final reflections

As aggression became clearer, and erotic feelings emerged, after much struggle she confessed to a habit of sitting on the toilet saying curse words. When she did tell me this, I remembered another patient who had told me the following "joke": After Hiroshima, survivors find a little old man sitting on a toilet, laughing, giggling hysterically and he says, "look what I caused!!!"

My association clearly revealed my perception of the destructiveness that until now had been defended against. It is not surprising that I could not find my notes of this particular session, and the sessions that immediately followed.

I now want to refer specifically to the stammering. For periods of time it was mild and in the background. She rarely referred to it, and I never did unless she did. On one occasion, telling me she was amazed that I really accepted whatever she said, she explained her mother forbade the expression of many things. She repeated her mother's injunction in the mother's language, then translated it. A few days later she commented the stammering had worsened. Agreeing, I suggested it dated to the moment when she had repeated in the mother's language: "This cannot be said." Elsewhere (Cairo, 2016) I have referred to this moment in the context of the use of various languages in an analysis. At a juncture where the physical manifestation of conflict became a focus of exploration, we could glimpse that speech was an act of violent expulsion of fecal explosive material.

We were able to formulate an understanding of this to which she responded in her most pensive, reflective, profoundly sensitive mode. Her stammering almost disappeared in the course of the analysis.

In the multilingual world of her childhood, the capacity to speak several languages must have acted as a protection, diffusing some of her rage in "spreading" it, so to speak, over several language systems. Also – silence can be replaced by switching between languages. The fact that the crucially dramatic separation at age 2 and a half is dated as the beginning of her stammering cannot of course be documented. But the time of her toilet-training coincides or at least overlaps with the time of that hospitalization.

The subject of money as the "vehicle" of the interruptions is complex. My excessive tolerance of the accumulating debt contributed to her idealization and perhaps was also a way of participating in the denial of the "dirtiness" of payments. The conflict is evident in the description of going to synagogue with father. A comment made in real awe, "I never saw a hand go in the pocket," revealed a denigration of transactions that involve money.

The breaks in the treatment were themselves a sort of expulsion, when I tried to set limits to the debt amount by forcing an interruption. The interruptions themselves were a sort of stammer, an incompleteness, a brusque, imposed silence.

The clinical material in the last sessions presented here presages the exploration of her attack on the parental couple, reflected also in her difficulty integrating words, and in her managing of money in a way that prevented the continuity of the analysis.

Finally, trauma may result in a rigid organization that would require a longer and deeper analysis which the interruptions prevented. Yet, I remain hopeful for Babette. I hope that eventually she will be able to separate the act, "psychoanalysis," from her analyst, me. That may allow her, in the future, to go on to an analysis with someone else.

I hope I have illustrated one personal way of exploring unconscious fantasy, in the context of a traumatic past.

Reference

Cairo, I. (2016). The place across the street: some thoughts on language, separateness, and difference in the psychoanalytic setting. In J. Beltsiou (Ed.), *Immigration in psychoanalysis: Locating ourselves*. London and New York: Routledge.

Chapter 11

Discussion of Dr. Irene Cairo's case

Babette, interrupted

Harriet I. Basseches

In her paper, Dr. Cairo presents an initial description of the sequencing of the treatment – a treatment that spanned many years with many interruptions. We thus are invited to understand the title of the case: "Babette, interrupted." Dr. Cairo's introduction also includes some identifying personal "facts" about the patient, which is followed by some early patient history including two early "traumas" and the beginning of a symptom, that of stammering, plus some analyst thoughts. The heart of the paper consists of process notes of five consecutive sessions from well into the treatment, accompanied by thoughts of the analyst which she shares with the reader, then a second set of notes from a month later, and finally the analyst's concluding reflections.

In preparation for my discussion of this very interesting case generously offered by Irene Cairo, I not only studied the clinical material but spent time thinking about how I listen to clinical material, here in written form. Specifically, I was trying to understand the role of unconscious fantasy in my conceptualization of what I was learning from Dr. Cairo's description of the analysis.

My first observation of my form of listening was that I experienced the entire presentation of the material not so much as separate elements either in type of information or of analyst point of view as distinguished from patient point of view, but rather as *the case*, and as a single unit. It is through the lens of this single unit – listening to the transference/countertransference duet – that I believe that an outside "third," the listener, can catch glimpses of the underlying fantasy. My second observation was that, almost without awareness on my part, as I listened to the unit, I nevertheless divided the material into manifest and latent content, and to some extent, into progressions or sequencing, i.e., how the telling moved forward. Throughout that process of listening, I was accumulating meaning. One might say, I was translating what I was "hearing" into my own version of meaning. Once I began to formulate meaning from the material, I gathered that meaning into concepts. It is at the level of the concept that I think the underlying fantasy emerges – whether expressed as a conscious wish as in a daydream or just as likely as a mostly hidden, unconscious, wish/idea. Further, I see the underlying fantasy as the motor for the action within and beyond the analysis itself.

I believe that the process of listening that I am describing is informed by my own theoretical knowledge as I have previously digested it, as well as my own experience in my own work with patients and previous listening experiences. I would go further to say that this form of listening is uniquely individual, characteristic of me personally even though others may have had similar educational preparation. Thus, any other person who would do the same exercise would approach the material uniquely as well, even if there were overlapping points of similarity. I say this because I am interested in how much agreement there will be between my designation of potential unconscious fantasy and others who would listen to the same material and identify their explication of unconscious fantasy.

Interruptions

I turn now to the substance of the presentation. To begin, the initial description of the sequencing of the treatment provides important information, and raises in the mind of this reader the question, what is the role played by the interruptions? What underlying fantasy do the interruptions represent?

I have several thoughts about the significance of the interruptions. I believe that Dr. Cairo thinks this element is important to the patient and to the treatment as demonstrated in the way that Dr. Cairo emphasizes it in the title of her presentation and in the presentation itself. I agree. The action (i.e., interruption) seems to speak to the patient's fears and cautions in relationships. At another level, in addition to a general distrust of relationships, and fear of intimacy, the patient's repeated interruptions can be viewed as a mode of communication. She may have been expressing her fear of committing – as if she must always be ready to run away from a perceived inattentive other or run to someone else for help because of the perceived limitations or unavailability of the other. This can be viewed as a repetition compulsion to repeat over and over a demonstrated escape route in order to master childhood painful (traumatic) experiences that led to overwhelming emotional states she would want to avoid. She gains a sense of control over even the chance for such a potential abandonment by being the abandoner rather than the one abandoned. In addition, if one remembers that she sent her younger sister to the analyst apparently in place of herself, following on the heels of the initial interruption which had come only three months into the treatment, there can be the meaning of testing the analyst to see how readily she will betray the patient. Or to put it another way, for her to see how much the analyst wanted her and would be loyal to her. When, then, one adds that her later interruptions occur over the manifest reason of lack of money, there are many interesting anal phase reasons that come to mind for this variant on the interruption theme. Examples are a wish that the analyst will allow her to come for free (entitlement) or not pay the debt over a long period, thus again testing how far the analyst will go to show her "love." Other meanings/wishes might include an attempt at expulsion/control over the analyst; a withholding of her "feces"/money as a sadistic gesture; casting herself as the poor, needy one, as a bid for some extra care; punishing the analyst for some perceived failure by the analyst, to name some possibilities. The analyst herself remarks about the idea that the money is "dirty," alerting us to the patient's possible disappointment in the therapist for taking the "dirty" money eventually.

The only leave-taking that – at least on the surface – *looks* as if it is out of the patient's control altogether is when the father stops paying for the treatment and sends the patient to a "very" Jewish therapist. Of course, here too, we do not know what the patient might have shared with the father that may have precipitated his turn-around decision. Without the actual session material surrounding these many interruptions to throw light on possible motives at the time, one can only make suppositions based solely on one's own speculation. Thus, speculatively, she might have wanted to have the decision not appear to be of her making so she would not be "blamed" or, to use her word, "judged" with contempt by her analyst. It seems possible that she might have wanted to submit to the father's will out of love for the father (an oedipal solution), but disguise her feelings, not to anger the mother/analyst when leaving her (an oedipal triumph). She could be saying, I must submit to my father because he controls all my bodily functions, perhaps an exciting idea.

Certainly, all the interrupting could speak to denial of the centrality of separation anxiety, presumably a critical issue for this patient. First, there is the wish to master her separation anxieties by taking control of them. Further, she might wish to leave the mother/analyst repeatedly as the "payback" to the pre-oedipal mother who left her repeatedly in early life. Such action could function as if as revenge toward a mother who did not want her enough and who was not there for her enough even though she was in such need.

With all those possibilities (and more which will be discussed below when considering the two significant traumas in the patient's early experience), it may be challenging to be able to capture the hierarchy of underlying fantasy here. Perhaps the wish would be that she had omnipotent control over who came and who went and that she would be the queen of leave-takings, and the belief that with that control, she would never be hurt.

Stammering, symptom

As with the temporal interruptions themselves, the stammering is interrupted speech and, like the physical interruptions, seems multiply determined.

The stammering, which began following the first trauma, suggests that the symptom, which had played a role in her life for a long time, was well ingrained and habitual. Also, the stammering proved useful as a concrete element of pain presented to the father so that he would agree to this treatment. In contrast to what she told the father, the patient told her therapist that her goal for treatment was to meet a non-Jewish man to marry. Those two contrasting explanations for treatment suggest an oedipal issue. While the roots of the symptom may be pre-oedipal in origin and closely connected with anal phase development, an oedipal cast had emerged. It may be that her conflicts over the forbidden oedipal wishes may have led her to think that the way out of her dilemma was to find a gentile/different loved one through her work with the "foreign" therapist – perhaps a fantasy of the therapist belonging to the "tribe" of the former loved maid Nisha. At the same time, on the more manifest content level, she was rebelling against authority, chafing at doing the bidding of the authoritarian dad, thus also making such a solution forbidden.

Three months into the treatment, she may have become frightened at her experience of commitment to working with the "foreign" analyst: perhaps a fear that her involvement could lead to her realizing or losing forbidden wishes. The kinds of fear I am talking about, for example, is her feeling that the attention she was getting from the analyst that she so wanted was making her feel disloyal to her own mother. Another fear might be that she feared this analyst might in fact help her to "marry a non-Jewish analyst" and fear a rupture with her family. Thus, she might have feared that something dangerous could happen here, possibly creating an ambivalence toward the analyst and the treatment. Perhaps, too, the early departure could have expressed her ambivalence about eventually giving up her stammer, signaling loss of the familiar. The fact that she returned to the treatment only after testing the analyst's loyalty to her over the younger sister suggests that the ambivalence was rebalanced in that instance after she was sure that taking the risk of counting on the analyst would be met with support.

One further thought to do with the stammer is the following: Holding back or stopping from going forward in speech might be an expression of a mixed feeling about saying what one thinks – for example, an angry thought or a thought felt to be too shameful. Since the stammering eased and almost disappeared by late in the treatment, we can assume that some large part of the conflict had been worked through. However, as the patient is only able to end the treatment by invoking another interruption rather than a mutual termination, the conflict, while lessened, seems to remain.

If I try to think of the underlying fantasy related to the stammering what comes to mind is the fear that she has terrible and shameful thoughts and impulses accompanied by the thought/wish that she would never have to spell these thoughts out. Perhaps, then, the stammer would have been preserved over time in the hope that it would ensure that her spoken thoughts could not jeopardize being loved and valued.

Turning to the two traumas, we can see many aspects that could create serious traumatic reactions.

Trauma 1 – hospitalization at 2 and a half without parental presence

The analyst's description of the patient puts great emphasis on language and, at least in the abstract, on words. The patient is fluent in many languages; silences and words are of importance in the analysis. Nevertheless, the patient describes listening as a young child to her mother on the phone and cannot "understand a lot of what she said" to her when the mother speaks in the mother's own language. This suggests that the mother's mother tongue is not in tune with the patient's linguistic facility, at this beginning language period – a puzzling phenomenon. To put it another way, one wonders what barrier might already have developed between mother and daughter that the child would not have first and most clearly understood her mother's own speech and language.

Also the symptom she adopts, a stammer, focuses on speech, albeit spasmodic speech. Moreover, the idea that a 2-and-a-half-year-old would be in a hospital situation, without understanding the speech, and bereft of any parental comforting, spoken or otherwise, seems shocking and cruel in the extreme. The 2-and-a-half-year-old toddler would presumably have limited speech as it is, and it is conceptually difficult to imagine a mother leaving such a child. So much of what may have been happening would not be verbalized and therefore would be largely unsymbolized, would make it very difficult to work through the issues for the child, or later adult. I would think that the damage done to such a child would leave that child with very great deficits and developmental disturbance, although the patient described does not seem as handicapped as might be expected. I am not sure what that means. Is this a screen memory? The child must have been very resilient.

Because there is much emphasis in the action of leaving and returning and because of the early traumas each involving the child being separated from parental objects, I have concluded that separation issues play an important role, a vulnerability, in this case. In addition, other thoughts include that the timing of the traumas would also have played a role as well. The first trauma could have been in the beginning or in the midst of toilet-training, which we learn was done by the non-mother mothering figure. There must have been confusion for the child as to where Nisha fit into the family frame. We do know that the patient had bed wetting problems and was afraid of the dark. The difficulties, however, led her to being permitted into the parental bed, placing her in between the mother and father and getting her much wanted attention. The patient volunteered to the analyst that those nighttime visits seemed to have linked in her mind to guilty feelings of being a voyeur. As for underlying fantasy connected with the coupling of nighttime fears and voyeuristic wishes with time in the parental bed, what comes most to mind is the possibility of confusing sado-masochistic erotic fantasies beginning here. If such fantasies were awakened, they might enter the masturbatory life, but be very challenging for her to express, even with her great linguistic skill.

Trauma 2 – crisis following tonsillectomy

Trauma 2 presumably would have happened at peak oedipal intensity. In itself, a tonsillectomy – even without complications – would be a frightening experience to a 6-year-old, as any invasive procedure would be. One wonders at the impact of such intense focus and pain on the throat/mouth being the locale of so much attention; the mouth/throat are associated with oral pleasures and with speaking. But the pain of this tonsillectomy became overshadowed by the frightening complications which undoubtedly induced terrifying fears associated with bodily damage. The little girl taking action on her own behalf seems heroic. One continues to wonder at the puzzling neglect by the parents and brother, and the child coming to associate her well-being and feeling of dependence on non-family members: first, Nisha, then the hotel concierge and, later, the analyst. Perhaps here would be the emergence of a family romance fantasy – that she did not really belong to this family but rather was from another different "aristocratic" family. The reference to the "aristocratic French Jews" whom she could not be among the way she could not be with her analyst in the analyst's private life brings the fantasy of her longing to be with the analyst and the French Jews to light. On the other hand, the family romance fantasy does seem linked to her adored Nisha, the maid/mother, whom the patient also links to the analyst. Thus, her family romance fantasy seems complicated, perhaps with many facets.

Here too could come the rescue fantasy which the analyst mentions, a fantasy which could have interchangeable elements as to who would rescue whom. These rescue fantasies could be based on her wish/need to be rescued, but also based on its opposite – her omnipotent wish that she was the powerful and real rescuer. The analyst describes her own feeling that the patient, though fantasizing herself as a hero, also as the unconscious fantasy of wishing her analyst would be the mother who would nurse the baby patient. Finally, there could be a continuance of fantasies about her submission to the other and its reverse: her dominance and control of the other. Such fantasies seem to be enacted by both her rebellion and then submission to the father's wishes and, also, her keeping control over the treatment timing.

Patient's transference and analyst's countertransference

The patient, despite her fears and oppositional actions, seemed open to Dr. Cairo. Thus some of the patient's transference wishes and ideas seemed reasonably accessible in the material Dr. Cairo provided. For example, she expresses her wish to have Dr. Cairo all to herself, reminding us through her possessiveness of her sibling rivalry, especially with the five-year-younger sister who had arrived in the family shortly before her own traumatic tonsillectomy. The birth of the sister and the patient's possible resentment of the mother's somewhat illusive attention shifting to the new baby could have ushered in a fantasy that it was because of the mother's devotion to the new baby that the mother was not there for her at the time of the tonsillectomy crisis.

In contrast to her freedom to express feelings of possessiveness toward Dr. Cairo, the patient expresses a negative thought that the analyst, if given the opportunity, would judge her. She explains that she avoids this imagined and unwelcome experience by claiming that she avoids making known to the analyst any of her own choices, which if known would bring the analyst's contempt upon her. Apparently there was an expectation that the analyst's position would be in disagreement with the patient's own choices. Thus, the patient has the fantasy that it was best not to have or at least to voice her choices. The contempt that the patient believed the analyst had toward her may have paralleled her belief in parental contempt; it could also be a projection of her own contempt toward the analyst/mother, which she tries to keep hidden. On that score, she competes with the analyst and perhaps feels that she is as good or even a better therapist than the analyst, the analyst merely being a "doctor who may have difficulty reading the data correctly." (This reference is made by the patient to the analyst about another doctor, but I had the impression that Dr. Cairo saw this as a displacement from the patient's feelings toward her analyst.)

She in turn acts amused toward the analyst, thinly disguising her frustration that the analyst will not answer her simplest inquiry that pries into the life and opinions of the analyst. It is as if the analyst will not let her climb into her primal scene bed, the way the parents had done, infuriating the patient. As an alternative it seems her wish is that the analyst be an independent woman devoted entirely to her unburdened by "other" children or husband – perhaps the way Nisha had seemed to the little girl, or perhaps in the fantasy of being the only child/baby to the analyst. On the other hand, the analyst felt that the patient did not fully trust the analyst, so she may also think of the analyst as unworthy, perhaps because of her taking the dirty money. This would be in contrast to the father who was admired because she "never saw a hand go in the pocket" (for money).

The analyst in her own countertransference is patient and positive toward the patient, even tender, empathizing with her and rooting for her. At the same time, the analyst has some sense – and perhaps uneasiness – about her patient's destructive potential.

From the patient's behavior and attitudes, one can imagine a child's fear of a parent acting amused or worse, disapproving of her expressed likes or dislikes and her expressed opposition to parental authority that does not mirror the parental preferences. That sounds consonant with her need to go along with parental choices regarding religion, the right therapist, and appropriate marital partner in order to avoid angering the parents or perhaps fearing some kind of rejection from them. As I stated earlier, however, her going along with the parental requirements might as well have fit with an oedipal solution of doing not so much what the parents wanted, but what she felt the father wanted of her, perhaps as she might have interpreted her role in the parental bed to suit her oedipal fantasies.

Taken together, these ideas picture the patient balancing on a tight rope of competing fantasies that leave her unsure where her best interests lie: with the father's approval of her in the Jewish husband's bed, and through that her staying close to the father in a dutiful role that actually is a pseudo grown-up position, or with the foreigner mother/analyst who she envisions will nurture her but she fears she cannot fully trust. Further, on balance, by maintaining her fantasy of the analyst's negative judgments, the patient might continue to fear that her analyst would hold her back or not know what the right way to proceed would be. These are the two main fantastical pulls, which externalize the growing up, as if the choices for her are made by others, and her choice is to submit.

Dr. Cairo hoped that the patient would have one more interruption and then a treatment with some other analyst. I picture that such a final, later piece of work would come with Dr. Cairo for yet another analytic engagement, so that the patient could better resolve her oedipal issues and allow herself to take responsibility for her choices and to mature fully. Thus, the analyst and I both see the patient as potentially able to analyze her inner conflicts and turn her fantasies into viable sublimated realities.

As discussant, I was asked by the editors to explain how I came to my descriptions of fantasies and further and more importantly to speculate how I understand that Dr. Cairo came to hers. In considering Dr. Cairo's lovely work with the patient, it seemed that she "read" – that is intuited – meaning from what her patient said, and did not say. I think she coupled these conclusions with her awareness of what followed, i.e., the next material volunteered by the patient after the analyst offered some interpretation. Another source of knowledge, especially of the unverbalized messages, was the actions of the patient and the analyst's discovery of her own actions, such as what she chose to say and not say. To this must be added her countertransference. For example, the times when the analyst "sensed" the patient's frustration behind her humor would be such an occasion. It is with all of these elements, along with the accumulation of her experience of the patient, that I think she came to her ideas about the underlying fantasies.

For myself, I would say that having followed the progress of the transference/ countertransference exchange, the development of my sense of the underlying fantasy was enhanced by my theories and by my identifications that resonated with my own experiences both professional and personal. As I was encouraged by the editors to give free rein to my own associations, I was able to be in touch with those latter influences as well as the material. It is challenging to contemplate how one learns of a person's underlying fantasies; in some ways it is more challenging to understand the "how" than it is the "what" of these fantasies.

I close with special thanks for the wonderful case material that Dr. Cairo presented that allowed me to give free rein to my own fantasies and associations.

Chapter 12

Noises and voices

Discussion on Babette, interrupted

Catalina Bronstein

Irene Cairo's very interesting clinical material gives us the opportunity to explore different ways of looking at and thinking about unconscious phantasies and the role they play in the analytic encounter.

As Grotstein proposed, virtually everything that is mental can be thought of as related to unconscious phantasy (Grotstein, 2008). Freud and Klein had a different conceptualization of unconscious phantasy. Even though Freud used the term "phantasy" rather differently at various stages in his work, he mostly spoke of phantasies as compromise formations based on wish-fulfilling activities belonging to the order of conscious or pre-conscious imaginary creations that arise when an instinctual wish is frustrated, such as in daydreaming (Bronstein, 2015a; Spillius, 2001). However, Freud also proposed a theory of primal phantasies, 'Urphantasie', in which some phantasies were seen to have a phylogenetic origin (Freud, 1916). We can speculate whether this concept of phylogenesis in relation to phantasy had an impact on Klein's ideas.

For Klein, phantasy is a basic mental activity present in a rudimentary way from birth onwards and even though it can also be used defensively, it is synonymous with unconscious thought (Spillius, 2001). Given that phantasies originate from the intimate connection between drives and object, they bring together affects and representations (Klein, 1946; Heimann, 1952). In Susan Isaac's words: 'There is no impulse, no instinctual urge or response which is not experienced as unconscious phantasy' (Isaacs, 1948: 80). Early embodied phantasies co-exist with those that belong to later stages of development and that are more organized and carry symbolic meaning, such as, for example, Oedipal phantasies. These early embodied phantasies could also be described, following Kristeva, as a 'pre-narrative envelope', as an 'emotional experience, both psychical and subjective, based on the drives in an interpersonal context' (Kristeva, 2000: 773).

This notion had already been assumed by Isaacs in her statement that 'meanings, like feelings, are far older than speech' (Isaacs, 1948: 84). I believe that corporeal elements that form part of the constitution of early 'raw', 'pre-symbolic', 'pre-narrative' phantasies interlock with the signifying process and greatly influence the emotional effect that can be experienced in the communication between patient and analyst (Bronstein, 2015a). While the content of the patient's discourse can carry symbolic meaning, early phantasies can affect the rhythm, the prosody, the 'semiotics' that accompany the account. In the case we are discussing, it seems to me that this rhythm is compounded by the stammering – the interruption in the formulation of words. I imagine that this might have produced a particular effect on Irene because in order to retain contact with the content of the associations, the analyst probably needs to adjust to the interruptions in the discourse. On the other hand, these interruptions form part of the discourse itself. I would like to suggest that whilst these earlier phantasies, expressed in the rhythm and flow of language, can at times come together with the symbolic process, they are often lived out in a split form that cannot be integrated but that still maintain an important influence on the patient's communications, in her coming and goings as well as in the way she might feel about herself and her objects.

Unconscious phantasy in the analytic session

Psychoanalysis aims at understanding the unconscious phantasies and concomitant anxieties that underline our patients' picture of both their internal and external objects as they are relived in the transference relationship. Defence mechanisms are part of these phantasies. One of the early defence mechanisms, projective identification, exercises a powerful effect on the analyst as it can lead to the actualization of the patient's unconscious phantasies and has a particular effect on the analyst's countertransference. Patients live out their defensive system in the session, often drawing the analyst into it, as Betty Joseph often described (Joseph, 1985).

There is an important difference between the idea that it is the patient's unconscious phantasies that are being projected into the analyst and one that sees the analytic process structured as a bi-personal field under the influence of unconscious phantasies that are determined by the relationship between patient and analyst (Baranger and Baranger, 2008). I think, personally, that there is an oscillation between these two possibilities. At times, we function mainly as recipients of the patient's projections – being affected by them but still being able to maintain a certain degree of objectivity that enables us to formulate an interpretation that reflects this dynamic – whilst at other times, we participate in the creation of a particular situation in which we share some basic unconscious phantasy with our patient. When this last situation remains undetected by the analyst it can lead to repetition and a sense of disappointment in both patient and analyst (Bronstein, 2015b).

It is only through the deep understanding of our countertransference that we can elucidate what role our phantasies and anxieties play in the analytic session. Given these complexities, unless we have access to the analyst's countertransference it is impossible to 'know' what the unconscious phantasies are that are being played out in the analytic relationship between another analyst and his/her patient. I see my discussion of Irene's case, therefore, as an exercise aimed at offering some ideas inspired by the clinical material but that might not necessarily reflect an accurate picture of this case.

As with the many different possibilities that arise when looking at a particular material, the analyst's interpretations can only point at one specific conflict that they feel is being relived at that moment in the session. Our interpretations arise mostly from configurations that Bion, following Poincare, called 'selected facts', by which he meant 'coherence and meaning that was given to facts that were already known but whose relatedness has not hitherto been seen' (Bion, 1963: 19). Therefore, the necessary over-determination of the patient's associations and constructions can never be completely reached by one interpretation. Thus, when I am addressing the different layers of unconscious phantasies that might be simultaneously operating in a particular session, it is with the understanding that not all of them will be reachable or available to exploration.

Irene tells us that Babette came for treatment at different stages of her life, always interrupting and returning after a period of time. Babette gave two reasons for her wish to have treatment. The first, that she was able to tell her family about, was because of her 'stammering'. She seemed to contrast this with what she felt was her real reason for coming, which was to be able to 'find a man', a sign that she wished to be independent from her father's imposition that she should find a Jewish man – like him – to marry. I feel that in this first statement there is already a presentation of the split within herself: a symptom (stammering) that she felt was acceptable to the superego (as its meaning was not revealed by the symptom) and the more 'secret' conflict involving her Oedipal struggle of which she was somehow more conscious. I think that these two reasons perhaps show the juxtaposition of two internal conflicts that she could not work out. One that was felt to be linked to an early trauma, as well as to a possible early traumatic relationship with her mother, and another that was more linked to the Oedipus complex, her own anxiety about the possibility of surrendering to the Oedipal longing for her father and her wish to move on in her life – to own her own sexuality and destiny. We could thus think that the 'rescue phantasies' that Irene mentions are a compromise solution, or an attempt to resolve these two main unconscious conflicts: early anxieties about the death of the self and object (connected to the body and to the early relationship to the mother), as well as anxieties of an Oedipal kind.

Irene describes the therapeutic encounter that started when Babette was 20 years old and that was characterized by her coming back to therapy, then to analysis, and leaving again at different times in her life. While the treatment was initially based on a twice weekly basis and lasted just three months, the second instalment was twice weekly for two years, the third (ten years later) was three times per week for four years and the fourth was three and four times per week for eight years. It seems to me, that while Babette managed to increase the frequency of both the sessions and the length that she allowed herself to stay in treatment before she interrupted it, she nevertheless had to repeat a pattern where she could not allow the analysis to reach a more organic and mutually agreed ending.

With hindsight, it is interesting that we are presented with the statement that the treatment had been 'interrupted' rather than 'finished'. In fact, when the patient's sister contacted Irene and asked for therapy, Irene told her that Babette 'was still her patient'. This made me wonder whether there is still a possibility that Babette will return and ask for more help, as well as the shared phantasy between patient and analyst of a continuum contact where the treatment is never ended, just interrupted. This would not be dissimilar to the stammering that involves an interruption in the flow of words. In these cases particular words cannot reach their natural ending so as to be able to move to the next word. Amongst these possibilities, we could perhaps think of this situation as one that was determined by a claustro-agoraphobic anxiety where there is a permanent juggling between distance and separation from the object, the result of a schizoid mode of being (Rey, 1994). But even more, I think it might also highlight an early anxiety about the death of the infant and of the object. Irene clearly pointed out the possible impact that early trauma had on her patient and perhaps endings were equated to potential death, whether it was about the end of a relationship or the feared end of a particular word that occurs once it is fully enunciated.

The third element that had an impact on me when I read this material is linked to what Irene describes as 'the power of words and language'. In my reading, I was constantly aware that for this patient the use of 'language' seemed to be constantly connected to a potential for confusion and with a subsequent need to separate and try to be in control of what could come out of her mouth. As if, perhaps, the anxiety was about the possibility of finding herself saying what could not be said, and a need to control the 'foreign', the 'unconscious' that could emerge at any moment and that was felt to be a threat to the patient and potentially to her family as well. This might have been represented by the foreign analyst, or by the non-Jewish foreign man, the foreign language as well as anything that was felt to be a dangerous or 'foreign' internal and external experience. At the same time, the foreignness was a source of attraction and, as Irene mentions, a vehicle for identification and idealization of her analyst.

Clinical material

I will try to follow the clinical material and convey my thoughts about it. Given that my comments are being made from outside the analytic encounter they should be considered just as the result of what was inspired in me by the material.

Reading this very interesting clinical material one of the things that had an impact on me was Babette's need to call her analyst to 'verify' the time of the **Friday** session. This session was on a day when she would normally not have therapy. In the message she left for her analyst, Babette said she did not need her analyst to call her back. I wonder whether Irene felt that despite this comment,

Babette needed to be called back, to feel that her analyst had heard her. This call and the associations the patient produced on Friday made me think about what Babette had said about wanting to hear her analyst's soothing voice, a voice that she later linked to Nisha, the nanny who looked after her physically and emotionally. At one point she says:

> In my family silence is a communication. When there were words it was terrible. That's when trouble started ... I also think your voice is different. Remember that time when I couldn't sleep, and in the night I would hear my mother's voice? I think your voice is soothing.... There was no voice like that in my childhood. There's always that shrill voice, angry or crying and maybe I thought, "Dr Cairo is too busy to call me" – my father was always too busy. My mother would speak on the phone and I wouldn't hear all the words, and she spoke in her language. So I didn't understand a lot of what she said.

It seems to me that she is expressing her very mixed, confused view of her objects. She is both trying to assess the relationship to her mother in connection to both the tone of her voice that – as she could not understand the words – would indicate whether there is an angry, upset, or indifferent maternal object. I wonder whether Babette was listening more to Irene's tone of voice than to her actual words.

On the **Monday** I thought that she was curious about her analyst. I think that there were two parallel phantasies being lived out in the transference. The experience of her analyst changing her time – in this case to actually accommodate Babette – led to confusion and anxiety. She might have needed to hear Irene's voice to feel reassured that she was neither angry nor crying, that she still had her usual composed soothing voice, the reassurance that the Nisha-analyst had not been transformed into the angry or upset mother. But then her analyst changes the session's time, exposing Babette to the awareness that Irene has a life outside the encounter with her patient, a life of her own. I felt that Babette was trying to deal with her rage with Irene for not 'talking', not telling her whether she saw the film she was talking about, challenging her wish to be in a state of mutual projective identification and thus canceling her longing for sameness. She is then confronted by an abrupt sense of separation. Perhaps Babette was searching for an identification that could ease her sense that her analyst had changed into a scary, mad mother. Perhaps at this stage the Oedipal constellation was being taken over by early phantasies (even of an early Oedipus complex) where she could no longer recognize the analyst, as if the maternal object now appeared to be strange and mad, no longer speaking in a familiar voice but producing instead 'noises' that were felt to be different from the ones that she knew. Babette is scared. I thought that she might be scared by the changes in her perception of her analyst. That she was not able to bring together the memory of the safe object with her perception of an unsafe object, with both remaining part of a conflict which is dealt with by trying to speak, to formulate words whilst having to control the communication by cutting it into pieces.

We could consider that Babette's early experience of hospitalization in a foreign city at the age of two and her later experience, when she could have died from a haemorrhage in a hotel in a foreign city, must have greatly contributed to her experience of feeling surrounded by either unavailable or unsafe objects with anxiety about what they could do to her as well as of what she could do to them. However, as Klein stated, 'no danger situation arising from external sources could ever be experienced by the young child as a purely external and known danger' (Klein, 1948: 39). The drive itself has a potentially traumatizing effect (Verhaegue, 1988). A situation might become traumatic when it is felt to trigger an unsustainable conflict between life and death drives, a conflict that threatens the ego with a potential defusion of the drives and its potential annihilation (Baranger et al., 1988; Bronstein, 2013). According to Klein, the workings of the life and death drives include their attachment to objects from the beginning of the infant's life. For her, internal objects cannot be thought of separately from either the mechanisms that create them or the underlying unconscious phantasies. Unconscious phantasies and internal objects can be defined as being in a dialectical reciprocal relationship. They come together as part of the same psychic experience (Bronstein, 2001). Phantasies about internal objects greatly influence the perception we have of reality.

In her anxiety that she could be exterminated from both within and without, Babette needs to rely on a safe object, on somebody who will reassure her that she will not be abandoned in this state of mind. I think that at the centre of this anxiety is the potential that her objects could suddenly change. This change might be caused not just by the numerous external changes and migrations that she was subjected to, but also by Babette's own changeable internal feelings and the movement between her love and hatred towards her objects. Any change could then be potentially experienced as dangerous, maybe bringing a sense that she could be left in a world where there are no safe voices, just strange noises that she cannot quite decipher. Changes then need to be cancelled out, forgotten or even disavowed. When Irene interprets that Babette is scared, Babette agrees. She then comments on the difference between the 'old city', full of noises. 'The noises on the street are different. So different from the silence. The silence is sad'. Irene then interprets that Babette is frustrated with her when she cannot get an answer and that the sadness is because of her analyst's silence. Babette says that perhaps her analyst is her French teacher, all elegant, always the same. At the end Babette has forgotten the change of time.

It seems to me that Babette is trying to work out a 'film', an image that she can get hold of, an image in the session which can be shared with her analyst, that makes her feel that her analyst is the same safe object she is trying to hold on to. But her analyst keeps changing, not just changing the session time, but changing in her patient's perception. I think that change means persecution, 'chaos' and potential extermination. It seems to me that Babette's struggle was compounded by her own potential persecutory guilt represented by a harsh superego that contributed to her fear of extermination.

Early anxieties about the relationship to the maternal object might have become accentuated by Oedipal strivings and through her experience of the effects of pubertal changes. Safety, represented by a need to accommodate and appease the different demands stemming from her drives as well as from her superego, could have led Babette to a compromise formation where words had to be interrupted and controlled, similarly to her need to control her passions (passionate love/passionate hatred and a longing for a passionate sexual relationship).

Rescue phantasies

In Freud's 1910 paper, 'A Special Type of Choice of Object made by Men,' he discusses rescue phantasies. Amongst several possible explanations for these phantasies, he mentions that the act of birth itself is the danger from which the individual wishes to be saved by his mother's efforts:

> Birth is both the first of all dangers to life and the prototype of all the later ones that cause us to feel anxiety, and the experience of birth has probably left behind in us the expression of affect which we call anxiety.
>
> (Freud, 1910: 173)

Freud proposed that one possible meaning of the rescue phantasy in a woman is the wish that she herself give birth to a child-her, that is, that the rescuer becomes her own parent. Britton discussed this in relation to the erotic countertransference and the offer to the analyst to see himself as a hero (Britton, 2003).

Babette describes her rescue phantasy in a Monday session. Irene proposes the idea that her patient was both idealizing her as well as feeling persecuted by her. She interprets Babette's wish to be a baby as well as identifying herself with her analyst. I think that this rescue phantasy allows us the opportunity to consider the different levels of phantasy that are operating at the same time. Babette seems to start the session by acknowledging how difficult it was to wait to see her analyst again. She remembers her analyst's suggestion that Babette did not want to have a voice of her own. It made me wonder whether Babette felt that her analyst could see that she wanted to project herself into her analyst and become her. This is followed by Babette's comment that she could not think because she had wanted to go to the toilet.

I think that Babette might have felt that Irene rejected her projections and her wish to identify with her analyst, to 'become' her analyst. Babette was possibly then confronted with a sense of internal urinary tension that she desperately wanted to evacuate, a potential 'infected' object that she wanted to eliminate as it prevented her from thinking. Having to confront the sense that she could not take possession of her analyst brought 'bad dreams'. I think that her desperate need to be identified with her analyst could be motivated partly by envy but also as a defence from paranoid anxiety that is stirred up when she feels they are separate. This anxiety is provoked by Babette's fear of her own hostility towards the maternal object, her wish to destroy and her fear of being destroyed (September 11), such as in her fear of subways, which she needs to use to come to analysis. Her daydream/rescue phantasy is one where there is a disaster which she survives for days and involves her rescuing a baby which she nurses.

I feel that all different levels of phantasy come together here: Babette's anxiety about getting trapped with and inside the maternal object into which she projected herself (the subway/linked to birth – but one that can become like a claustrum from where she can also control the object, following an idea by Meltzer (1990). 'There is a disaster' which protects her from having to acknowledge her death wishes in which she kills everybody else except mother and baby. She becomes identified with her heroic mother and looks after the baby/her. As if, in this construction, she can bring together simultaneously, an idealized relationship between mother and baby, a narcissistic phantasy where she embodies both of them and the triumph brought about by cancelling the parental intercourse, as everybody else seems to have died or disappeared. Perhaps I see this as connected to the 'various languages' being spoken in the analysis: the language of the body, the infantile phantasies, the unknown mother, a foreign mother who could be crazy or suicidal, who might wear the perfect suit but who can also be so different. Thus, a mother who can make her feel at the mercy of noises that cannot be deciphered, but is also the idealized mother.

When following the movement of the phantasies in the session, I ask myself why these associations appear at certain moments in the session. It seems to me that Babette is both reliving the conflict between mother and baby, but at the same time she is also able to create a metaphor, one that is a condensation of the conflicts she is experiencing in relation to her analyst. She is frightened of her own drives that stem from inside the subway-mind and of her analyst's condemnation, but she is also seeking help and able to bring this material to her session.

I find it extremely interesting that the stammering almost disappeared in the course of the analysis. I think that this is proof that the analysis reached the different levels of phantasy and enabled a more coherent and integrated ego, which must have helped Babette to find her own language.

References

Baranger, M. and Baranger, W. (2008). The Analytic Situation as a Dynamic Field. *International Journal of Psychoanalysis*, 89: 795–826.
Baranger, M., Baranger, W. and Mom, J. M. (1988). The Infantile Psychic Trauma from Us to Freud: Pure Trauma, Retroactivity and Reconstruction. *International Journal of Psychoanalysis*, 69: 113–128.
Bion, W. R. (1963). *Elements of Psycho-Analysis*. London: Heinemann.
Britton, R. (2003). *Sex, Death and the Superego*. London: Karnac.
Bronstein, C. (2001). What are Internal Objects? In C. Bronstein, (ed.), *Kleinian Theory. A Contemporary Perspective*. London: Wiley, pp. 108–124.

Bronstein, C. (2013). Nobody died! Trauma in Adolescence. In E. McGinley, E. and A. Varchevker (eds), *Enduring Trauma through the Life Cycle*. London: Karnac, pp. 43–62.

Bronstein, C. (2015a). Finding Unconscious Phantasy in the Session: Recognizing Form. *International Journal of Psychoanalysis*, 96: 925–944.

Bronstein, C. (2015b). The Analyst's Disappointment: An Everyday Struggle. *Journal of the American Psychoanalytic Association*, 63: 1173–1192.

Freud, S. (1910). *A Special Type of Choice of Object made by Men*, S.E., 11 (pp. 165–175).

Freud, S. (1916). *Introductory Lectures on Psycho-Analysis*, S.E., 15 (pp. 1–240).

Grotstein, J. (2008). The Overarching Role of Unconscious Phantasy. *Psychoanalytic Inquiry*, 28: 190–205.

Heimann, P. (1952). Certain Functions of Introjection and Projection in Early Infancy. In M. Klein, P. Heimann, S. Isaacs and J. Riviere (eds), *Developments in Psychoanalysis*. London: Karnac, pp. 122–168.

Isaacs, S. (1948). The Nature and Function of Phantasy. *International Journal of Psychoanalysis*, 29: 73–97.

Joseph, B. (1985). Transference: The Total Situation. *International Journal of Psychoanalysis*, 66: 447–454.

Klein, M. (1946). Notes on Some Schizoid Mechanisms. In *Developments in Psychoanalysis*. London: Karnac, 1989.

Klein, M. (1948). On the Theory of Anxiety and Guilt. In *Envy and Gratitude*. London: Hogarth, 1980, pp. 25–42.

Kristeva, J. (2000). From Symbols to Flesh: The Polymorphous Destiny of Narration. *International Journal of Psychoanalysis*, 81: 771–787.

Meltzer, D. (1990). *The Claustrum. An Investigation of Claustrophobic Phenomena*. London: Karnac.

Rey, H. (1994). The Schizoid Mode of Being and the Space-Time Continuum (Before Metaphor). In H. Rey, H., *Universals of Psychoanalysis in the Treatment of Psychotic and Borderline States*. London: Free Association Books, pp. 2–30.

Spillius, E. (2001). Freud and Klein on the Concept of Phantasy. In C. Bronstein (ed.), *Kleinian Theory: A Contemporary Perspective*. London: Wiley.

Verhaegue, P. (1988). Trauma and Hysteria within Freud and Lacan. *The Letter: Lacanian Perspectives in Psychoanalysis*, 14, Autumn: 87–106.

Chapter 13

Not quite a princess

Janice S. Lieberman

> They saw at once that she must be a real princess when they had felt the pea
> through twenty mattresses and twenty feather beds. Nobody but a real princess
> could have such a delicate skin.
>
> (Hans Christian Andersen)

Karen, a 30-year-old divorced woman, living alone and employed as a secretary
at an advertising agency, entered treatment presenting herself as helpless and
speaking about herself in a way that made me think of her as quite childlike and
dependent. She was referred to me by the analyst of her friend Zelda who was
then completing a four times a week analysis. Zelda seemed to be considerably
more developed and an unlikely peer of Karen. Karen came into treatment
hoping to become more like Zelda, especially since Zelda had recently become
engaged to a wealthy doctor. Karen expected me to offer her suggestions and
to tell her what to do in all areas of her life. She was, however, able to tolerate
the fact that I did not behave with her as her mother, Zelda, and most of her
female friends were accustomed to doing. The following is a summary of the
beginning and some of the middle phase of her treatment, a span of about four
years.

Karen's (heretofore K) presenting problems were numerous and diffuse. She
reported experiencing low self-esteem in every area of her life and complained
that her life and her job were boring; nothing interested her. She believed herself
to be unattractive and ungainly and was especially self-conscious about her small
breasts and heavy legs. She described her relationships with both men and
women as self-destructive. She was frigid during sex and wondered if this was
due to the trauma of an abortion at 19 and of an operation for pre-cancer of the
cervix at 25. She believed her genitals to be damaged. She was unclear as to why
she had married a man she had experienced as unattractive and unappealing. He
had rejected her by leaving her for another woman. They were divorced after
four years of marriage. Four years after the divorce, she was still feeling hurt and
greatly traumatized and missed the status of marriage. She felt herself to be an
abject failure and hoped that psychoanalysis might enable her to feel up to

finding a husband and possibly a job that she liked; yet she was pessimistic, for she considered herself to be a "basket case."

Despite K's bleak self-description, I found her to be lovely, well-dressed, well-spoken, and of some intelligence. She was able to reflect upon her problems in a psychological manner that was pseudo-sophisticated and probably not that accurate, but that did not at all reflect the low intelligence with which she felt herself to be endowed. However, the wish that treatment provide her the outcome Zelda received from *her* analyst was rather naïve and concrete, and I suggested that she begin treatment twice weekly in order to assess whether an analysis, which the patient had asked for, was appropriate. I found no defects in her ego functioning. She had a number of stable though ambivalent relationships. Her superego was well established. She was reliable and appropriate. The material that emerged seemed to reflect conflicts at *every* phase of development. At that point, no particular phase seemed central. Although her diagnosis was unclear to me, the extent of her problems made me believe that a thorough analysis was needed, that psychotherapy would not be enough. (I was not aware that I had somehow been led to believe something that K's mother had told her and was a central part of her conscious and unconscious self-image: that *all* people had problems but *she* had *more* than *most* people!) K made the financial arrangements that would enable her to come four times a week and within a few weeks the analysis became the central focus of her life. She appeared to be highly motivated and interested in the analytic process.

The beginning of treatment was quite confusing. I found K difficult to listen to and to understand from the point of arriving at any dynamic understanding of the origins and chronology of her problems. Her ability to experience or to communicate any emotion was minimal. She was intellectualized and obsessive. Her voice was tight and trying to listen to. I experienced it as withholding and having an anal-retentive quality. Her initial associations had to do with feelings of loneliness and obsessive thoughts about being excluded and unwanted by friends. She interspersed these with associations about her feelings of ineptness about buying clothes, changing her hairdo, going for exercise, trying to improve her figure and her ungainly legs. She communicated this in a manner that made it difficult to understand from the point of view of its inner meaning. It was shallow and superficial. For the most part I listened and did not respond to her many requests that I give her advice and support as she believed was the practice of her friends' therapists.

Analysis of K's defense of isolation of affect yielded some changes. Her constricted tone of voice altered, and strong affects, especially depression and rage, emerged. It became apparent that her original listlessness and incapacity to work or to take charge of her life was related to a stubborn refusal to work or to seek a better job. She experienced having to work as a "comedown." Themes of entitlement, envy of others, and the fantasy that others "just got what they wanted, automatically," emerged. She experienced for the first time on a conscious level tremendous rage at her parents, especially her mother. She believed, and for a long time led me to believe, that she had been the victim of a most unempathic mother. However, her unabated rage at her mother, her continued use of her sessions for discharge rather than for understanding, her unwillingness to examine what was inside her, and a basic lack of movement in her life as well as in the treatment led me to re-evaluate the efficacy of empathic reflection, a technique I was using at that time with narcissistic patients. I undertook, with some trepidation, an active phase of defense analysis, which then resulted in a clearer understanding of her underlying dynamics. She manifested intense jealousy of her older brother, feeling less preferred because she was not a boy (*"boys* got *everything automatically"*), and feelings of jealousy, rage, and being excluded when her father paid attention to her mother. Attempts to have her parents repair old wounds she believed they had inflicted upon her were made in the form of requests for money and gifts, which, when given, never seemed to satisfy her. Not having a husband, never earning enough money to support herself adequately, and being forever miserable were the penance she paid to her superego for her jealous and rivalrous feelings. They reflected the vengeance she took on her mother: her parents could never feel released from worry and financial responsibility for their grown daughter. K's greatest pleasure was to meet her father for lunch in order to discuss with him how he would pay for her most recent debts while mother remained at home.

I began to understand her initially meek and unassuming posture to be similar to that of the princess in *The Princess and the Pea*. At the beginning of this fairy tale, the princess appears, soaking wet from a rainstorm, at the door of a woman who takes her in and gives her a bed. On the couch-bed, K tried to demonstrate that she, too, was a *true* princess, by the volume of her complaints and her exquisite sensitivity.

The following dream (presented to me typed, with a drawing) from the first few months of treatment reflects K's fragility, extensive use of defense, her hopes for the analysis as well as the trauma of her abortion:

> I was among a group of people and was pregnant. Eight out of the ten women were pregnant. We were in and around an empty swimming pool. The pool was deep and at the shallow end it gradually and gently sloped up to meet the ground. The colors were soft pastel shades of blue and white. The dream had a warm soft quality to it. I was relaxed and happy (content) about being pregnant. It all seemed natural.
>
> Then I had to pack my luggage. There were three suitcases of varying sizes that all neatly fit into one another. They were lovely old-fashioned bags made of thin cardboard-like material. They were white and delicate with pretty pale (and faded) blue "fleur-de-lis" on them. They reminded me of dainty, lovely old hat boxes that a Victorian woman might carry. Yet the locks were missing and most of the hooks were missing or didn't work. There was white tape around the edges to hold the bags together but it was coming off. This didn't upset me. There was also a woman there to help me

pack. During the packing I was standing on a mound of dirt. I seemed to be somewhat behind the mound, and about halfway up. [Drawing of the mound]

When the white tape didn't stick, we left the white bags and went around to the brown suitcase – strong, sturdy and practical. The mound was thick and dark (it was firm and reminded me of shit or manure but it wasn't offensive). I didn't actually pack anything because there weren't any belongings in the dream but I remember opening both suitcases. The white one I opened almost fully and it was empty and the brown one I only started to open so that the inside wasn't visible. In the dream everything seemed natural and flowing –nothing upset me. I just did what I had to do. I was young (about 19 or 20 – which is how old I was when I was pregnant) but I wasn't young in a negative or immature way – just inexperienced. I felt good.

K was the second-born of a middle-class Jewish couple with upper-class social aspirations, always living beyond their means. The first child, S, a boy, was two years older than K. He was nicknamed "the Hero," for he was mother's idol and could do no wrong. K was so envious of him that she hardly ever spoke to him or interacted with him, although it is quite apparent from the transference that she was at all times acutely aware of him.

K was nicknamed "the Princess" when she was born, an appellation that she considered to be a misnomer, but which seemed rather appropriate in the early years of her analysis! She believed that she was expected to grow up and marry a wealthy man as her life's work. Father wished no more children after the first was born. K and her younger brother, M, born when she was three, were conceived because mother pricked a hole in her diaphragm, a rather characteristic way that mother had of managing family affairs. Early in treatment, K reported tender feelings toward M and felt identified with him in mother's neglect of him. Later on, M came to share S's fate in being envied and the butt of K's contempt.

The following represents K's *perception* of her parents: Mother was described as conflicted and confused about who she was and unhelpful to her daughter in providing her a clear notion of who she was, where she belonged, and her value, especially as a female. Mother tried to adopt the Catholic values of the wealthy members of their village; yet she was the daughter of an Orthodox Jewish businessman with whom K's father was always unfavorably compared. Mother's concerns were material ones: money, clothes, jewelry, and gifts. Mother dominated father and criticized him for never earning enough to suit her needs. She was also described as playing the flirtatious, dumb coquette when she wanted something from father or another man. Needless to say, K internalized the harsh aspects of her parents' relationship, thinking of and treating others as objects. Mother's having to go to work when K was a teenager was regarded by the entire family as a sign of father's inadequacy as a provider. Mother was experienced by K as truly the Queen of the household, and her every whim and concern was to be respected and immediately obeyed. Father always stood up for mother in this respect. There was little room for anyone else, except occasionally for S's academic and financial successes, which mother then aggrandized. K experienced her mother as controlling and self-involved.

Mother's body was described as skinny, flat-chested, and girdled. In one of her first sessions K said:

> I don't like kissing my mother or holding her. I don't feel warmth from her. She tells me that she loves me. I don't believe it. Maybe it's the way she loves a son or daughter – clinging but not relaxed – she makes me uncomfortable. Mother's a manipulator. That's one of the things I dislike the most.

In the transference, I was at times experienced as pushy, controlling, and trying to "one up" her when I made any statement the slightest bit ahead of statements she had already made about herself. This would then enable her to become angry and avoid any close or tender feelings toward me, thus repeating with me the defensive sequence that had originated with mother. K used anger to defend against symbiotic and homoerotic longing for me. "I've become a frustrated lonely old maid. I bring all my problems here. All I am is a mass of functioning problems. Before my analysis my problems were latent; now they are blatant!"

Father was experienced more positively than mother and as more reasonable and helpful. I believe that K's ability to form a working alliance with me was based on these early positive experiences with father. K perceived herself as favored by him over her brothers. He was seen in two ways: (1) as passive; and (2) potentially explosive and dangerous, for he had a bad temper. This was enacted with me in the transference when K became explosive over some small thing. He was quite critical of her during her adolescence and seemed to be using angry defenses to avoid experiencing the sexual feelings her developing body aroused in him. Father would give all to mother, but begrudgingly support his daughter. Thus, even when she saw herself occupying a favored position, she still did not get what she wanted.

A number of key memories of early childhood were consistent with what I observed about K's character formation as an adult: As a toddler, she was prone to climb out of her crib and run out of the house. Rather than lock the door, her mother, on the advice of the pediatrician, tied her to the crib with sheets. After a while, when put in the crib, she would automatically raise her leg to be tied. Her loss in her struggle with her mother for autonomy resulted in the inhibition of aggression, her defense mechanism of turning against the self, and planted the seeds for the emergence of her adult traits of passivity, masochism, sexual compliance, and masked rebelliousness. K as a 2-year-old child detached from her mother by never showing her neediness and her wishes for tenderness. She learned and used curse words and mother would repeatedly slap her or wash her mouth out with soap. She would not give in. The physical contact she longed for with mother came in these forms. She continued throughout her life to struggle in this ambivalent manner with her mother, with female bosses, and with me in her sessions. At the age of 2, she also withheld her bowels and would not submit. She suffered from constipation and a spastic colon when she entered treatment and refused to seek medical relief. For most of her adult life she would not work to her fullest at her jobs. She at times would not cooperate by working in her analysis and withheld feelings and fantasies about me. She cried on the stairwell *outside* my office, but hardly ever *in* sessions.

K: I'm angry at mother. Had weird dreams over three nights. In between feeling angry at mother, I was doing the crossword puzzle and thought of her – she does them – and I had a warm feeling – she has to be bright if she can finish one of those things – I was unpleasant to her on Saturday – I don't talk to her and don't want to – Saturday morning she woke me at 9:30 – "Sorry, did I wake you?" – "No ... yes" – then she just ran down a list of what was going on – it made me angry – an uncle died – "I don't have his daughter's address," she said, "So call me for it when you send her a note." I was mad she was *telling* me to do it. It bothers me she *told* me to do it. Of course it might not have occurred to *me* to send L a card. It was two days after Valentine's Day that I thought of sending them to my nieces.

JL: On the one hand, your mother tells you to do things and you are angry; on the other hand you don't remember to do it.

K: Yes, if I *have* to do it. Borderline things I don't do. Mother tends to do them. I resent her telling me to do it, but I don't do it. It's *my* decision – mother is close to his daughter. *I'm* not.

As the session continued, I had to ask for the dreams referred to in the beginning and not reported – a habitual resistance. When I interpreted this, I was experienced by her as pushing her to remember the dreams she withheld.

DREAM: Visiting a villa in Italy (*where Zelda went on her honeymoon*); a street or waterway – embarrassed because I got my period and was bleeding on towels.

ASSOCIATIONS: Upset because friend M unavailable on weekends because she dates men (*session is on Monday, JL's office is Italianate in décor, but no reference is made by K to this*); sick of getting her period – a drag being a woman; wants to be pregnant; angry at mother; blames mother for this stuff; why did she have to have a second child? "My life is nothing but pain and work."

K: My mother takes control – she thinks for me – she speaks for me – she takes over so much that I'm not able to develop – I was just thinking about sending Valentine's cards to my nieces – it's the first time it occurred to me and it's too late. It takes me longer to make these decisions – I am so used to mother telling me what to do – if she leaves me alone I'll do it – I don't want her to know she can tell me to do it – I feel guilty about being nasty to her – she doesn't know why – I want to tell her I'm not a child and I don't want to be told what to do.

JL: This conflict with mother arises as you speak of your feelings about being a woman, having your period.

K: Mother never told me what to do – she neglected to talk to me about things of importance – only this etiquette bullshit – she's incapable of it – she's too fucked up about sex to talk about it – he doesn't know or care – I can accept that – but to come down on me about this other shit – it annoys me – it also annoyed me that she raved about the present my brother S and his wife A gave her; they are visiting her; his friend is getting married – *not* what I want to hear! God dammit! She tells me to call S, but *he* can call *me* if he wants to see me. I feel like I am screaming at her, but I'm still afraid of her – when I'm direct with her, she's a witch – like with my boss L – when I'm direct with her, it makes matters worse – the best way to deal with her is to have nothing to do with her.

K's chronic pattern of feeling angry and avoiding dealing with others was being worked through and understood.

K reported that on the occasions when her boss L criticized her, treated her badly and asked her to change, she kept control by refusing to do so and by hating her. "If I were to give in, I might like her and that would be too confusing. I'd also risk further rejection." The meaning of this remark was to be explored further. K seemed to comprehend that she used hate defensively and was guilty over masochistic aspects of her childhood relationship to her mother. This emerged in a dream of a woman who undressed her, solely for the woman's pleasure, while a man observed. She then remembered a childhood game. She pretended to be Annie Oakley and would tie herself to her bed; then she would feel anxious that mother would find her this way and punish her. "Was she masturbating?" "Yes ... no ... I don't remember." Among the further associations was the memory of mother tying her to her crib and the memory of mother slapping her face when she chewed on her bonnet string. "Giving in" seems to involve some unconscious sexual fantasy, as yet inaccessible to her.

K experienced intense jealousy of a younger woman, J, in her department at work "who does everything right," just like her older brother did, and is therefore well-treated by her boss L. J is at times also experienced as her young brother.

K: L helps J because she's below me – she expects *me* to write perfectly.

K: I feel that I am being a waitress for J and a slave for L, like with mother. J is favored like my brother. I'm not treated as though I'm capable of doing anything. L doesn't give me anything – no raise, no respect. I'm not considered; people just don't care. I share an office with J. She's not that friendly – acts like she is better than people. She bugs me. I wonder why I was so angry toward her recently. I came in Monday morning and wanted to kill her. She's like my brother S – he was the intelligent one. He treats me like a kid – he's always in charge, in control, superior.

(*After keeping her phone disconnected three nights in order to avoid speaking to mother, who might call*):

K: I say they really don't like me. They're really sick. It's really sick of my mother to love my older brother so much because he was the first. It has nothing to do with the individual. It blows my mind. There's no reason for it. Because he's a boy and born first. I think because I'm realizing that – they have no reason not to like me. I'm angry they could never recognize me or talk to me.

K was jealous of S because he had *visible* accomplishments that mother could brag about. Mother treated her as if she were an idiot. She was the only child in the family who did not have a penis. Her older brother was favored and M was given more attention because he was an infant. She fantasized that everybody else got what they wanted (mother's love, a penis) *magically*. Only *she* did not. She recalled lying in her bed one night. She overheard her mother in the next room saying goodnight to her brothers. Her ballerina doll (a long-legged, long-armed doll) was on her dresser. All of a sudden, the rubber bands holding the doll together snapped and the doll fell apart. She fantasized that she was an angel who comforted her. There are multiple meanings to this memory, which I understand as a screen memory. The doll's snapping is a projection of K's internal rage, her jealousy and feelings of exclusion. The angel represents a good mother, but also K's extensive use of the defense of fantasy for dealing with painful situations. Much analytic work had to be done before K could deal with similar situations by asking for the attention she needed; she had to work through her characteristic manner of comforting herself with fantasy and further withdrawal. In the transference she complained that stress from her analysis caused her to develop acne, leaving scars on her face. This was the analyst's fault. It was an outer reflection of her horrible inner self. In response to my question about what she would like from analysis (after she complained that she had gotten nothing from me), she screamed, "I want *physical* changes."

In the second year of treatment, K became pregnant by a married lover. This affair was a displacement of the paternal transference. She at first welcomed the pregnancy in that her fears that she was infertile from her earlier abortion were disconfirmed. Strong fantasies of having the child as a way for the lover to leave his wife and marry her seemed to be derivatives of an earlier wish to have a baby with father. Her lover's rejection of her was met with denial. Instead, she harbored the fantasy of their reuniting long after it seemed possible.

K's contempt for her mother was experienced over and over with me when she pointed out my "incompetence" and my "stupidity." She sought to revenge mother and at one time wished to revenge me by reporting me to the "authorities" for her failure to reach her analytic goal of finding a man.

K was able to get her mother to pay attention to her by provoking her to punish her. She felt that mother favored S and sought revenge for this by refusing to comply with her mother's demands. Her mediocre performance in school led to a low estimation of her abilities by both parents. Mother dealt with her disappointment in her daughter by taking over. As an example, one time she substituted her own artwork for her daughter's in a contest. Early in treatment, K repeated this interaction with me by working very hard at doing nothing in order to get me to do the analytic work for her. Feelings of longing for me were masked in the non-caring, sulky, defensive, and non-cooperative attitude that originally provoked her mother to behave in an even more critical, sarcastic, and competitive manner. In treatment, K became aware of having longed for a close relationship with her mother, as she re-enacted the defensive "not caring" with me in the transference.

Mother's criticism of her daughter's ungainly legs reinforced her poor body image. She was made to exercise her legs and was sent to charm school to learn how to walk. Mother told her that her walk was elephantine. She recalls with much pain a "roast" held by her boyfriend's fraternity brothers in which they ridiculed her legs by holding up two ham bones. A hypercathexis of her legs as a symbol of her defective body and unlovableness has held to an unwillingness to be in sexual situations and to be seen by anyone else. K did not develop the breasts she hoped would compensate for the fact that she did not have a penis. She felt fully deprived. Her surgery for cancer of the cervix prior to her husband's abandonment of her, her two abortions and abandonment by the men who had impregnated her, reinforced this negative self-perception. She had a dream of "a messy kitchen drawer" which we understood as her view of her genitals.

K similarly maintained a low estimation of her abilities in domestic, academic, and vocational areas. She thus did not pursue the acquisition of many skills and important knowledge. This served the unconscious function of spiting her mother, whom she blamed for her inferiority.

K: I'm damned if I'll take a writing course because my boss wants it (*training she knew she needed*).
JL: Do you recall you just told me that as a child you never got out of the ring to really ride and just went round and round because you were so angry at your mother for forcing you to take riding lessons? You said that you would have liked to have advanced, but refused to learn out of spite. It seems that that is being repeated here.

It became increasingly evident that K was a capable person who spitefully and angrily held herself back in all areas of her life. She felt sentenced to work, to be in therapy, and to go out and look for a man. She viewed these as great humiliations.

K was prone to making sarcastic, biting, devouring complaints about my giving her too much to handle (force-feeding). She would "spit" back what I would say.

K: So what good does that do me now?

JL: You want change to occur instantly. When it doesn't, you become furious. You do not allow yourself the pleasure of step-by-step gratification. You want it all at once.

The patient tended to "bite the hand that feeds her," causing the hand to withdraw. She most probably made her mother withdraw and lost the attention she craved. The biting was derived from wishes to bite the breast. (I had to analyze my own wish to withdraw in order to stay "with her" while being "bitten.")

She demanded that I prod her to associate, that I *make* her produce.

K: I want *you* to tell me. Why be in analysis if I am to do it myself?

JL: You seem to know what to do but withhold it and get furious with me for not taking over for you as your mother did.

At times she would stubbornly and spitefully withhold associations. At times she would stop and look at her watch as soon as we seemed to be getting somewhere (particularly as tender feelings were touched upon). She would become silent or, if it was late in the session, get into a rage and storm out the door. The interaction with her mother during the time she would run out of the house and have to be tied to her crib was being relived.

P: I don't give a damn.

A: If you don't give a damn, how come you're so angry?

At one point in treatment, every "What comes to mind?" led to an automatic "It's my mother" – which symbolically relived her automatic foot-raising when tied to her crib. She *defiantly* gave me what she thought I wanted – a Pavlovian response on the couch-crib.

Masochistic hypochondriacal complaints and narcissistic wishes for bodily perfection appeared to derive from an unconscious fantasy that her mother was responsible for her "castration" and her general defectiveness. A key memory that came up quite often was that her mother ignored for days her complaint that her ear hurt and that she had to be hospitalized for a mastoid infection. She accused me of not believing her when she thought she needed knee surgery (after telling me she had walked 20 blocks to my office!).

K: All that I've gotten from treatment is holes in my face (*from acne*). My body is ruined (*from stress*).

One prominent character resistance was to "play dead" and to unconsciously withhold observations about herself, so that she could then have the pleasure of responding provocatively to my interventions with "So what!"; "*I* knew that all along"; "So why do you wait till *now* to tell me?"; and "All you give me is *more* problems."

In the sessions following my absence for summer vacation one year, she appeared for the first time in a long time to be friendly to me and spoke of her growing trust in me and of her increasing dependence upon her analysis for solving her problems, indicating a shift in transference. She reported having the following dream:

> A battlefield – the Germans were coming – I was in a brick house – lying there – a mother and child there. The Germans were making sure they shot everybody and figured we were dead. I was scared. A German took a knife and cut a sliver from my finger to see if I was alive. I was fully awake when it happened. When he cut it, I remained perfectly still and detached myself from that pain. It amazed me that I was so quiet, pulling it off so well.

The patient's associations were to the incompetent doctor-analyst-mother who cut a hole-vagina in her leg (penis); to clean an abscess; to having her parents take care of her as they did; to being taken care of in analysis; and to her experiencing of work as "all pressure."

A: What is vivid is that you're a *live* person pretending to be dead.

On the surface, the patient often expressed oral dependent wishes to be taken care of by a (mothering) husband. She expressed these wishes in her associations to this dream after her analyst's absence. In this dream, her wishes were *characterologically* expressed by her stubborn, withholding, withdrawing, and masochistic stance. This had as its unconscious aim the eliciting of a sadistic, castrating response from others. In the dream, wishes to keep her pain from the German reflected her habit of crying on the stairwell outside my office rather than *in* sessions. She has reported that as a child, she was "damned" if she would ever let her mother see her cry. Her dreams and associations enabled us to reconstruct that she was too angry at mother to get close to her or show her any feelings that might help mother to really understand her. A year after she had this dream, she described her mother as using "Gestapo tactics."

Due to the working through of some of her hostility and spite, K then began to fantasize participating in a ménage à trois or having a homosexual relationship. These fantasies both frightened and excited her.

K: Maybe because I wasn't breast-fed and have a desire to suck someone's breasts, maybe because mine never grew big, I never had my mother's to go to and I never developed my own. The fantasy is to have a gorgeous body and to have a sexual encounter with another woman where I'm the aggressor. I can't fantasize anybody doing anything to me. There is a wish to be the other woman – to touch her breasts and thighs.

At the time these fantasies emerged in the treatment, she came to sessions in sexually provocative, scanty clothing, and was concerned that she be "noticed" by those in her office. A heterosexual relationship she began at this time was understood as a defense against homosexual wishes for me. She suggested that I treat her boyfriend, thus trying unconsciously to create a triangle that could stimulate her sibling rivalry, homosexual rivalry, and Oedipal rivalry. She spoke at the time of her extreme possessiveness and jealousy.

K: I can't stand the slight rejection. The idea of a man I like even *being* with another woman – even in a car driving. It could be my mother who was never with me – as though if someone is not with me every minute and letting me know I was the most important.... There was only one time when my father singled me out.... Yet when I'm singled out, I feel uncomfortable – I can't believe someone loves me.... How I hate my mother.

At that time she "revenged" me with her boyfriend and tantalized me with minute details of her sexual encounters.

Fantasies from the *Oedipal phase* of her development led to her taking on a number of character attitudes that have also served as resistance to the treatment. For example, by "playing dumb," she could be "daddy's girl." This has led to her "not thinking" in sessions.

K: My assets (*intelligence*) are what my parents hate.

As the painful affects of the past were remembered, re-experienced and understood, a number of changes in K's life were noted. She began to date and realistically assess men in terms of their suitability for her. She began to view herself as attractive and intelligent. She began to invite people to her apartment, to socialize, and made plans to share a summer house with some friends. She saw some women friends socially, but still experienced difficulties in these relationships due to her unconscious contempt for women, her unconscious fear of the emergence of homosexual feelings, and her more conscious jealousy and experiencing of women friends as trying to gain power by forcing her to do what they want to do in the choice of shared activities. She continued to progress in her work in advertising copywriting.

K dreamed that she was given a large apartment with many rooms that was structurally sound but involved lots of work within the rooms and possibly the help of an architect and a super (in her dreams, this was usually me). Above her apartment, in a much better place, lived her sister-in-law. Associations were to analysis, conflicts about continuing in analysis (was it worth the money?), and fixing up her own apartment. There appeared to be further involvement in the working alliance and hope.

A: This is the first one in which you've dreamed of *yourself* as making the repairs, even with the help of an architect or a super.
P: It's the first one that *needed* repairs – it had to be completely re-done – so dirty and disgusting – rats and mice running around – I couldn't do it – it

was impossible to do it on my own – my sister-in-law A didn't do a damn thing – my brother did it – I resent it – *I* have to work.

A: So though you know now that you're capable of working and doing this type of work, you'd prefer to be like A, who does nothing.

P: No – A's an extreme – I don't mind doing something – but I mind doing *all* of it – it's a drag to find shades. I'd like a little help – I have a new project – putting prints on one wall – it takes forever to get it done – it would be nice to find something to take care of it.

A: It seems that you have in your head a model of a woman who sits, like A, as *you* appeared in your other dreams, and of a man who works like S.

P: I don't mind doing it but I'd like someone to take me out on a Saturday night *after* I do it. I don't think I have the desire to be *totally* independent and self-sufficient for the rest of my life.

A: You seem to believe on some level that if you become self-sufficient you will always be alone; whereas if you hold back and don't make changes and improvements, a man will come along.

At this point in the analysis, I considered this patient to be the "middle phase of treatment." Her major conflicts were being relived and worked through. Treatment was slow because her masochistic, self-destructive character fought its progress and her parents were enabling her. There was some potential for a negative therapeutic alliance. The patient's passive, withholding tendencies and her unwillingness to take the initiative often resulted in her not offering up connections that she could have made on her own. The major task of the analysis at that time was to deal with the character defenses that resisted the treatment by way of interpretation so that the core of the infantile neurosis could be reached. If the character won, treatment would lose.

Chapter 14

Mirror, mirror on the wall: who's the fairest of us all?

Comments on Janice Lieberman's case: "Not quite a princess"

Carolyn S. Ellman

In reading Dr. Lieberman's paper, I felt I was back in the days of the controversies over penis envy (with Freud (1931), Horney (1926) and Klein (1932)) debating whether penis envy is basic or is a defense against some primary anger and longings related to the woman's wish for a baby and envy of her mother. Here is a woman that comes for analysis with all the anger and rage at her mother that seemed aimed at what she perceived as her defective body. Freud would have had a ball! Her mother loved her brother more because he had a penis! Her mother gave him everything and idolized him! He was wonderful! The patient (a girl) was terrible, stupid, defective, and sicker than the rest of the family. The mother made fun of the patient's legs (after all they were extensions that were ugly – not like the brother's beautiful penis). The mother had caused her to lose her penis (she dreams of the Nazis coming and taking off a sliver of her finger) and says her mother used "Nazi tactics" in raising her. Not only are these the accusations that Freud listed as to why the girl turns away from the mother (Freud, 1925) but also in this patient's case this mother traumatizes the patient during a crucial phase of development by destroying her autonomy.

The patient describes how because she would get out of her crib and run to the front door, the mother tied her to the crib so she could not get out. This is a powerful traumatic moment to come to know. It brings understanding that the patient's rage about not having a penis and envying her brother started much earlier in her very poor relationship with her mother. The mother's apparent lack of empathy for this little girl is so striking that it raises questions about what happened in these two children's first year of life. She and her mother have never been able to bond to help her to establish a separate sense of self and trust in the world. We see someone stuck in extreme envy without a sense that she can do anything about it. In the patient's mind, the mother/analyst has to make everything right. The mother is the cause of all that is bad. She has given her a vagina/ hole, making her defective and now she feels the mother/analyst has to find a way to compensate her. The patient is railing against the analyst that she is the cause of all her problems and it is her job to get her a husband/baby and make life right. She has to give her what Zelda her friend got from her analyst (a rich husband).

However, being a student of Horney and Klein I believe that penis envy is secondary to envy of the mother and I did not have to wait long in this case to start seeing some of these fantasies emerge.

Two months into the treatment, the patient has the following dream (which I am duplicating here because I think first dreams are extremely important):

> I was among a group of people and was pregnant. Eight out of the ten women were pregnant. We were in and around an empty swimming pool. The pool was deep and at the shallow end it gradually and gently sloped up to meet the ground. The colors were soft pastel shades of blue and white. The dream had a warm soft quality to it. I was relaxed and happy (content) about being pregnant. It all seemed natural.
>
> Then I had to pack my luggage. There were three suitcases of varying sizes that all neatly fit into one another. They were lovely old-fashioned bags made of thin cardboard-like material. They were white and delicate with pretty pale (and faded) blue "fleur-de-lis" on them. They reminded me of dainty, lovely old hat boxes that a Victorian woman might carry. Yet the locks were missing and most of the hooks were missing or didn't work. There was white tape around the edges to hold the bags together but it was coming off. This didn't upset me. There was also a woman there to help me pack. During the packing I was standing on a mound of dirt. I seemed to be somewhat behind the mound, and about halfway up. [Drawing of the mound]
>
> When the white tape didn't stick, we left the white bags and went around to the brown suitcase – strong, sturdy and practical. The mound was thick and dark (it was firm and reminded me of shit or manure but it wasn't offensive). I didn't actually pack anything because there weren't any belongings in the dream but I remember opening both suitcases. The white one I opened almost fully and it was empty and the brown one I only started to open so that the inside wasn't visible. In the dream everything seemed natural and flowing –nothing upset me. I just did what I had to do. I was young (about 19 or 20 – which is how old I was when I was pregnant) but I wasn't young in a negative or immature way – just inexperienced. I felt good.

This dream is striking because it hardly seems the dream of someone who hates her femininity and is longing for a penis. First of all, 8 out of 10 women are pregnant and that seems to be a blissful thing. My first association was that there was going to be another abortion. At this point the patient had only one! The warm, soft quality in the opening part seems like a connection to the mother in a very tender way. When she has to pack her luggage, it feels that it is the beginning of the realization that she has to give up her baby. The three suitcases remind me of the three babies that her mother has. The suitcases are very delicate and very feminine. Again, this woman finds some parts of being a woman very beautiful. The locks are messy and most of the hooks are missing seems related to her possible fears that her uterus is defective and she will not be able to hold a baby. Is it defective because her mother's envy has ruined it? She has to leave the pretty white bag. Was it a female child that she was carrying? We learn later that she had this lovely princess doll that was held together by rubber bands and fell apart and she wanted to nurture it back to health. She winds up with a brown suitcase in the dream that is strong, sturdy, and practical. This image does not seem to have any female sexuality but maybe being asexual helps her to cope in her relationship with her mother. She cannot pack anything because there are not any belongings. It seems that all the babies are gone. But what about the affect in the dream? She is calm and happy. She just did what she had to do. The abortion has left her with an anal baby standing on a sturdy mound of shit.

This dream prompts me to wonder about the patient's self-described hatred of being a woman and envy of her brother. This is a story of an envious attack on the mother's body (Ellman, 2000). She wants to empty out her mother's body (the pool is empty) and put feces in it. She wants to soil all the lovely white and dainty things that represent the early mother and rob the mother of all the babies she had inside. The affect in the dream is happiness. She does not care if she has nothing to put into her suitcases as long as she can make the mother miserable and destroy her happiness. She desperately envies her mother's babies and her mother's insides but is willing to have a miserable life if she can also ruin her mother's life.

Many other aspects of the case reinforce the idea that envy of the early mother and wanting everything she has is much more the central issue than envy of the brother and penis envy. She actually started treatment with the demand that she get what Zelda has, not something that she sees a man having. She becomes more aggressive as she demands over and over that Dr. Lieberman stop asking her to do any work but instead give her everything she wants. After all, in the patient's fantasy Dr. Lieberman has everything in her body that the patient envies. Why does Dr. Lieberman keep asking her for associations and dreams, and wanting her to participate in the treatment when the patient consciously believes she is damaged? Day after day the patient wants to tell Dr. Lieberman how terrible *she* (Dr. Lieberman) *is*, how *she* is to blame for everything bad happening to her. In my mind, this is the patient's envious attack on the analyst's mind. She behaves as if she wants to empty the analyst out (just like the pool) so that Dr. Lieberman has nothing left to give her, and there will be nothing left to envy. They both will be left with only shit that is being flung back and forth.

Soon after this dream the patient tells her the traumatic memory about being tied to the bed. I wonder if the patient is provoking Dr. Lieberman to live out something related to this memory/fantasy. One has to wonder about the sadism in the mother that would lead her to treat the child this way. Perhaps this mother could not tolerate her daughter's needs, and possibly felt in competition with a daughter. The mother seems to want to force a submission from her child. Instead we see a child fighting for her sense of self by withholding her bowels in order to not give in. She suffers from constipation and a spastic colon, and from then on she seems to refuse submitting to authority anywhere. She does not work to her fullest at her jobs and definitely does not work to her fullest in treatment. She does not want to let her mother hold or kiss her, and refuses to show her mother when she is upset, by never crying in front of her. We clearly see a picture of a mother–child relationship that is filled with struggles over autonomy with the daughter saying "no" to almost every request the mother makes (such as giving her a phone number of one of her nieces). But, the battle with the mother is not over only autonomy and who is the mother's favorite. The battle is about how can she extract more than anyone else through a masochistic surrender? In these regressed and masochistic battles (that she seems to be playing out in most parts of her life), there is a tremendous amount of envy of the mother's position, both hating her and wanting to be her. The mother overpowers the child in her tying her to the crib and reinforces the powerful image she has in the child's mind.

Apparently, the patient's mother also wanted to be treated as a princess and was angry with the father. She is described as materialistic and wanting money, clothes, jewelry, and gifts. We are told that the mother dominated the father and criticized him for never earning enough to suit her needs. She also could be flirtatious when she wanted something from him and he in turn always stood up for her. The mother had to go back to work when K was a teenager and apparently this was seen as a terrible failure on the father's part. We see the daughter emulating the mother in these ways. She wants to marry a rich man and she does not want to have to do anything. On one hand there is the identification with the aggressor since the patient emulates the mother's terrible behavior toward Dr. Lieberman and others. On the other hand there is intense envy of everything the mother is able to get. After all, the treatment starts with this very strange request. *I want what Zelda* (her friend) *has!*

In the course of the treatment we see more themes that are related to the envious spoiling of whatever the other woman has. She dreams about a villa where Zelda went for her honeymoon and the patient is bleeding over the towels. She has to show Zelda that she got her period and does not have a baby. Is this Zelda's fault also? Does she fantasize Zelda does not want her to have a baby?

She has a dream of a woman who undresses her solely for the woman's pleasure while a man observed. On one hand this could be the mother enjoying humiliating her in front of the father so that the mother was clearly the winner but it could also be the beginning of the patient starting to show that some of her rage is not only about her inadequacy but the rage at the mother for having a man, and her own hidden wishes for sexual gratification and a baby. It also strikes me as a more libidinal investment in the treatment with a fantasy of the analyst's interest in her.

The patient remembers an interesting memory of pretending she was Annie Oakley and tying herself to her bedpost. She did not want her mother to know about this. This activity was her turning passive into active by being the one who tied herself to the bedpost and not the other way around. While Annie Oakley was great with a gun (so in that sense she had her own penis), she also took Frank Butler away from his wife and married an older, successful man. The hidden nature of her wishes to defeat her mother has many different forms but seems to only show itself in rage and not wanting to submit at the beginning of her treatment.

Towards the second year of treatment, the patient develops acne and fantasizes that the analysis has caused this. I think this is a sign of movement in the treatment. It is as if the patient's wishes to have her vagina seen are transferred to her face. Instead of being the beautiful woman she wants to be who will steal the father and have his baby, she is deformed and ugly. The analyst has done this to her. The analyst has put feces, dirt, and pus into the patient. The analyst wants to make the patient less attractive and less loveable so that the analyst can have everything, and she nothing. The woman undressing her solely for the woman's pleasure now includes a more active conflict that is expressed in a bodily symptom.

During the second year of treatment, the patient got pregnant with a married man who she hoped would leave this wife. There was a foreshadowing of this in her first dream where the intense envy of the mother and the wish to rob her of everything suggested she would act out against another woman and then punish herself by aborting another baby. The fantasy of aborting a baby is related to her wish to kill off something in her mother and then both identify *and* punish herself by killing off life inside of her. The intensity of K's wishes, causing her acne, leads her to attack Dr. Lieberman, calling her "incompetent and stupid." Did she think the analyst had children, grandchildren? How much did she envy the mother's pregnancy with her younger brother and want to destroy the baby?

She talks at this point not only about how her mother took over her life and tried to control her but subtly demonstrates the mother's competitive wishes by putting in her own artwork for a school project instead of the daughter's. It is hard to know the extent to which the patient's passive-aggressive withholding behavior could provoke the mother to take over the patient's work or how competitive the mother really was with her daughter. However, what seemed apparent was that the daughter was hiding her own wish to compete in her self-demeaning behavior and in supporting the mother as the winner. Underneath this seemed to be her wish to rob her mother of everything. The extreme inhibition where she did not try to excel in any domestic, academic, or vocational area is profound. She was both submitting to the mother and keeping the mother constantly involved with her by having to care for this child who was always needing help. The patient reports, "all that I've gotten from treatment is holes in my face (*from acne*). My body is ruined (*from stress*)." Her reports seem like a punishment for her horrific wishes. By remaining incompetent and passive, the patient could disown her own destructiveness and at the same time believe the other person is the aggressor.

What is in it for the patient to play dead? She is deprived, her genitals are ruined, her face is ruined, and she cannot have a baby. Dr. Lieberman and her mother have taken all away from her for their own greedy purposes. When the early relationship with the mother is disturbed, it becomes an impossible task to want what the mother has, or to safely identify with the mother without feeling one has devoured her and taken all of their contents for one's own. The lack of differentiation in this patient suggests a deep confusion about boundaries. So much of what she accuses Dr. Lieberman of seems to be related to her own deepest wishes. The ego cannot tolerate this type of envy and destructiveness in the self without feeling one has literally killed the person that one is most dependent on. In these situations, there is more projective identification because it is impossible to contain, to tolerate, these feelings. Everything bad must be in Dr. Lieberman/Mother. They have the envy. They are competitive, they want to keep it all for themselves. It is striking that the patient can say all of these things without any apparent guilt or feeling that she is in any way destructive. She really believes she lives in an environment of people wanting to hurt her. If she starts becoming in touch with her own desires, she will come to realize that it is she who wants to rob someone else of what they have. With patients like this it is so hard for them to move into really doing something for themselves. For a long time, the best they can do is say to the therapist, "You have nothing to give to me that is worthwhile," and in that statement they try and negate all the pain they have of wanting it all. I pointed out in my paper "The Empty Mother: Women's Fear of their Destructive Envy" (2000) that the fear often takes the form of worrying (and an unconscious fantasy) that the mother will do something destructive to the daughter's insides. That seemed to be a constant theme for this patient.

It may be the third year of the treatment when the patient has a dream in which she survives a Nazi invasion by having a slice of her finger cut off without showing any pain. The fantasy that one day she might have had a penis that was cut off seems part of the idea that one can have everything, and her Nazi mother wanted to take it away and use it for herself.

Perhaps in the third year, we start to see some of the patient's sexual fantasies emerging as she fantasizes participating in a ménage à trois or having a homosexual relationship. She says:

> Maybe because I wasn't breast-fed and have a desire to suck someone's breasts, maybe because mine never grew big, I never had my mother's to go to and I never developed my own. The fantasy is to have a gorgeous body and to have a sexual encounter with another woman where I'm the aggressor. I can't fantasize anybody doing anything to me. There is a wish to be the other woman – to touch her breasts and thighs.

She comes into sessions in sexually provocative, scanty clothing and wants Dr. Lieberman to treat her boyfriend in order to create a triangle. She tantalizes Dr. Lieberman with minute details of her sexual encounters.

This is an important turning point in the treatment because the patient is actually expressing some positive desire for the female body, a desire that involves a fantasy that is not one of emptying it out of all its contents. Rather than rejecting the mother/female body, she wants to touch it and enjoy it and be the one who is powerful. She wants Dr. Lieberman to know she can enjoy sex and reverses the situation in the dream where the people used her for their own pleasure; now she wants to use them for her own pleasure. She wants someone else to be the onlooker. She wants to taunt Dr. Lieberman the way her mother taunted her. Here, the patient is no longer stuck in a passive-aggressive masochistic revenge position but is actively seeking out ways to become the person that is envied. She no longer thinks of herself as damaged and defective in every way, but in a dramatic moment, says, "*My assets* (intelligence) *are what my parents hate.*"

We must remember that this patient said that every single thing about her was damaged and that she was the weak link in the whole family! Here are the beginnings of her fantasies that secretly her father loved her but could not show it because of the terrible mother who wanted everything for herself (mirror, mirror on the wall, who's the fairest of us all?). Now we see her fantasy of being the one who is envied!

In the final dream in this sequence she talks about "a large apartment with many rooms that were structurally sound." This image ends the sequence of her belief that her womb/body had been destroyed by the mother's attack, suggesting that reparation has occurred and that her womb has the ability to hold a baby. Perhaps she imagines that she will even be able to take care of it. In this, the fantasized mother is no longer a threat. The patient says that she does not mind fixing up an apartment and doing some of the work but, "I'd like someone to take me out on a Saturday night *after* I do it. I don't think I have the desire to be *totally* independent and self-sufficient for the rest of my life." She no longer seems to be merged in a relationship with a mother where she is withholding in her effort to force her to do everything for her, nor separate from a mother and having to do everything for herself. She seems to have some beginning idea of doing some things for herself and also getting help, of relating to another in a way that is not sado-masochistic. The idea of having her own body/apartment is a big step in differentiation. Some of the lovely things in the first dream relate to the hidden wishes that have been there for a long time, to fix up some home in a beautiful way and fill it with babies.

Now, I would like to comment on the transference and countertransference in this difficult case. In spite of the constant demands and pressure on Dr. Lieberman to take care of this patient and the abuse that was aimed at her, the analyst and analysis survived and the patient seems to be progressing. At first the patient presents in this demanding childlike way with unrealistic demands for the analyst to get her a husband and do everything that the referring analyst had done for her friend. She does not seem to have an idea that she has to work in the treatment. Is it this reason that Dr. Lieberman thinks of her as "a princess?" Hour after hour the patient is either raging at her mother or not wanting to talk, associate or tell the analyst her dreams. The analyst at first believes that she can be different from the patient's mother and friends, and not be forced to take care of her, but this is an attempt to convince herself that she will not be forced by the patient into an enactment. The analyst is working much harder to win the patient over than she thinks. She tries to be empathic with her not being well taken care of by her mother but then when the patient is not giving her associations, she starts her defense analysis. The patient desperately wants to put all the bad into the analyst and not look at herself. At this point she is not aware of her fantasies because she is projecting everything into the other. The analyst is being forced to be more active (which is effective with many people in the patient's life who are induced to take care of her). The analyst experienced her as "withholding and having an anal-retentive quality" and she felt the patient's remarks were "shallow and superficial." So the analyst resorts to analyzing the defense of isolation of affect, which produces depression and rage. We are not surprised at this since the patient has narcissistic problems, making it hard to interpret to her. The patient experiences the analyst as pushy and wanting to one up her and the patient starts blaming the analyst for her problems. The patient says, "before they were latent, now they are blatant."

The patient has the memory of being tied to the crib and how she then went into a phase with her mother where she never showed tenderness and used curse words, which led to her mother to wash her mouth with soap. We cannot help but feel that the more Dr. Lieberman wants her to associate and interact in the treatment, the more the patient is acting exactly with Dr. Lieberman as she did with her mother. She withholds dreams and Dr. Lieberman has to ask for them. One of the dreams she withholds is about the menstrual blood that is on the towels in her friend's hotel. She says she is sick of getting her period but she is using her not being pregnant to torture the analyst with the fact that she has not had a baby with her and cannot stand what the analyst is withholding. Dr. Lieberman tries to interpret these withholding tendencies but the envy in the room causes the patient to belittle all interpretations. She is constantly blaming her analyst for what she does not have and believes she is a victim of an unempathic mother/analyst. It would be hard for the analyst to be empathic because she is constantly being told how terrible she is. We are not told how Dr. Lieberman manages not to retaliate or the nature of her countertransference fantasies, but she survives these attacks.

The patient's traumatic memory of being tied to the crib might have elicited more empathy but the patient's attacks on the analyst prevent the very love and attention she yearns for. Part of this is due to envy because the mother/analyst being able to give love leads the patient to envy her even more. Part of this seems tied to the lack of trust this patient feels toward anyone she perceives as trying to render her dependent. In her mind dependency means giving over control to the other and the other having everything.

The patient seems to accelerate her masochistic hypochondriacal complaints. She says: "All that I've gotten from treatment is holes in my face (*from acne*). My body is ruined (*from stress*)." Basically she has projected into Dr. Lieberman all of her sadism. And the fantasy is of Dr. Lieberman penetrating her and damaging her. Any attempt to interpret this leads to denial or the patient saying she knew all of these things before. She tries to make the analyst feel useless the way she once felt. Stupid, inadequate, incompetent and useless...

In the midst of this the patient gets pregnant again. She starts an affair with a married man. We do not know if she thinks the analyst is married but now she more actively wants to take something away from her. She is not only trying to destroy her mind but there is more of a feeling that she wants what Dr. Lieberman has in her life. It is not only Zelda and the woman at work who are getting things. It feels as if the transference has intensified and she fantasizes taking any man Dr. Lieberman may have.

The fascination with women's bodies and also the analyst's sexuality shows itself first in the patient dreaming about a woman undressing her in front of a man and then later the fantasy of a ménage à trois where she would be the woman using the other woman for her purposes. We watch as an unconscious fantasy of robbing the mother's body is acted out by wanting to rob some other woman of her man and have his baby or a baby with the mother. The symbols of the patient's body become more and more differentiated as she moves from being totally obsessed with her mother's body to having some feeling that her own body can be desirable and that she can get sexual pleasure from the other. She thinks about having someone suck at her breast and having a beautiful body, which seems to be the first indication that she wants to be the powerful woman who is envied. Even though she still cannot give Dr. Lieberman any credit for these changes this is a big change for this woman as her fantasies have become less destructive. It also follows that her dream about having an apartment that has structure and is something she owns is a sign of some beginning sense of self.

This treatment started off with the patient in many ways unable to think and associate as she pushed for an enactment with her rage and disappointment with her mother/analyst. She tried to engage Dr. Lieberman in a sado-masochistic relationship by either withholding from her by not working in the treatment or by blaming the analyst constantly for all her problems (which she said were getting worse because of treatment). She was trying to make Dr. Lieberman into her "non-empathic mother." By containing these projections as the analyst survived these attacks, the treatment became more libidinal and the patient was able to start fantasizing that the analyst wanted to "use her" for the analyst's sexual fantasies by psychically undressing her with questions. The patient's fantasy life revealed in time more hope that her insides had not been destroyed by her sadistic wishes toward the mother and she then tested it out by getting pregnant again. The working through of this patient's destructive fantasies toward her mother's insides helped her to feel more whole and able to own her own body as capable of repair and further growth (as shown by her dream about the apartment). As one watches the fantasy life of this patient grow, we also see the beginning of psychic structure and internalization.

I thank Dr. Lieberman for giving me the opportunity to read about her incredible work with this patient. Working with someone who has such envy is very difficult and she seems to have been able to withstand the assault and help this patient finally allow herself some real pleasures. Also the Oedipal issues in cases such as this are on an early level and finding a way to have real triangulation will take some time. At this level, envy and jealousy are barely differentiated and outdoing another woman is more out of envy than wanting a real relationship with a man. This case shows the power of fantasy in a more primitive patient. The concrete nature of the fantasy of being envied or envying someone else can lead to a deprived, masochistic life out of the fear of acting out the terrifying fantasy of their destructiveness.

References

Ellman, C. S. (2000). The empty mother: Women's fear of their destructive envy. *The Psychoanalytic Quarterly*, *69*, 633–665.

Freud, S. (1925). *Some psychical consequences of the anatomical distinction between the sexes*, S.E., 19 (pp. 243–258).

Freud, S. (1931). *Female sexuality*, S.E., 21 (pp. 225–246).

Horney, K. (1926). The flight from womanhood. In K. Horney (Ed.), *Feminine psychology* (pp. 55–70). London: Routledge.

Klein, M. (1932). The effects of early anxiety situations on the sexual development of the girl. In *The psychoanalysis of children* (pp. 194–239). New York: Dell, 1945.

Chapter 15

The broken doll

Discovering the unconscious fantasy in the case of Karen

Ilany Kogan

The role of unconscious fantasy in mental life has been recognized as having primary importance in psychoanalytic theory and practice. Freud (1901, 1908, 1915, 1919, 1927), followed by later psychoanalysts, stressed the powerful role of unconscious fantasy in the creation of dreams, parapraxes, and neurotic symptoms. According to Freud, fantasies are wish fulfillments arising from instinctual frustrations due to repression.

The Kleinian approach presented by Susan Isaacs (1948) at the Controversial Discussions of the British Psychoanalytical Society introduced radical changes in this concept. Unconscious phantasies[1] are not limited to repressed phantasies, but are the mind's content, which underlies from birth onwards the entire structure of mental functioning.

In modern North American ego psychology, Jacob Arlow's conception of unconscious fantasy remains the most influential (1969a, 1969b). In contrast to the Kleinians, Arlow maintains that unconscious fantasies are composed of elements with fixed verbal content that have an inner consistency, that is, the fantasies are highly organized. Arlow uses the term "fantasy" in the sense of a daydream, and finds it of greater relevance to speak of "unconscious fantasy function" (Abend, 2008, p. 126) as a constant feature of mental life. He groups fantasies around basic childhood wishes.

Arlow explores the interaction between fantasy thinking and the perception of reality. Whereas unconscious fantasy activity supplies the "mental set" in which perceptual input is perceived and integrated, external events, by contrast, stimulate and organize the re-emergence of unconscious fantasies. The result is a composite mixture of the two inputs. It is not only the id, but also the ego and the superego that play a part in the formation of unconscious fantasies, which are compromise formations.

Arlow's ideas have been recently reassessed by Shapiro (1990, 2008), Levine (1993), and Moss (2008). Levine elucidates the ways in which "unconscious fantasy" intersects with various theories of psychoanalytic technique. Moss and Shapiro represent what is euphemistically called "two person" and "one person" psychologies. Moss finds Arlow's proposals, and especially his way of discerning the encroachment of "unconscious fantasy" upon conscious experience, emotionally non-participatory and epistemologically suspect. Shapiro, in contrast, greatly appreciates Arlow's approach. He believes that it is useful for analysts to consider the notion of "unconscious fantasy" as a universal disposition, a later mental representation that underlies behavior and thought and is potentially organized in a linguistic format. He suggests that we can discover unconscious determinants of the patient's mind by grasping the patterned fantasies that dictate distorted behavior based on childhood views of the world. Shapiro contrasts this view with the current views that fantasies emerging during the clinical session are "co-created."

Recently, Bohleber et al. (2015) have done excellent work in attempting to achieve a better integration of the concept of "unconscious fantasy." For this purpose, they have developed a model to study the differing and diverging conceptualizations of "unconscious fantasy." They have deconstructed them in various steps, and, basing themselves on various dimensions, they have sought to identify their differences and similarities.

In this chapter I will use the clinical case presented in the previous chapter by Dr. Janice S. Lieberman to discover her patient's unconscious fantasy. From the point of view of the object relations theory, we can search the patient's unconscious fantasies in the enactments of internalized object relations in the transference and in the countertransference oscillations (Schafer, 1997; Kernberg, 1988). In contrast to this view, I believe that to focus mainly on the patient–analyst relationship will take us away from finding the unconscious fantasy. Basing myself on some of Arlow's premises, I will explore unconscious fantasy from the following prisms: (1) the specific verbal elements which may serve to reflect the patient's unconscious fantasy; (2) the external events which triggered the unconscious fantasy, which, in turn, affected the patient's perception of external events; (3) the elements of drive and defense contained in the patient's unconscious fantasy; and (4) the partial encroachment of the patient's unconscious fantasy upon her realistic ego.

Dr. Lieberman describes parts of an analysis from its beginning up to the middle phase of treatment (approximately four years). Her description includes the patient's anamnesis, dreams, and behavior, as well as transference and countertransference processes. Dr. Lieberman's account impressed me with its frankness and admirable sincerity. I was also impressed with the holding ability of a sensitive analyst who accompanies a difficult patient on her painful analytic journey, as described in this fine work.

Dr. Lieberman begins with her first impressions of the patient: Karen is a 30-year-old divorcée who lives alone and works as a secretary in an advertising agency. She appears rather childlike. Karen came to treatment with the expectation that analysis would help her to find a wealthy husband, as it had her friend Zelda. Karen's presenting problems were many and diffuse, including a damaged self-esteem and a lack of interest in life and work. Karen suffered from a damaged body image, complaining particularly about her small breasts and heavy legs. She also complained about her frigidity, and believed her genitals to have been damaged by the trauma of an abortion at age 19 and by surgery for pre-cancer of the cervix at age 25. Karen's husband left her for another woman after four years of marriage, and now, four years after the divorce, she is still greatly hurt and traumatized by it. Although her parents called her a "princess," she had low self-esteem and regarded herself as a "basket-case."

The analyst's initial perception of Karen was more positive than Karen's own perception of herself. The analyst found her to be a lovely, intelligent woman, with no defects in her ego functioning and with a well-established superego. Dr. Lieberman's positive impression of Karen changed once analysis began. This is seen in Dr. Lieberman's description of her difficulty listening to Karen's "tight" voice and in helping Karen overcome her intellectual, obsessive defenses. She notes that Karen's withholding of her emotions has anal retentive quality. Although Dr. Lieberman does not mention her diagnosis of the patient, I think that the change in the analyst's countertransference feelings led to a change in her evaluation of the patient's pathology and to a subsequent change in technique. Apparently, at first, Dr. Lieberman believed that her patient was suffering from a narcissistic disturbance (Karen was both a "princess" and a "basket case"), and therefore used a technique of empathic reflection, which she usually employed with narcissistic patients. However, as analysis progressed, she realized that she was dealing with a personality disturbance with narcissistic traits. Therefore, she changed her technique from empathic reflection to an analysis of the patient's defenses.

The analyst became aware that Karen was "not quite a princess," but rather a patient who is "difficult to reach" (Joseph, 1975). It was indeed difficult for the analyst to make contact with the aspect of the patient's personality that needed the experience of being understood, as Karen had split off her needy and potentially receptive parts, attacking them with her destructive parts. The change of technique enabled the therapist to reach those needy parts and to integrate them more fully into the patient's ego (Joseph, 1989).

I The specific verbal elements which may serve to reflect the patient's unconscious fantasy

Language furnishes many clues to the nature of unconscious daydreaming that accompanies altered experiences of the self. Sharpe (1950) states that "The verbal imagery corresponding to the repressed ideas and emotions, sometimes found even in a single word, will yield to the investigator a wealth of knowledge."

I will explore Karen's dreams and childhood memories in an attempt to uncover her unconscious fantasy. I would like to suggest that some of the specific verbal elements of the dreams can help us in this regard.

I will begin by focusing on the first dream which the patient brought to analysis at the beginning of treatment. The patient presented this dream to the analyst on a typed sheet of paper that included a drawing. Below is the therapist's description of this dream:

In her dream Karen is pregnant, and she finds herself around an *empty* [my italics] swimming pool with another ten women, eight of whom are pregnant. She has to pack, and finds three empty suitcases, white and delicate with pretty pale-blue "fleur-de-lis." But these empty, delicate bags with royal symbols have no clasps, and can break at any moment, because they are held together around the edges with white tape. Karen does not use the fragile, white suitcases, preferring a sturdy brown suitcase, which seems strong and practical. She is packing while standing on a mound of dirt, which reminds her of shit or manure.

The mound of dirt appears in the drawing on the paper on which the dream was typed.

I found Dr. Lieberman's description of the dream most interesting. The analyst informs us of the results of the joint exploration of the dream with her patient. In her opinion the dream reflects the patient's fragility, her extensive use of defense, her hopes for the analysis, as well as the trauma of her abortion. However, we are told nothing of the associations which the patient made in connection with the dream. Thus, we are left "empty handed" with regard to Karen's associations, which could have been useful for discovering her unconscious fantasy.

I will now refer to some of the specific verbal elements of the above dream which may provide clues to Karen's unconscious fantasy. For example, I was struck by the word "*empty*," which Karen used to describe both the swimming pool and the suitcases. In my view, this word may reflect an unconscious fantasy of being depersonalized, of feeling empty, dead. Dr. Lieberman's assumption that the dream reflects the trauma of Karen's abortion (the empty bags symbolizing Karen's empty womb) is thus plausible. In addition, the empty pool may symbolize the psychoanalytic womb from which Karen has to be reborn, and, as there is no amniotic fluid in it, she will emerge from it as a dead fetus, a mound of dirt. A further dream which Karen brought to analysis may also reflect her being depersonalized by becoming a dead object. In her dream Karen describes a brick house with a mother and child inside. Germans came, made sure that they shot everybody and figured that she and her mother were dead. One of the Germans took a knife and cut a sliver from Karen's finger to see if she was alive. Although fully conscious when this happened, Karen remained perfectly still and detached herself from the pain, which apparently was how she remained alive. In her associations, Karen describes her mother as using "Gestapo tactics."

The analyst maintains that Karen is an alive person pretending to be dead. I believe that this dream reflects Karen's unconscious fantasy of being depersonalized, which served as a defense against pain and thus had survival value.

Karen's unconscious fantasy of being depersonalized may have resulted from her childhood experience of feeling like an inanimate object in her mother's hands. The analyst describes how Karen's sadistic mother tied her to her crib to prevent her from climbing out of it and running out of the house. When Karen cursed, her mother would wash her mouth out with soap. These traumatic experiences may have had a deadening effect on the toddler, and Karen had to feel like a lifeless object in order to be able to withstand her mother's cruel treatment of her.

A memory from Karen's childhood sheds additional light on Karen's unconscious fantasy of being a dead object. Karen describes lying in bed, holding her doll and overhearing her mother in the next room saying goodnight to her brothers. All of a sudden, the rubber bands holding her doll together snap and the doll falls apart. Although in her conscious fantasy she is an angel who comforts the fragmented doll, I believe that in her unconscious fantasy she herself is the broken doll, a broken, inanimate object.

In my view, the patient's specific verbalizations – the "empty" containers and the "broken doll" – show distortions of her sense of self with momentary lapses in both her sense of reality and reality testing that had an impact on her life, as I will demonstrate later on.

2 The external events which triggered the unconscious fantasy, which, in turn, affected the patient's perception of external reality

I believe that the traumas in Karen's adult life – the abortion at age 19 and the surgery for pre-cancer of the cervix at 25 – may have reactivated her unconscious fantasy of not being a person, which she had used in her childhood to fend off feelings of pain, humiliation, and anxiety.

The psychoanalytic model of trauma, which posits two events – a later event that revivifies an original event, which only then becomes traumatic (Laplanche & Pontalis, 1973) – can help us to understand the reactivation of the unconscious fantasy in this case. Because they were linked to past terrors, the present traumas of the abortion and the pre-cancer surgery took on the quality of childhood fears and nightmares. Faced with what she experienced as the destruction of her fetus and her genitals, Karen may have felt threatened by the destruction of the boundary between inside and outside, between reality and fantasy (Auerhahn & Prelinger, 1983). Perhaps she felt that in undergoing the abortion she had "killed" her fetus and had evacuated it as a mound of dirt (which, in the above dream, appears outside of her body). In my opinion, Karen unconsciously imagined that she herself had been "murdered" by her mother and evacuated from her mother's body as a pile of shit. According to Freud (1917), the fecal mass or "stick" foreshadows the genital penis, the production of stools becomes a prototype of childbirth (the infantile sexual theory of giving birth through the anus), and excrement in the rectum anticipates genital coitus. The unconscious fantasy of being depersonalized, a pile of shit, may perhaps be connected to Karen's childish theory of being born from her mother's anus.

It is possible that, faced with the traumas described above, Karen could no longer tell whether excitation was of internal or external origin, and was therefore overwhelmed by feelings of helplessness and fear – the famous "*hil-flosigkeit*" described by Freud (1917). The "unfortunate encounters" (Green, 1973) between fantasy and traumatic events in reality can be terrifying because the communication from inside to outside is damaged to the point that inner spaces are no longer able to contain the inner world (Janin, 1996). The abortion, which may have made Karen feel that she had murdered her fetus, became the embodiment of the worst fantasies of her inner reality, overwhelming her with the realization of her own potential destructiveness.

I believe that the unconscious fantasy of being a broken doll influenced Karen's perception of her recent traumatic experiences. The abortion and the operation became destructive acts performed by persecutors who intended to break her, and they lost their quality of being helpful medical procedures. This, in turn, reinforced her distorted sense of self, of being depersonalized. Thus, traumatic reality may have reinforced the imprints of the past, which insidiously spilled into and permeated the present (Kogan, 2007).

3 The elements of drive and defense contained in the patient's unconscious fantasy

Freud (1912) traces the onset of neurotic illness primarily to a disturbance in the quantitative relationship between drive and defense. In his elaboration of the precipitation of neurotic illness in adult life, Arlow (1969a) adds that this onset is found in the consonance between the realistic situation and the specific, unconscious fantasy which it reactivates.

The unconscious fantasy, like the neurotic symptom, includes a combination of drive and defense. Karen's unconscious fantasy of being a dead object, psychically numb (Kogan, 1990), may have incorporated the defensive use of identification with the aggressor, which she employed on different occasions to fend off feelings of humiliation, anxiety, or reproach from the superego (Aichhorn, 1925; A. Freud, 1946). Karen, who was treated cruelly by her mother, may have mastered feelings of humiliation and pain by identifying in fantasy with her persecutory, murderous mother. Perhaps the abortion reactivated Karen's unconscious fantasy of identification with her mother, which transformed her into the mother who had killed her fetus. This fantasy may have been reinforced by the surgery for pre-cancer of the cervix, which created anxiety with regard to her further ability to become pregnant, transforming her into the murderer of all her potential fetuses.

It is possible that Karen's unconscious fantasy of being her mother's broken doll included her libidinal attraction to the mother as well as her defense against it. We can see Karen's homosexual attraction to her mother in Karen's following dream: A woman undresses Karen solely for the woman's pleasure, while a man is watching. Karen's associations deal with her conscious homosexual wishes. The analyst stresses that in the transference, the patient uses her anger to defend herself against the symbiotic and homoerotic longings which she (Karen) feels toward her.

Karen used her homosexuality, her sexualized search for the gratification of oral needs from an idealized mother (Kernberg, 1975) to defend herself against her frustrated oral and dependency needs from her mother.

I also believe that Karen used her homosexuality to deny a completely unacceptable inner reality. She fled from an internal reality filled with hatred and repudiation of the maternal object to an external reality that incorporated an ideal maternal figure, embodied by a female lover. This is a kind of "suspended animation" (Winnicott, 1935) – an attempt to omnipotently control the bad internal object by denying its existence by means of flight to another external reality. As a result of her attempt to erase the internal object with which she identified, Karen also erased her own self and became depersonalized, dead, and empty inside. Karen's search for a homosexual partner can be viewed, in Khan's (1979) words, as a compulsive attempt to conceal and partially substitute for the absence of the feeling of being alive. By means of this manic defense, she even tried to reverse deadness into aliveness (Kogan, 2003a), but with little success. Using homosexuality, Karen tried to create a sense of herself, though at the expense of the self, leaving her sexuality fragmented and infantile (McDougall, 1978, 1986). From Kohut's (1971, 1977) perspective, this was a desperate attempt to re-establish the self's integrity and cohesion in the absence of an empathic response from an important other.

4 The partial encroachment of the patient's unconscious fantasy upon her realistic ego

Arlow (1969a, 1969b) maintains that fixation in a childhood experience and its repetition later on in life point to the existence of an unconscious fantasy. He also states that the intrusion of fantasy upon conscious experience may, at times, be so overpowering as to seem relatively independent of the influence of perceptual data.

Dr. Lieberman tells us that Karen remained fixated in her sado-masochistic experience, and developed a stubborn, withholding, withdrawing, and masochistic stance, with the unconscious aim of eliciting from another a sadistic, castrating response. In the transference, Karen re-enacted the sado-masochistic pattern of behavior which had existed between her mother and herself. Karen's sado-masochistic tendencies may have originated in her cruel childhood experiences – being tied to the bed and slapped by her mother – which were followed in time by Karen automatically extending her foot so that her mother could tie it to the crib. These experiences may have been accompanied by libidinal excitement (Freud, 1919). In the transference, the masochistic position toward her mother can be seen in Karen's response to the analyst's question of "What comes to mind?" which led to the automatic accusation, "It's my mother." Dr. Lieberman suggests that by attempting to give the analyst what she thought the analyst wanted her to say, Karen symbolically relived her automatic extending of her foot for it to be tied to the crib. Karen's sadistic position was expressed through her responses to the analyst's interventions with "So what!" or "I knew that all along," which annulled everything the analyst said. The analyst felt "bitten" by Karen, who encroached into her "perimeter of safety" (McLaughlin, 1995), and she found it difficult to continue working with her.

The sado-masochistic relationship between patient and analyst can be seen also in Karen's above-mentioned dream, in which the cruel German cuts a sliver from her finger. In the transference, Karen perceives the analyst as the persecutory, castrating Nazi mother, while she, the mother's victim, plays dead, withholding her emotions in order to survive. But, at the same time, Karen is also the German persecutor who castrates the mother, and turns her into a dead object. (These images made me wonder whether Karen's family had any connection with the Nazi persecution of Jews in the Holocaust, as she is tormented by Jewish-victim and Nazi-perpetrator images.)

In the context of the above dream, the analyst calls Karen's reactions of "playing dead" – withholding her emotions – a "prominent character resistance." Although this reaction is indeed a resistance to treatment, I suggest that "playing dead" in this case is an "enactment" (Bohleber et al., 2013; Kogan, 2014) of the unconscious fantasy of being an inanimate object in the relationship. In my view, this unconscious fantasy had an impact on the way Karen perceived her therapist: For Karen, the analyst was not *like* her cruel mother, but *actually was* her cruel mother, thus giving the sado-masochistic relationship with the analyst a life-threatening quality. As the unconscious fantasy of being depersonalized encroached upon the "potential space" (Winnicott, 1971) that exists between the ego's perception of reality and unreality, Karen could either be "murdered" by her mother/analyst, and turned into a broken doll, or she could "murder" her, thus transforming the mother/analyst into a dead object.

An interesting question arises in this case analysis: Why is Karen unable to part from her mother, the persecutory introject that caused her so much pain and suffering? I believe that Karen is trying to preserve the relationship with her persecutory mother even at the cost of her own health. Guntrip (1968) writes eloquently about this problem: "Why do human beings maintain an internal object-relations world at all, especially if it is a bad one? What greater danger is being avoided in electing to face the dangers of internal bad objects experience?" (p. 207). One answer to this difficult question is that by parting from the bad introject, there is a danger of losing oneself in a vacuum of experience, and this vacuum is even more frightening than the object itself (Fairbairn, 1943; Green, 1974; Guntrip, 1968; Kogan, 2003b).

Towards the end of the chapter, Dr. Lieberman informs us of a number of impressive changes in Karen's life that resulted from her work in analysis. Karen began to date and assess men in terms of their suitability. She perceived herself as more attractive and intelligent. She began to invite people to her apartment and to socialize. She advanced at work.

I believe that one of Karen's biggest problems, which has yet to be worked through in analysis, is that of someday becoming a mother. We are told that

Karen, now about 34 years old, recently became pregnant after having an affair with a married man, and again aborted the baby. We do not have any information about Karen's feelings with regard to this second abortion. There is a dream from this period in which Karen is given an apartment which requires much repair work. The repair work is dirty and disgusting, as rats and mice are running around. In my view, the apartment may symbolize Karen's womb, and the rats and mice, the live children running around, who should be exterminated. I believe that Karen's inability to give life to a child is connected to her unconscious fantasy of herself being a piece of dirt, a disgusting, dead object.

Dr. Lieberman describes Karen as aggressive, complaining about her acne, and screaming that what she wants from her therapist is "physical change." The patient's forceful appeal to the therapist that she heal Karen's wounded face can be understood as a cry for help to heal her wounded psyche (Kogan, 1987). Moreover, by asking for "physical change," Karen may unconsciously be requesting to be transformed from an empty bag or a doll in pieces into a live human being. In my view, Karen is demanding that the analyst fill her body, her inanimate container, with life, or sew the pieces of the doll together and breathe life into it.

In conclusion, I suggest that the elaboration during future phases of analysis of the patient's unconscious fantasy of being depersonalized may eventually enable Karen to finally release the bad object from her unconscious (Fairbairn, 1943, p. 336; Guntrip, 1968, p. 345) and revive her inner deadness.

I want to thank Dr. Lieberman for her wonderful clinical contribution, as well as for her elaborate weaving of the joint explorations of patient and analyst. Moreover, I want to thank Drs. Ellman and Goodman for requesting my elaboration upon the unconscious fantasy in this clinical case, a topic which I find fascinating and worthy of examination.

Note

1 The spelling of the word "fantasy" is heterogeneous in psychoanalytic literature. Kleinians use "phantasy" to denote unconscious phantasies, and "fantasy" for conscious ones. North American analysts mostly prefer the spelling "fantasy," which I too use in this chapter.

References

Abend, S. (2008). Unconscious fantasy and modern conflict theory. *Psychoanalytic Inquiry*, *28*, 217–230.

Aichhorn, A. (1925). *Wayward youth*. New York: Viking Press.

Arlow, J. A. (1969a). Unconscious fantasy and disturbances of mental experience. *Psychoanalytic Quarterly*, *38*, 1–27.

Arlow, J. A. (1969b). Fantasy, memory and reality testing. *Psychoanalytic Quarterly*, *38*, 28–51.

Auerhahn, N. C., & Prelinger, E. (1983). Repetition in the concentration camp survivor and her child. *International Review of Psychoanalysis*, *10*, 31–46.

Bohleber, W., Fonagy, P., Jimenez, J. P., Scarfone, D., Varvin, S., & Zysman, S. (2013). Towards a better use of psychoanalytic concepts: A model illustrated using the concept of enactment. *International Journal of Psychoanalysis*, *94*, 501–530.

Bohleber, W., Fonagy, P., Jimenez, J. P., Scarfone, D., Varvin, S., & Zysman, S. (2015). Unconscious phantasy and its conceptualizations: An attempt at conceptual integration. *International Journal of Psychoanalysis*, *96*, 705–730.

Fairbairn, W. R. D. (1943). The repression and the return of bad objects. In *Psychoanalytic studies of the personality* (pp. 59–81). London: Tavistock, 1952.

Freud, A. (1946). *The ego and the mechanisms of defense.* New York: International Universities Press.

Freud, S. (1901). *The psychopathology of everyday life*, S.E., 6 (pp. 1–310). London: Hogarth.

Freud, S. (1908). *On the sexual theories of children*, S.E., 9 (pp. 209–226). London: Hogarth.

Freud, S. (1912). *Types of onset of neurosis*, S.E., 12 (pp. 27–38). London: Hogarth.

Freud, S. (1915). *Repression*, S.E., 14 (pp. 141–158). London: Hogarth.

Freud, S. (1917). *On transformations of instinct as exemplified in anal erotism* (1917–1919), S.E., 1 (pp. 125–134).

Freud, S. (1919). *The "uncanny,"* S.E., 17 (pp. 217–252). London: Hogarth.

Freud, S. (1927). *The future of an illusion*, S.E., 21 (pp. 3–56). London: Hogarth.

Green, A. (1973). *Le discours vivant. La conception psychanalytique de l'affect.* Paris: P.U.F.

Green, A. (1974). L'analyste, la symbolisation et l'absence. *Nouvelle Revue de Psychanalyse*, *10*, 225–252.

Guntrip, H. (1968). *Schizoid phenomena, object relations and the self.* London: Hogarth.

Janin, C. (1996). *Figures et destins du traumatisme.* Paris: Presses Universitaires de France.

Joseph, B. (1975). The patient who is difficult to reach. In P. L. Giovanchini (Ed.), *Tactics and techniques in psychoanalytic psychotherapy* (Vol. 2, Countertransference) (pp. 205–210). New York: Jason Aronson.

Joseph, B. (1989). Psychic equilibrium and psychic change. In *Selected papers of psychoanalysis, New Library of Psychoanalysis* (*9*, 1–222). London and New York: Tavistock/Routledge.

Kernberg, O. F. (1975). *Borderline conditions and pathological narcissism.* New York: Jason Aronson.

Kernberg, O. F. (1988). Object relations theory in clinical practice. *Psychoanalytic Quarterly*, *57*, 481–504.

Khan, M. M. R. (1979). *Alienation in perversion.* New York: International University Press.

Kogan, I. (1987). The second skin. *International Review of Psychoanalysis*, *15*, 251–261. In *The cry of mute children* (pp. 46–69). London and New York: Free Association Books, 1995.

Kogan, I. (1990). A journey to pain. *International Journal of Psychoanalysis*, *71*, 629–640. In *The cry of mute children* (pp. 69–87). London and New York: Free Association Books, 1995.

Kogan, I. (2003a). When words are used to touch. *Psychoanalytic Psychology*, *20*(1), 117–130. In *The struggle against mourning* (pp. 47–69). New York: Jason Aronson, 2007, under the title "Lust for love."

Kogan, I. (2003b). On being a dead, beloved child. *Psychoanalytic Quarterly*, *72*(3), 727–767. In *The struggle against mourning* (pp. 123–157). New York: Jason Aronson, 2007.

Kogan, I. (2007). *The struggle against mourning*. New York: Jason Aronson.

Kogan, I. (2014). Some reflections on Ian McEwan's "Atonement": Enactment, guilt and reparation. *Psychoanalytic Quarterly*, *83*, 49–70.

Kohut, H. (1971). *Analysis of the self*. New York: International Universities Press.

Kohut, H. (1977). *The restoration of the self*. New York: International University Press.

Laplanche, J., & Pontalis, J. B. (1973). *The language of psycho-analysis* (D. Nicolson-Smith, Trans.). London: The Hogarth Press and the Institute of Psycho-Analysis.

Levine, F (1993). Unconscious fantasy and theories of technique. *Psychoanalytic Inquiry*, *13*, 326–342.

McDougall, J. (1978). The primal scene and the perverse scenario. In *Plea for a measure of abnormality* (pp. 53–86). New York: International University Press, 1980.

McDougall, J. (1986). Identifications, neoneeds and neosexualities. *International Journal of Psychoanalysis*, *67*, 19–31.

McLaughlin, J. (1995). Touching limits in the analytic dyad. *Psychoanalytic Quarterly*, *64*, 433–465.

Moss, D. (2008). Two readings of Arlow's "Unconscious fantasy and disturbances of conscious experience": One old and one "green." *Psychoanalytic Quarterly*, *77*, 61–75.

Schafer, R. (1997). *The contemporary Kleinians of London*. Madison, CT: International University Press.

Shapiro, T. (1990). Unconscious fantasy: Introduction. *Journal of American Psychoanalytic Association*, *37*, 38–46.

Shapiro, T. (2008). Ubiquitous daydreams and unconscious fantasy: A reassessment of Arlow's "Unconscious fantasy and disturbances of conscious experience." *Psychoanalytic Quarterly*, *77*, 47–59.

Sharpe, E. F (1950). Psychophysical problems revealed in language: An examination of metaphor. In *Collected papers on psychoanalysis*. London: Hogarth.

Winnicott, D. W. (1935). The manic defence. In *Through paediatrics to psycho-analysis: Collected papers* (pp. 129–144). New York: Bruner/Mazel, 1992.

Winnicott, D. W. (1971). *Playing and reality*. London: Tavistock Publications.

Chapter 16

Unconscious traumatic fantasy

Dori Laub and Nanette C. Auerhahn

Severe trauma wipes out the mind, resulting in a massive erasure of thought. How is it represented, recovered, or reconstructed after elision? We broach the topic by following the threads of our imagination as we contemplate traumatic experience. We can cognitively know about trauma, but trying to imagine it leads to prompt withdrawal. We start to imaginatively enter the gas chambers but emotionally refuse to stay. Overwhelming feelings lead us to slam the door, functioning like signal anxiety that stops us from experiencing further. We freeze in our tracks, no matter the effort. The best we produce are two-dimensional images without affect and without movement. Can we assume the existence of unconscious fantasies that take our imagination further than we know? The disabling affects we briefly experience are without content and without images.

If we carefully observe what happens, we discern changes in what goes on with and around us. The familiar and safe acquire different, newer meanings. We are gradually drawn into conflictual narratives lived through again and again, always convinced of their authenticity and truth. If we are involved in a thera-peutic relationship, it becomes the container of these narratives which drive and give shape to transference – countertransference enactments that come to be at the center of the therapeutic process. At that point, traumatic affect is no longer known, experienced, or remembered, but re-enacted and relived, because trauma is neither thought nor felt but experienced as present and immediate. Action and not imagination become the mode of its transmission, intimate interaction the locus of its occurrence. The space for self-reflection and observation is encroached upon and severely reduced by the relived traumatic experience's intensity, to disparate islands of self-recognition and self-experience that lack continuity, narrative cohesion, and an ongoing presence. Insights reached earlier are gone, without leaving a trace. There is nothing on which to fall back or build to enhance insight and self-awareness and to keep traumatic re-enactment at bay. Whatever gains are made are prey to the fragmenting impact of traumatic affect floods.

The myth of Philomela as an alternate myth to that of Oedipus

The myth of Oedipus has been a central organizing myth for psychoanalysis, framing understanding of how we know what we don't and shouldn't know. It is about how we take possession of forbidden knowledge. It also has come to represent the acquisition of language, occurring at the age when the brain has matured so as to allow secondary process thought, fantasy, and declarative memory and symbolizing the child's initiation into triadic relationships and all that the Father represents (cf. Lacan, 1977). The myth has been useful as a way of understanding creation of the dynamic unconscious and critical for the conceptualization of conflict and defense. But it limits our understanding of trauma and deficit, for which a different myth is called for. We nominate that of Philomela.

The most famous rendering of the myth of Philomela is that of Ovid (1955). In the fifth year of her marriage to Tereus King of Thrace, Procne asks her husband to let her see her sister Philomela who resides in Athens. Tereus travels to Athens to bring Philomela to Thrace to visit, but lusts for her upon seeing her. At the end of their voyage, he forces her into a cabin in the woods, rapes her, and cuts out her tongue when she refuses to remain silent. Unable to speak, Philomela weaves a tapestry that tells her story and has it sent to Procne who, enraged, kills her son by Tereus, boils him, and serves him as a meal to her husband. Procne and Philomela confront Tereus with the boy's severed head, making Tereus aware of his cannibalism. He pursues them with an axe. In desperation, they pray to the gods to be turned into birds to escape Tereus' revenge. Procne is transformed into a swallow, Philomela into a nightingale, and Tereus into a hoopoe.

Looking at the structure of the narrative, we see a theme repeated twice: There are two events of which someone is unaware. In the case of the rape, the person who does not know is Procne. In the case of cannibalism, it is Tereus who is unaware that he has eaten his son. In each instance, something happens that changes ignorance into knowledge. Procne learns of Philomela's rape from the latter's weaving which tells the story. Tereus learns of his cannibalism when Procne and Philomela present him with the severed head. The first carrier of knowledge, the weaving, is an artistic representation. The second, the ingestion and presentation of the boy's head, are enactments. Like the weaving, the murder, boiling, and ingestion of Tereus' son bring what happened to awareness.

Aristotle, in his analysis of Sophocles' play *Tereus*, based on the myth of Philomela, refers to the weaving that tells the story as the "voice of the shuttle" – an example of a poetic device that aids recognition of what has happened earlier in the plot. Literary critics have seen in the weaving a metaphor for the artistic process. Little has been written about the similarly communicative functions of the cannibalism and presentation of the severed head. But all bear on the topic of this chapter: the manner in which trauma that has not been represented nevertheless is communicated and made known to self and other.

The Oedipal triangle is about initiation of the child into language and creation of the dynamic unconscious. The myth of Philomela is a metaphor for the vicissitudes of trauma that eludes language. In the moment of trauma, the mind dissociates and is severed from the speech centers of the brain that go off line as it were, creating experience that is recorded in sensorimotor percepts not remembered in words. (Perhaps the child's severed head is an eidetic presentation of severance from language.) Traumatic experience makes itself known through semiotic as opposed to symbolic presentations (cf. Kristeva, 1980) that emerge in re-enactments in life and enactments in therapy.

In the Oedipal myth, the hero is split horizontally, with what he does not know being repressed "below" into the unconscious. The myth provides a paradigm for repression and for the distinction between the conscious and unconscious selves. In trauma, the traumatized self is dissociated from the apparently normal self in a vertical split that disconnects the conscious mind from unsymbolized and unmetabolized trauma. We see this in the myth of Philomela: After the rape, the survivor's traumatized self, Philomela, is hidden from the self, Procne, that attempts to live in the normal world, not thinking about or even knowing what has occurred. The conscious self cannot process trauma that has not been represented, narrated, or shared with a witness. Severing of the connection with language and reason is depicted many times over in the myth even as its manifest content narrates eventual movement into voice and communication. The death of language is symbolized in the cutting out of Philomela's tongue most obviously, but even in her transformations. Early Greek sources have Philomela turning into a swallow, which has no song. And although most depictions of the nightingale in art and literature are of female nightingales, female nightingales do not sing – only the males do, undercutting ubiquitous use of the nightingale as an archetypal symbol for the oppressed woman who finds her voice in a beautiful, sorrowful lament that stands as a metaphor for art and literature. (See Hartman's (1970) and Klindienst's (1984) discussions of this trope.)

If trauma is cut off from language and hence the symbolic, how does it emerge? A first reading of the myth suggests that symbolization leads to action and denouement. But while artistic creation is the idealized means for processing, communicating, and transforming experience (not just trauma), the less "tasteful" aspects of the myth typify the way trauma emerges in life and therapy – as bodily enactments that engage and involve the other/therapist. The vicissitudes of trauma follow the path of action/enactment first (including swallowing/insertion, digestion/metabolization) and only then creation of a narrative. That is the argument of our paper.

Cannibalism is an apt eidetic representation of the metabolization of traumatic experience and symbol for the paradigm shifts in psychoanalysis, as it has considered trauma, from repression to dissociation and from cognition, interpretation, and insight to affect, psychoanalytic process, and relational repair (Bromberg, 2011). The actions of Procne, Philomela, and Tereus are re-enactments that bring trauma into conscious awareness via mutually responsive actions. The therapeutic relationship can be understood unconsciously as canni-balistic. (Indeed, Winnicott (1958, p. 276) noted the parallels between the good mother who is "cannibalistically attacked" and the therapist who, if not "eaten, worn down, stolen from" remains "outside … people's reparative … activities.") Patient and therapist make room internally for the other, each inserting and pro-jecting himself into the other, imbibing the other's representational world, and allowing each to chew over, taste, and know what the other has experienced and transmitted. Enactment is the primary language of PTSD; the unconscious fanta-sies that propel it teleologically can only be known through deciphering such enactment with an observing mind which retains the capacity for reverie and imagination. This may occur verbally to a certain extent, but it is the shifts in the enactments that indicate to what extent the unconscious fantasies have become known to patient and therapist. While it might appear that the therapist is a passive bystander to the traumatic, at times self-destructive, derailments of the patient's life, in fact he remains a participant observer deeply affected by these enactments; his affective resonance and psychic mental functioning are crucial to their understanding and resolution as they coalesce into fantasies and emerge into narratives. While the fantasies appear to accurately describe the behavioral enactments, they do not exist prior to the enactments but are woven afterward. Trauma is unsymbolized and unthought. True fantasy is characterized by a mobility and reversibility (Dowling, 1985) lacking in traumatic imagery and thought which is instead frozen, static, and unmoving. Sensorimotor experience results in enactments that bring representational thought about trauma into being if distilled by a witness who imagines and thinks when the victim is unable to (Bion's alpha function.) Traumatic fantasy is a co-construction of patient and therapist after the fact of enactment that describes the enactment and that exists as a representation once it is formulated and "given back" to the patient. (An image comes to mind of a parent who first chews a piece of food before inserting it into the mouth of her infant.) The fluidity of primary process helps us grasp that the myth of Philomela is told backwards: *First there is enactment, then there is weaving.*

Aborted therapy: re-enactment of an unconscious trauma fantasy in a mother–daughter pair

A three-way struggle between patient, mother, and therapist took center stage at the beginning of defining the therapeutic contract, obliterating everything else. The central concern for the 29-year-old and her mother was obtaining ADHD medication. Multiple appointments were set but never kept. The daughter was psychotic but refused to take antipsychotic medication; the mother looked for strategies to force her to do so. Finally, mother made it to an appointment, albeit late. She brought her flight tickets to her home country, to see her dying sister, to prove that what she was telling was true, as if she was unsure of what she knew. She asked whether the therapist had received her autobiographical email, which he had not. She wanted to show him her iPhone to prove that she had sent it. It provided a contradictory, vague history punctuated by extreme events, vividly detailed. A picture of a brutal marriage emerged with a violent husband who staged a mock "suicide" by putting a noose tied to the ceiling around her neck and a chair under her feet. She took all the blame, confessed her guilt, and he "spared" her life. Only upon discovering her husband molesting their 11-year-old daughter did she divorce him. She described catching him upon unexpectedly returning home and seeing her husband holding their daughter in a condition indicative of molestation. She screamed at the daughter that this was inappropriate, to which the latter responded, "But, Mom, we snuggle every day." She picked up the phone while her husband hit her, pushed her downstairs, and threatened to jump off a bridge with the children if she called 911. Years later her daughter remembered his "sharp body part pressing in her back" and called him "father child molester." Restraining orders and police visits became regular features of their life. Yet, she never pressed charges, not only because of fear for her life, but also because she was unconvinced of what really happened. The daughter was hospitalized numerous times, but mother did not think of her as sick. The mother could not imagine the outrage, disgust, guilt, and betrayal that permeated and eclipsed her daughter's feelings, but lived her own terror. Regarding her children, she could only enumerate their symptoms and speak about her protective actions. There was no space for conscious imagination or reflection.

There was no order to the mother's narrative, no unfolding or evolution. Resolute, prompt action to manipulate and control was called for. The unconscious fantasy enacted by mother and daughter involved gaining the upper hand as the only way to ensure life. Everything else faded into the background. To fit the trauma script, the therapist was cast as the ruthless perpetrator who had to be outsmarted even at the cost of truth and the therapeutic enterprise. The mother had written the autobiographical email while under its spell, failing to send it while not registering that fact. Or perhaps she knew she had not sent it, but told him otherwise, as part of wrestling with him to spare her life. The husband seemed immune from custom and law, in possession of absolute power as though the abuse transpired in a world separate from regular life, with its own rules. Only after discovering incest did the mother act, able to change external reality but not the internal traumatic world that had been set in motion. At age 23, the daughter chose to live with her father. One night at 5 a.m., she ran out of his apartment to a train station where she called 911, but refused an interview for fear of humiliation. Between 2006 and 2011, she was hospitalized yearly. During a 2012 hospitalization, she was sexually assaulted by another patient, after which she cut her hair, started wearing male clothing, and did not want to be a woman. There were 15 more psychiatric hospitalizations. Now she does not leave home, refuses to come to appointments, and sleeps much of the day.

The mother–daughter post-traumatic trajectory impresses with the increasing malignancy of the traumatic condition and persecutory objects; the latter, along with defenses (often obsessional) mobilized against them, *are* represented in fantasy. Fantasies of persecutory objects stand in the place of an erased mind and absent empathic other who *cannot* be represented or thought, only inferred via enactment and (often somatic) symptoms, e.g., difficulties falling asleep and feelings of death, persecution, falling apart, etc. The failure of symbolization of the traumatic experience and absent empathic other cannot be told, only shown.

Return of the perpetrator: re-enactment of an unconscious traumatic fantasy in a married couple

Patients in their fragmented traumatic states cannot accrue insight or knowledge. After affect storms, there is the ability to make connections and discover patterns in one's life; however, such ability vanishes when one is again impacted by traumatic experience. At times patients can be cognizant of their re-enactments, but unable to stop them or withdraw from their spell. Re-enactments can occur unexpectedly.

The patient was a married woman in her forties. Between the ages of 4 and 8, she was repeatedly raped by her stepfather, who offered her for sex to friends. Her mother claimed to notice nothing, and when the girl tried to tell her, accused her of imagining it all. Mother offered her for sex to men as a teenager, telling her to "be nice" to them. All her adult life she suffered from severe PTSD symptoms and somatizations (pneumonias, bladder infections, sinusitis, and muscle spasms) that led to heavy medication and unnecessary hospitalizations and surgeries. She kept herself extremely busy, doing chores for the family such as buying all the Christmas presents everyone gave. This culminated in her ending up in an accident, with her car in a ditch beside the road. Motorists who helped extricate her told her they were surprised that she had not been killed. Not long thereafter, her husband could not wake her in the morning and took her to the ER. She was taken off all her medication and gradually developed an organic psychosis with paranoia and hallucinations. Because her therapist had hospital privileges, he could be the treating psychiatrist, which proved to have immense benefits because she trusted him. He gradually increased some of her medications and symptoms cleared within a week. A stronger therapeutic alliance had been forged. They had been through something together, which could be put into words and mutually acknowledged, no longer an unconscious fantasy.

One morning the patient received a phone call from a man who claimed to be with the IRS. He told her she had committed tax delinquencies and was going to be punished unless she paid immediately. He gave her a number that was the IRS and advised her to keep her phone open, so that their conversation could be taped. She failed to inform her husband of the situation because she was so absorbed in it, terrified for her life. She was instructed to deposit $4000 to a bank account she was given. After she did that, the man "spoke to a supervisor" and asked for $3000 more. There were penalties and back taxes that had to be paid. After she fulfilled the second request, $12,000 was demanded. When she responded that she could not come up with that amount, he settled on $3000. She went to the bank to carry out the transaction, by which time it was 4 p.m. She informed her husband, who raised no questions about the legitimacy of the requests. When she told him that two men were coming to the house to deliver papers documenting the deal, he expressed fear about their visit, as if he, too, fell under the spell of the abuser, without being able to think. It was only when the transaction was over, and $10,000 had been withdrawn, that it dawned on them that they had been defrauded!

The patient was furious that her husband refused afterward to take the matter seriously. She had been terrified and now felt abandoned and alone. The experience was like reliving the times she had been raped by her stepfather and his friends. She had felt helpless and weak facing a tyrannical, absolute, murderous power. When she had turned to her mother for help, the latter had trivialized the situation. Her husband was re-enacting mother's disbelief and indifference in her mind. A recent phone message her mother left, in which she sounded drugged, distant, absent-minded, not really speaking to her, triggered the same state of mind – a muted rage and malaise that lasted for more than a week.

The therapist had to empathically experience with the patient that the abuser was back and that her mother refused to notice. He experienced surprise, restlessness, and excitement in realizing that she was reliving her original traumatization, and it was these affects that he had to convey to her in a way that felt authentic, intimate, real, and present, bringing home the message that he was not the trivializing, drugged, headachy, and absent mother. It was insufficient to provide an emotionally positive experience, to just acknowledge that the patient was remembering the original traumatization. Simply making connections between memory and current experience was not enough. Such a corrective emotional experience would remain side-by-side with her unacknowledged re-traumatization and hardly touch it; it would not undo, neutralize, or balance it. New object relationships do not cancel out old, internalized, bad object relationships. What is necessary is a new experience with an "old" object, the original internal object (cf. Katz, 2014) elaborated in the therapeutic work, which allows for change to happen. The therapist had to create a larger holding environment, a framework in which he was fully present, to receive the testimony of a disaster that patient urgently wanted to transmit. She did not just remember, but relived her traumatic experience – not as an event from the past but as a moment in the present which she experienced in the here and now.

Traumatic blackout

"Traumatic blackout" is the term we use for the moment or stretch of life (which can be long-lasting, even permanent) during which overwhelming traumatic affect takes center stage and leads to a shutdown of thinking, self-reflection, reality testing, and conscious remembering. It is as though symbolization and dialogue with the internal other halt. A metaphor that captures this state is that of a lively, pulsating, interactive wakefulness turning suddenly dark because a light switch has been thrown. Conscious awareness is constricted and free associations limited. What is known is primarily informed by unconscious traumatic affect and takes a variety of shapes determined by factors such as survivors' closeness to the traumatic experience (Laub & Auerhahn, 1993).

Both of the foregoing patients were trauma victims who experienced the traumatic affect in transference enactments and in life re-enactments. In therapeutic relationships and life situations in which an internal therapeutic dialogue is present, it is as though a dim light has been re-established in which the vague outline of things can unconvincingly be seen, side-by-side with the relived, re-enacted traumatic experience. Therapeutic presence and holding provided by a therapeutic alliance facilitate emergence and enhance stability of reality in the shadow of traumatic affect.

A dimension that determines the shape of what comes to be known is the reality situation that triggers the traumatic memory and affect. In the case of the defrauded woman, it was the totalitarian persistence of the perpetrator who did not relent in accusing her of crimes that triggered the traumatic affect. He presented a situation that was totally false as true and real without flinching. Conviction in the truthfulness of his distortion triggered the paralyzing memory of her abuse which was dismissed as fantasy by parents. When no longer in the presence of the perpetrator, after she had paid him $10,000, she felt free to reflect and realized the fraud she had fallen victim to. It is not about throwing a switch and turning on the light again or reaching an all-illuminating insight that does away with neurotic distortions, but about the gradual, incremental internalization of a therapeutic presence, the re-establishment and solidification of an internal partner to dialogue with, which allows for restoration of reflective space that can withstand the impact of traumatic affect.

Intergenerational transmission

If we return to the myths of Oedipus and Philomela and use the latter to reread the former, we are alerted to a backstory that has largely gone unheeded: Euripides, in *Chrysippus*, tells the story of how Laius, father of Oedipus, kidnapped Chrysippus, son of a royal family in which he was guest and tutor, in order to violate him, causing the gods' revenge on Laius' family. Thus the myth of Oedipus may be read not only as referring to triadic relationships and the nuclear family, but also to the vicissitudes and emergence of intergenerational trauma. Laius, within a family setting, violated a son, setting the stage for the re-enactment by Oedipus of violation of the incest taboo. Furthermore, reading forward, Oedipus' sons, Eteocles and Polynices, killed each other in a battle for power after which Oedipus' uncle, Creon, took the throne and refused Polynices burial rites. When Polynices' sister Antigone defied this edict, Creon had her buried in a rock cavern where she hanged herself, whereupon her fiancé, Creon's son, stabbed himself to death. What had started as a sexual boundary violation in one generation became murder, incest, and suicide in subsequent generations. What we had first posited as contrast – Oedipus as metaphor for the acquisition of forbidden knowledge, Philomela as metaphor for the acquisition of traumatic knowledge – might be more illusion than reality. Perhaps the family romance, penis envy, and the Oedipal complex, all so vitally connected to the Oedipal myth in psychoanalysis, may be more screen memory than bedrock – screen for trauma, that is. The blinding and self-mutilation of Oedipus, for example, representing in psychoanalysis castration anxiety, may symbolize the parasympathetic (vagal) state of withdrawal and detachment that characterizes the dissociative response of the traumatized individual who shuts down metabolically and "strives to avoid attention to become 'unseen'," like the traumatized child who "disengages from stimuli in the external world" and is "observed to be 'staring off into space with a glazed look'" (Schore, 2007, p. 757). Both myths may be mined for what they tell us about intergenerational trauma. With Philomela, it is no accident that the sister who does not know is the one who kills her son from a horror and melancholia that cannot be worked through because it is not her own experience, while with Oedipus it is the third generation, his daughter and Laius' granddaughter Antigone, who tries to end the cycle of violence by burying the dead, i.e., giving them their due and reinstating processes of mourning, something that usually requires three generations for resolution. Finally, the affliction passed from one generation to another because of trauma is devastatingly illustrated when a mother, Procne, out of grief and terror, forgets her son and mothering function, thereby unraveling the links by which one generation nurtures and gives life to another. It is apropos that the perpetrator, Tereus, is the son of Ares, god of war.

The patient grew up in Israel. Both parents lost family in the Holocaust. Mother had fled with her parents to the Soviet Union, discarding her own mother's body after the latter died of typhus. Knowledgeable and intelligent, she was self-centered, punitive, and harsh. Father was not allowed to move around the house so as not to dirty it. Nothing the son did was good enough. Frequently he returned from school to find a locked door on which he banged and banged. A neighbor would invite him into her apartment for lunch. The boy repeatedly implored his father to leave his mother so that they could live together, but father felt incapable of leaving, explaining that after the Holocaust, he had become a broken man. Sometimes father and son came to blows. The Holocaust experience of extreme victimization, random, willful use of absolute power, and complete absence of empathy reigned in the life of this family, in spite of its members' intelligence, creativity, and work discipline.

The son participated in the Yom Kippur War. Death was all around as soldiers were killed left and right. He had to extract the wounded from a vehicle that had been destroyed by a shell. He fell asleep on guard duty and woke up to the sight of dead enemy soldiers who had tried to sneak up and attack his position but were intercepted and killed by guards who had not fallen asleep. He wrote to his father that now that he had had his own firsthand experience of death, he understood the Holocaust. Death was inside him, causing him to feel that he had died in the war and was only going through the motions of being alive.

The patient had many close friends and was admired by colleagues, but repeatedly became involved in one-sided friendships with women who used him as a sounding board, never showing interest in him. He felt hurt but kept silent, feeling damaged and not worth anybody's attention. During sleepless nights he demeaned himself, feeling abused and enraged, torturing himself with inadequacies and mistakes. It was liberating to realize in therapy that he had internalized his persecutory mother. He could identify her voice alongside his own, realize how they overlapped, and increasingly separate them, becoming less depressed.

It is not difficult to locate in this man's emotional life the presence of an extreme traumatic experience, endured by the previous generation. Although many of his experiences can be understood as related to neurotic processes, there is an additional layer of immediacy, totality, and absence of ambivalence that is Holocaust related. Mother was the primary carrier of this emotional information. The Yom Kippur War, during which Israel's extinction was a probability, solidified the imprint of his death encounter and recognition of the Holocaust in his self. How does the therapeutic enterprise engage such compelling life experiences?

The process goes beyond cognitive knowledge to mutual discovery by patient and therapist of something that neither had known before. Such discovery lies in details – in the particular experiences, relationships, and feelings of the patient. It was in his own derogatory words to himself that he could recognize his mother's demeaning tirades. It was only in hearing them that therapist and patient could recognize an internalization which neither knew of ahead of time, just as they did not anticipate the way in which his relationships with egocentric women mirrored his relationship with his mother.

Re-experience with the therapist of details is crucial for rewiring the patient's affective experience. It is for this reason that we have supplied so many details about patients' re-enactments and are struck by the lack of biographical details in some of the literature on trauma (e.g., Bromberg, 2011). While getting the story has been eschewed in part because of the accurate recognition that repetition of one's traumatic history can cement rather than heal pathological functioning (Ogden & Minton, 2006), the baby has been thrown out with the bath water. The therapist must know details and must live through with the patient that which the latter repeats in the present. The meal is not eaten by the patient alone. (Winnicott (1958) notes that the mother must hold the situation in time so that the infant can work through the consequences of experiences in a process comparable to digestion, and that it is the analysis of oral sadism in the transference that lessens persecution in the patient's inner world.)

Testimony as a paradigm for therapy of extreme traumatization

The foregoing patient talked about how deserted he felt. Friends are present only if they need something from him. There is asymmetry in his life, with no place for his pain. Someone viciously attacked him professionally, precipitating a desire for revenge stopped only by friends' intervention. He suffers from repeated waves of intense anxiety connected to the emptiness and deadness that he feels. The Israeli soldiers of 1948 decided to die before being killed. Yigal Alon died in 1948 at the age of 30, whereas his biological death occurred only in 1986. In spite of Alon's important political positions, he fell silent after the war. The patient has been fascinated with the "living dead" for 25 years. All the dead that remained alive fill him with fear, causing him to tremble. He cannot remember a dream, but is thinking about bodies lying in the field – sleeping or dead soldiers. There is something casual about this image. They are just lying there, their death inconsequential. Perhaps there is slight movement of one of the corpses. It is cold. Such lonesomeness. Why is he terrified?

ANALYST: Is it like reliving a memory?

PATIENT: (*angry*) This doesn't help. You may be accurate, but it is abstract, clinical. You are far away.

ANALYST: You want me to stay close, in touch with what you feel. You felt you died in the Yom Kippur War. You saw so many bodies just lying there. You imagined yourself to be one of them, hardly noticed, alone.

PATIENT: But what am I so terrified of?

ANALYST: Of remaining unnoticed, taken for dead, left behind in the field.

PATIENT: Perhaps. I can hear that.

In the next session, when the analyst reminds him of his anger when told that he was reliving a memory, another incident from the Yom Kippur War comes to mind. It was toward the end of the war, and he was sleeping on his tank. Suddenly, Egyptian soldiers who had climbed on the trees above him started heavy fire toward the soldiers below. Tens were killed instantaneously. His friend Beni jumped into the tank and closed the lid, leaving him outside. He screamed for him to open it, but Beni could not hear and thought he was dead. Eventually Beni opened the lid and let him in. The earlier, casual image of soldiers lying there, unnoticed, were those left as dead.

During the following session, the patient admits to feeling better. He must undertake the huge task of ensuring that his radical political statements be heard and taken at face value. What he has to say must be heard as testimony, as newly discovered knowledge. It must "lacerate the eye and perforate the heart," terminology taken from Judge Benjamin Halevi's verdict at the Kfar Kassem trial in Israel in the 1950s. Over 40 Israeli Arabs returning to their village had been shot by border police after imposition of a curfew that they had not been informed of.

Halevi used this term to clarify how an illegal order can be recognized. The term referred to a situation in which life cannot continue as usual: What had happened cannot be contained because the sense of normalcy had been destroyed. The patient feels that he has been saying this all his life to no avail. He knows that the Jewish people were defeated in the Holocaust despite their acts of resistance and that the Israeli army was defeated in the Yom Kippur War, despite its ultimate victory. The analyst's statement that he was reliving a memory felt like an attempt to contain his experience by telling him that it was no more than a repetition. What he was feeling at that moment was current, new, sharp, and wounding – not a reproduction. He had felt erased by the interpretation, his sword broken.

The analyst responds that had he gone inside, he would have found the patient alive and screaming, not dead. The patient follows with another memory from the Yom Kippur War: It was chaos. He lost his tank and was picked up by another tank. One night the crew was sleeping near the tank. He woke to the sound of loud rumbling. The tanks were leaving. His new tank was already gone. Not having been a regular crew member, he had been forgotten and left behind. As the tanks were moving away, he was afraid that he was being left alone in a desert infested by enemy soldiers. It took more than five minutes of frenzied screaming before one of the passing tanks noticed him, stopped, and picked him up. He himself was the dead soldier in his imagery.

When he expresses his radical opinions, other professionals treat him as though he does not exist. On some level, he agrees with them. When his opinions negate their work, when it lacerates their eye, this leads to violence against him or to his erasure. He prefers the peace that comes with the silence of his death to the violence that breaks him up so that he can only seek revenge. Acceptance of erasure, of his death, eventually brings him peace. He has no right to be alive anyway, harboring violent wishes for revenge. The feeling of being dead is frequently expressed by survivors of extreme traumatization. This patient's terror of being left behind as a soldier believed to be dead is linked to his wish to be left in peace as dead and to terrifying memories of when this almost happened.

The therapeutic process resonates with testimony in which a narrative that did not exist previously is created by the surprising discovery of emotional and cognitive knowledge one didn't know one had but which emerges when two people are totally present to each other. The witness in the listener must actively engage the patient's reverie, imagining with him and for him, in order to create knowledge which does not yet exist consciously or unconsciously. What do exist are discrete sensory fragments, broken up percepts of trauma fiercely lodged in the brain, exerting pressure and demanding an accounting. They do not jell into a cohesive narrative. An internal observer is needed for the fragments to become libidinized, merge, and form a narrative gestalt. Therapeutic engagement brings about creation of an internal witness in the intimate, shared holding space of testimony. Such engagement happens when the therapist empathically experiences, together with the patient, the traumatizing experience that the latter testifies to.

Extreme traumatization, be it genocide or childhood sexual abuse, defies knowing because at its core lies failure of the empathic human dyad. The experience of human responsiveness comes to be nonexistent. A responsive "thou" to one's basic needs no longer exists. Faith in the possibility of communication dies. Intrapsychically there is no longer a matrix of two people – self and resonating other. When the perpetrator is in full control, when the empathic other has totally failed in the external world, the internal, empathic thou as a generator, container, and addressee of self-dialogue ceases to exist. According to Amery (1980), "The experience of persecution was, at the very bottom, that of an extreme loneliness." There is no one, either outside or inside one self, that one can communicate with or tell one's story to; the story remains untold. Speaking to one self – i.e., the internal dialogue through which experiences become mentally represented, symbolized, verbalized, and narrativized – comes to a halt.

The self as interpreter of experience and creator of meaning can no longer function once impacted by massive psychic trauma. The ensuing absence of internal dialogue means that creation of internal knowledge of the traumatic experience is impossible. The survivor is absent to it, coming upon trauma "one moment too late," so that trauma remains an "unclaimed experience" (Caruth, 1996). The survivor suffers from traumatic imprints of visual, auditory, and physical sensations as well as strong affects that remain outside the narrative structure or story of experience as it is remembered. He is under a continuous conscious and unconscious barrage of these imprints that present themselves as enactments, flashbacks, and somatizations that colonize life, leaving no room for other experiences. The survivor experiences a powerful urge to tell his story – to remember, putting the disjointed fragments together into a whole. This can only happen when he finds his witness – a totally present listener who is receptive and willing to re-experience his traumatization with him anew.

It is at this juncture that the therapist needs to help the patient re-establish the witness position in his self by becoming his passionate witness. The patient temporarily anchors his self-witness position in the therapist until the trauma narrative, as he is able to testify to it, is complete and he is able to reclaim that position for himself. Reinternalizing the witness position constitutes the therapeutic process in the psychotherapy of extreme trauma and may need to be repeated again and again, until such position is firmly established in the survivor.

References

Amery, J. (1980). *At the mind's limits: Contemplations by a survivor of Auschwitz and its realities* (S. & S. P. Rosenfeld, Trans.). Bloomington, IN: Indiana University Press.

Aristotle. *Poetics* (16.4).

Bromberg, P. M. (2011). *The shadow of the tsunami and the growth of the relational mind.* London: Taylor and Francis Ltd.

Caruth, C. (1996). *Unclaimed experience: Trauma, narrative, and history.* Baltimore: Johns Hopkins University Press.

Dowling, S. (1985). A Piagetian critique. *Psychoanalytic Inquiry*, *5*, 569–587.

Hartman, G. (1970). *Beyond formalism: Literary essays 1958–1970*. New Haven: Yale University Press.

Katz, G. (2014). *The play within the play: The enacted dimension of psychoanalytic process*. New York: Routledge.

Klindienst, P. (1984). The voice of the shuttle is ours. *Stanford Literature Review*, *1*, 25–53.

Kristeva, J. (1980). *Desire in language: A semiotic approach to literature and art* (T. Gora, A. Jardine, & L. Roudiez, Trans.). New York: Columbia University Press.

Lacan, J. (1977). *Ecrits: A selection* (A. Sheridan, Trans.). New York: W.W. Norton & Co.

Laub, D, & Auerhahn, N. C. (1993). Knowing and not knowing massive psychic trauma: Forms of traumatic memory. *International Journal of Psychoanalysis*, *74*, 287–302.

Ogden, P., & Minton, K. (2006). *Trauma and the body: A sensorimotor approach to psychotherapy*. New York: W.W. Norton & Co.

Ovid (1955). *Metamorphoses* (R. Humphries, Trans.). Bloomington, IN: Indiana University Press.

Schore, A. N. (2007). Review of "Awakening the Dreamer: Clinical Journeys" by Philip M. Bromberg. *Psychoanalytic Dialogues*, *17*, 753–767.

Winnicott, D. W. (1958). *Through paediatrics to psycho-analysis*. New York: Basic Books.

Chapter 17

The dawn of unconscious phantasy

Robert Oelsner

Introduction

In this chapter I wish to explore the early stages of the development of unconscious phantasy seen as the very origin of thinking. In order to do so I will first briefly remind you of some of Freud's statements and the extensions made by Melanie Klein and Wilfred Bion and a vignette of a young girl whose rich phantasy work will give us a background to contrast with the cases of two severely disturbed boys I will present in the clinical section. Both boys' precarious psychic functioning may help illustrate the oscillation between an arrest and the dawn of unconscious phantasy.

My professional experience began with adolescent schizophrenics in the time that pioneers like Klein, Herbert Rosenfeld, Hannah Segal, and Bion developed tools to make their treatment possible applying the classical psychoanalytic frame and method. Since then I have felt motivated to delve further into this challenging territory (Oelsner, 1979, 1983, 1985, 1987a, 1987b, 1991a, 1991b, 1998, 1999, 2002, 2003, 2007). With the help and inspiration of Donald Meltzer (1986), whose work and personality completely blew me away, I also became interested in studying the continuum between primary autism and a range of infantile psychotic illnesses – here in America referred to as "autistic spectrum" – which can be best understood on observing the thread and the disruptions of their unconscious phantasy.

Unconscious phantasy[1] along with infantile sexuality, the Oedipus conflict, and transference are the pillars of our psychoanalytic theory. As we know, in the beginning Freud thought that the unconscious was made up of "forgotten" memories of actual sexual seductions that occurred in childhood. He also realized that forgetfulness happened, as the subject did not really *want* to remember those events and deployed a force to counteract the memories from emerging into consciousness. He called the mechanism that achieved this *repression* and the force employed *countercathexis.* His next discovery was that the repressed memories were not facsimiles of actual events in childhood, but of the *interpretation* of them, which created a modified version of the real events but actually became part of what he coined *psychic reality*. "If hysterics refer their symptoms to imaginary traumas, then this new fact signifies that they *create*[2] such scenes in their phantasies, and hence psychic reality deserves to be given a place next to actual reality" (Freud, 1916, p. 144). Furthermore, in the Lecture XXIII Freud (1916–1917) goes on, saying,

> Among the occurrences which recur again and again in the youthful history of neurotics – which are scarcely ever absent – there are a few of particular importance, which also deserve on that account, I think, to be brought into greater prominence than the rest. As specimens of this class I will enumerate these: observation of parental intercourse, seduction by an adult and threat of being castrated.

He will call these unconscious memories *primal phantasies*, stating that they are universal and probably date back to the infancy of our species rather than to one's individual childhood.

Klein built on Freud's concepts of psychic reality what became a fourth metapsychological point of view, namely the dramatic point of view. Anna O's reference to her "private theater" (Breuer, 1893) seemed quite fitting with Klein's internal world, a space within the mind made of self and objects playing evolving dramas, the inspiration for which came to her observing little children play imaginary stories with their toys. Amongst these imagined unconscious dramas, one that stood out was the "primal scene."[3] According to Klein unconscious dramas are ongoing with its dramatis personae and storylines. The unconscious system is, for her, in constant interaction with the external reality through projections and introjections. Internal reality helps to make meaning of the events in the external world and external reality modifies and enriches the internal reality as introjection also occurs. This Kleinian view explains the therapeutic action of psychoanalysis and clearly defines Klein's model of the mind as part of a two-person psychology, which is often overlooked in circles less acquainted with her work.

A common misunderstanding occurs when the ordinary meaning of *fantasy* as the opposite of *reality* is confused with the psychoanalytic concept *phantasy*. The latter should be used only to indicate the product of the *subjective interpretation of reality*, a large portion of which is unconscious. When I interpret to a patient that his phantasy of, say, the weekend break is that I was tired of putting up with him and express that through leaving him, I don't mean to say that he is wrong. On the contrary, I am focusing my, and hopefully his, attention to his subjective unconscious experience in order to open a window into the exploration of the source of this take in his unconscious. Phantasy with a "ph" is strictly related to the aforementioned concept of psychic reality, the other reality we all live in, which is as real and effective, if not more, than the external one.

It is not my purpose to make a summary of the evolution of the concept of unconscious phantasy which has recently been treated in the enlightening articles on this topic by Hannah Segal (1994), Elizabeth Spillius (2001), Riccardo

Steiner (2003), James Grotstein (2008), David Bell (2012), Catalina Bronstein (2015), and the list goes on.

This preamble should lead us to my personal version of the contributions by Wilfred Bion (1962a, 1962b, 1963, 1965, 1967, 1970), whose psychoanalytic epistemology is all about the matter of how we come to thinking.[4]

The birth of thinking

Bion, as Freud, maintains that we are born with some innate phantasies or set of predispositions to make sense of actual experiences. As said before, Freud called these primal phantasies and thought of them as phylogenetic memories. Bion instead called them "pre-conceptions," something like an expectation of an experience which when impacted by an approximate matching stimuli create some meaning, a conception. Meltzer[5] once said that rather than "I can see a cat" one should say, "I am cat-perceptive." As an example, the pre-conception of a something that will fit into the mouth and satiate the need to suck and also to nurse is necessary for the baby to make sense of the encounter with the breast and originate the conception of the breast not just as an anatomical organ but also as an experience. Babies need to be "breast-perceptive" to benefit from their relation to their mothers. Likewise, mothers need to be "baby-perceptive," to have what in everyday speech we call maternal instinct, Bion called reverie, and Winnicott (1975) referred to as primary maternal preoccupation.

The role of the mother in understanding and satisfying the baby's needs is quite crucial for the pre-conceptions to find their mates (Oelsner & Steinberg, 2016). But also the experiences of frustration when an expectation is not satisfied stimulate the mind to think of the experience in its absence – which Freud (1900) in his early work coined "thought identity" as opposed to "perception identity." The experiences of satisfaction and of frustration lead to representations of gratifying good objects and also of frustrating bad objects. Gradually these representations of objects populate the baby's mind and are felt to have a concrete existence in psychic reality and a powerful effect in the personality. They interact with its early ego and become a part the inner (private) theater of the mind with a storyline that begins to unfold, which is the baby's interpretation of reality. In its inchoate state, phantasies are quite simple and radical, objects being good or bad, idealized or persecutory and the baby is alternatively a good, happy, satisfied baby or a bad, angry, frustrated one. Love and hate, hope and despair seem to have their roots in this early stage of development. This initially simple and clear-cut drama helps the baby to orient itself towards and against experiences with objects, which over time will become richer and more complex. Thus early phantasies are representations of experiences, which require the existence of innate pre-conceptions and of external reality coming together. Only the representations and the evolving drama are necessarily internal as they are a function of the mind.

In conclusion, according to this model of the mind, thinking has its origins in the internal world with its pre-conceptions, which are constantly enriched and modified by the external reality to become conceptions. This is also what Klein's internal objects really are and explains how both in life and in psychoanalysis they undergo modifications. When modifications cannot occur we speak of fixations and of repetition compulsion and hope that our psychoanalytic approach can help patients to open to the refreshing processes of projections and introjections.

Unlike what you are given to find when you carry out systematic baby-observation, by the time patients, young and old, come to our consulting rooms the early stages of unconscious phantasy can only be inferred from the totality of the clinical material, particularly through paying attention to the ways the analyst as an object is being experienced in the meeting. The experience largely depends on the projection of the patient's expectations or pre-conceptions. The stability of the analytic setting gives one a privileged position to observe how all this has happened and reoccurs. From this point of view psychoanalysis is less of a therapy for the sick and unhappy and more an instrument to study and enhance thinking. The point can fairly be made that any psychopathological picture is due to failed thinking processes. Mechanisms of defense, for instance, are in theory smartly invented phantasies but in practice end up failing.

Infantile sexual theories, as another example of unconscious phantasies, help the child to get some version of the relation between the parents enough to be able to imagine what they do in the other room. However, infantile sexual theories are never the right ones for lack of sexual maturation and experience yet to accrete.

In the Kleinian/Bionian model, not only representations of actual events but also modalities of psychic functioning, relations, experiences, and affects with objects are the stuff of which unconscious phantasies consist and largely effect our organ of consciousness. Transference processes are in this regard manifestations of early phantasies that were never entirely given up but only overwritten by new modes of thoughts and relations. The analysis of very young children gives us the privilege to observe the process of unconscious phantasy closer to its origins and also closer to the surface of the mind. The infantile sexual theories and phantasies have not yet been challenged and repressed by adult reasoning into the depth of the unconscious.

Patty, age 5, prior to a holiday, climbed, turned, and hid behind the seat of my high armchair. She also mentioned she would go on a trip. And then said something about her dog and her cat going nuts when she was away. "They might even die," she added. I interpreted that on the high chair she was now me and I was the dog and the cat she believed would react and might die as she went away. She threw herself on the couch and showed signs of great anxiety. She also said that she'd rather not go away at all and stay here. She started to wrap herself up in a blanket and said that she was very tired. I said that she wanted to stay here, sleep with me, as she often wanted to do at home with her parents, so as to make sure that I will not die when I sleep with my wife – the cat and the dog – in her absence. She started pulling her hair in a dramatic fashion and screamed: "Oh no! That would be tragic!" And immediately added: "that will not happen because people do not die in bed and they don't die in the night. They made it that people die only in the morning!"

It was not difficult to see that her going away for a holiday had for her a similar meaning to going to sleep and freeing up Mommy and Daddy to be together in their bed. Her jealousy and anger made it that in her phantasy she sentenced them and me, as the cat and the dog, to death, which she also felt would be tragic, as she would be left alone. Therefore, she created a defensive phantasy or two. For once, she would not go away at all. (At times she would also not leave the parents' bedroom and sleep with them all night.) Then, the idea that people do not die in bed or during the night – or when she goes on holidays for that matter – was now a denial of the phantasy that made her so anxious.

It takes much more time and work to unveil these kinds of phantasies in grown-ups as external reality oftentimes only buries them deeper in the mind.

The dawn of unconscious phantasy in clinical practice

I will now present some case material of two far more disturbed children in which one can observe both the failure and the formation of unconscious phantasies in *statu nascendi*.

Tyler[6] is the 10-year-old son of a well-educated European family. He is tall, well built with an attractive face, pale blue eyes and long black hair. He invariably arrives with a dark cap that covers his head down to his eyebrows and ears. His gait is sometimes ungainly. He speaks in a sort of flat, unmodulated nasal tone, often making unusual noises.

A recent physical attack on his father moved the parents to bring him to therapy. Due to a difficult birth he had to be sucked out with vacuum extraction after 24 hours. He was breastfed until the age of three as that was the only way his mother felt she could have him close. He refused any other type of food and was always hostile to his father. He has his rituals and would flare up uncontrolled if things did not go his way. He has gone as far as biting and hitting his mother when contradicted. Toilet hygiene, washing his hair, cutting his fingernails, eating and doing simple chores are extremely problematic if not impossible for him to follow.

Although he crawled at 9 months, talked at 12 months, and walked at 18 months, when he entered nursery school at age 3, his teacher reported that he seemed unrelated to other children, distractible, and at times "in his own world."

This is now the therapist's actual report:

> For the first several months, Tyler would enter the room and begin reciting information about computer games, which I had great trouble following. He'd circle the room as he talked, leaping up on the couch or a chair as he

went. He sometimes lay on the rug, pressing the side of his face to the air vent, and he'd often comment on the texture of things in the office – "it's hard" or "it's soft." He often seemed not to hear me when I spoke. He dictated stories, which really were lists of things. He played a kind of fort-da game with me, going behind the couch, and I spoke of his figuring out if I would be there or not when he looked. He also figured out the contours of the space in my room – close to me, far from me. When he was most in contact with me, I felt that he was establishing the physical parameters of our time together. But often, I would feel deadened by his circling, his lists, and the flatness of his voice. I tried to think about how to initiate something more spontaneous and more connected.

Over time, Tyler became more engaged with me, even "falling in love" a bit, writing me notes when I was away on break and sending them to my office, emerging from his solipsistic world. I became very encouraged for a period of time when he seemed to be developing a fantasy game in which he and I were the grandparents of some stuffed animals in my office. At that time, he was also more responsive to comments or observations I made. However, I found that the fantasy game also became stuck and began to get quite repetitive. It seemed to stall around an anticipated violent death of the stuffed animals' parents, a fantasy from which he could not extricate himself. Eventually, he stopped this game, but without a sense of resolution.

He returned, at that point, to the making of lists and recitation of the attributes of video game characters.

Discussion

This boy seemed to have had a troubled transition from the womb to the external world. Being sucked out of his protected environment must have been a violent and painful experience, the stimuli of the outside world coming as an overwhelming shock. Only his clinging to the mother's breast as an extension of the umbilical cord would reconstitute the symbiotic unit. Father – and at times mother as well – was likely held responsible for this terrible eviction, hence his attacking them. We hear that he had made some headway early on regarding crawling, walking, and talking. But soon his talk turned into a flat idiosyncratic speech. Likely all of his early development was either based on mimicry, or rapidly regressed to ritualized meaningless movements and sound emission or lists of words, much easier to handle than the complexity of emotions. It also seemed that anything that would go into his body, like food or sounds, or removed from it, like washing his hair or cutting his fingernails, were strongly resisted as all that disturbed the peaceful existence in the womb.

He would not really play in his sessions but rather explore the texture of the place or react to the texture of the voice of the therapist. The cap that covered his head down to the ears likely had the function of muffling all sound stimuli. Any progress in his contact between him and the therapist would soon be undone.

Her words being turned into agrammatical lists that he would recite may be indicative of the method employed to learn to use words at the age of 1. His fixation to a ritualized fort-da type of interaction was likely a way to simplify his universe of experience to a bare minimum. It seemed that coming to life was the hateful thing that needed to be ironed away.

We can leave Tyler for now, the boy who could not forgive his parents for the fact that he had been born, and turn to our next child whose disturbance seemed rooted in the early stages after birth in which the encounter with an object that calls for the baby's attention, and a baby that discovers it, are essential.

Maxie, an appealing boy with blond hair and big blue eyes, was 6 years old when I first saw him. His mother brought him to therapy for his odd behaviors. He often ran from one corner to another in the home and at school, and would approach strangers with questions and remarks as if he did not have the category of strangers. He "daydreams" – says mother – "and believes he is a car or a robot and acts as such."

He is the only child of a couple who 10 years ago came to Seattle from the East Coast, transferred by the company they have been working for. Mother said that she noticed her pregnancy when she started missing her menstrual periods. Maxie was born three weeks early, but could go home with his mother after a couple days. She noted that he would fall asleep at the breast and could therefore not get enough food. He was transferred to the bottle and that seemed to work well. Mother knew she had to go back to work soon after his birth and was shy of engaging with him for fear of not bearing to give him up for full days to a nursery. She was depressed then and still looks so now. He was eventually sent to nursery at 4 months old.

At school he has been reportedly isolated, in his own world, talking to himself, making mouth noises and running in circles in the playground.

Maxie's father decided that he would not hinder, but also not cooperate with, his son's therapy for he believed there was nothing wrong with him.

Maxie first came into my office without any sign of anxiety or emotion. He quickly started to run around and climb onto furniture. He behaved more like a little monkey than a child. However, he easily allowed me to bring him down when he put himself at risk of falling. When he settled down he produced two things. First he glued two squares, blue and yellow, onto a white sheet of paper. Then he glued a red square on top of the yellow one (Figure 17.1). No comments. Next he did a drawing of a robot/monster, which he immediately crossed out many times (Figure 17.2).

For some time he would bring dozens of books with stickers of all kinds of robots and monsters whose names and characteristics he was all too familiar with. He would cut them out and then stick them to places on some pages designed for them. That was all he would do and talk about while at the same time he also became one of them. There was little contact with me and he would barely listen to my comments or questions. After some months when this activity seemed clearly unproductive, I encouraged his mother and him to keep these

Figure 17.1

books out of the sessions. He then changed and would at times cling to me, either sitting on my lap, or wrapping his legs around my neck and shoulders or using my lap as a footrest. I felt I was little more than another piece of furniture or climbing device with the exception of brief periods when he would ask me to tightly hold his hand or wrist for almost the entire hour.

Figure 17.2

Discussion

Maxie was undrawn (Alvarez, 2016) to his mother and the breast but did well on the bottle. The lack of responsiveness to a live object was seemingly there from the start. Perhaps the mother had herself some problem to notice him as a live baby since the time in the womb, being that her report about the pregnancy was only about the physiological sign of missing menstruation. Her subsequent shyness to engage him and her depression must have left Maxie identified with a flat, depressed mother.

He seemed to feel that he was part of a bi-dimensional world of inanimate robot-stickers and monsters-stickers that could only cling to the surface of objects. He would therefore stick to my body surface or ask me to stick to his. Both at school and in his sessions he would stay in his idiosyncratic world, like the picture of his remote mother. His lack of emotionality, flatness, and unresponsiveness was probably not only an identification with his depressed mother but also the result of his not having been called into existence by her (or the father). His preference for the odd stickers rather than engaging with or responding to me reminded me also of his unresponsiveness to the breast while latching on to the bottle. Holding on to his sticker-figures was most likely an expression of his view of objects without an inside to take him in. Meltzer (1975) called this type of narcissistic relation "adhesive identification," an idea he took from Esther Bick (1968, 1986).

In therapy

For the first eight months I would invariably find him curled up in a fetal position underneath his mother's chair in the waiting room. When I opened the door I had to call him and then very slowly would he emerge, stand up or crawl, make several stops and finally come with me into my office. I said to him that he felt like a baby coming out of Mummy's bottom. But once in the session he would assemble airplanes, machines, or robots with Lego blocks. After a short while he would fluctuate between sticking to me and going into his odd separate world where I could not reach him.

I will now report in detail a session, 9 months into therapy, Maxie at 7 years old. As I go for him to the waiting room he is stuck looking at the cover of a magazine on my shelf without reacting to me. So, I have to wait and then he runs in before me. (Since I looked at just him I regretfully missed the theme of the cover until the session was over.) As he runs in, he exclaims that I should not ask him what he was doing there. He opens his box, takes his pad and pencil and makes the first drawing in a rush: Pipi (Figure 17.3, left) and Spiderman (Figure 17.3, right) – Spiderman known to us from previous sessions to be for him a highly persecutory figure.

Figure 17.3

Next he draws a hero that is good and can help: MhYTi Heros (Figure 17.4), he says and writes down.

I say that that he feared me to be one of the very bad figures, hence his not wanting me to talk. Am I Spiderman that might attack him?

He responds that Spiderman makes big webs. He hurries to lock up both drawings and the pad in the box. He starts his running back and forth, making short leaps in the air each time he arrives at one of the sides of the room (which is quite small). He speaks mostly gibberish though, here and there, I can recognize some words like "hero," "flying," "I'll hit you," etc. After a while of his doing this, I say that he feels in danger of being caught in Spiderman's web and only running like crazy and jumping or finding a mighty hero who can prevent that from happening. At this point I can tell that Maxie is hallucinating webs and other terrifying images. However, he does not look anxious. (I chose not to give a transference interpretation as I felt that he was in another world.)

He barely looks at me and keeps running. This takes a good part of the hour during which I feel dropped. I say, finally, that he is caught now in some imaginary place that only he can see, and I do not exist. And also that he can always take his imaginary world away with him. No missing Robert or Mummy. (Mother, he and I know, is about to leave on a trip for a week and will not be able to bring him to his sessions.) He goes to my computer and pushes the

Figure 17.4

keys, which some time back we agreed was not for him to play with. He looks to see if I react. I then tell him that he is concerned that when he goes to his imaginary world and leaves me, I might do the same and leave him (which actually I need to struggle against, as his withdrawal has a powerful effect, nudging me to slip away too). He pushes the buttons to have me come back to him, I say.

He now goes to the armchair, puts himself head down and legs up, makes some movements and falls to the floor hitting his forehead. He gets up and seems to feel no pain.

I say that in the imaginary world he went to, nothing should fall (my way of saying he is in the outer space away from the gravitational attraction of the Earth).

He goes on running again and eventually stops, exhausted.

I ask him when it is that Mummy goes away and he won't come to see me. (I wanted to bring the matter into his awareness, as it seemed to me it had provoked his retreating.) Although he does not respond, the question seems to touch him and he looks at me.

I say that sometimes Mummy is not there with him and sometimes Robert is not there with him. And, that he has played in the hour that he wasn't there, leaving me alone. That is also what he expects will happen when Mummy leaves and he won't come for a week.

The session ends and I walk him to the waiting room, where mother confirms that he will have to miss the upcoming week. He grabs a New Yorker from the magazine table and shows me the cover: two girls are sitting with their back turned to each other. Each one is looking at her computer screen with a Playmobil kind of figure on it, and their hands playing on the keyboard, oblivious of the toys that are lying around on the floor and of the view of the garden with a swing-set and a ball and nobody there. They seem to be in their respective own worlds.

Since the session had finished and we were back in the waiting room I only mention to him that they are not looking at each other. But he shows me the detail I overlooked, and says they are both having the same type of computer game on their screens!

I bid him goodbye and say I will see him in two weeks.

After he left I looked at the cover in more detail. The ironic title the artist gave it is "Playdate."

Discussion

Maxie is no longer in his Mummy's bottom. He has now been fully evacuated through her anus. But life in the outside world has its hazards. He is in a trance looking at the magazine. In his unresponsiveness when I collect him, he is turning his back to the real world (and to me for that matter). Is he perhaps convinced that if he tried to look for/at me he will find me turning my back on him?

If so, then the scene of the two girls represents the two of us as well as him and his Mummy, and him and his uncooperative Daddy. Neither feels drawn to each other or willing to call each other's attention.

His behavior should not surprise us since we heard that after birth he fell asleep at the breast and also that his mother shied away and was depressed. But he needs me to wait and not slip away. When he does relate to me fleetingly he seems to imagine that I am enraged – bad Spiderman – having been kept waiting and will now go after him, trapping him into a web of words. He also brings up a second object, one that is good and can help. I failed to acknowledge that he had hopes to find in me a MhYTi Hero to rescue him, instead interpreting only his persecutory version of me/Spiderman.[7] This he takes for a fact, locks all the drawings away and flees to his MhYTi world, dropping me on the way. He is busy there, having become an imaginary hero that can not only run but also fly and hit and beat his bad persecutors. He creates this mighty reality by hallucinating it, turning once again his back to external reality altogether. Yet after a while – and he must have feared my drifting off as a response to being ignored – he pushes my buttons to have me come back, which I do as a reaction to his getting into my computer. But his falling off the chair and hitting his head indicates, it would seem, that he had already gone too far away and only his fall brings him back to reality for an instant. And I was not there to catch him. Note his drawings with all figures up in the air. His reaction to his feeling dropped has him flee once again the painful world without protective objects he came to exist in, with an uncooperative father and a depressed mother. At that point I decide to bring him back with my question, to remind him that he is about to lose both his Mummy and me for many days, in an attempt to broach the matter. This seems to awaken him to his pain again. At that point the hour is over and once in the waiting room he does this amazing thing of picking the cover of the two isolated girls turning their backs to the world and to each other. Quite evocative of the atmosphere of our session. He is capable of finding – not in his mind but in my waiting room – the right image to convey what just occurred!

Maxie's father – for what I know – is himself a withdrawn character, would never play with him and lives literally on his screen. Left with a scarcity of helpful objects, real Mighty Heroes, Maxie had to invent them in his hallucinated reality. Yet for moments he has managed to relate to me as he did at the end of this session, which gave us some hope that he could experience and introject me as a heroic, mighty father who could stay put with him regardless.

Conclusions

As we come to the end of this chapter a few comments may take us back to the title, "The dawn of unconscious phantasy." The purpose of this contribution is to focus on the conditions needed for unconscious phantasy to be called into existence, and its impairments and oscillations. Unconscious phantasy is an ongoing function in the mind – like the function of dreaming – essential for representing one's view and experience of the world one lives in. It therefore is the very foundation of thinking. In order for unconscious phantasy to develop there has to be a baby with the innate expectation (Bion's preconception) of objects to meet him. Likewise, there needs to be a mother (and a father, as Maxie proved) to give the preconception its realization to create an idea and a script (phantasy). Exchanging with the world of objects that projections and introjections modify serves to enrich and complexify its content and meaning.

But, as both Tyler and Maxie showed in their respective therapy hours, the function of developing unconscious phantasy may be arrested early on. Tyler's being violently sucked out of a muffled womb had him hate the bombardment of the experience of the world. His clinging to his mother – breastfed until the age of 3 – did not help him to transition to the outside world, but rather fixated him in the delusion of still being inside. Whenever the stimuli (frustrations being powerful stimuli) could not be borne he would either fall apart or move back into his autistic capsule. Like Maxie, in order to be there he would at times resort to strip off the meaning of words and thoughts and phantasies by turning them into list-recitation or mechanical motions, the evidence for which was his strange gait and his running around aimlessly. Finally we need also to consider a possible innate factor, like the lack or feebleness of pre-conceptions may arrest the development of the thinking/phantasying mind since its inception.

While Maxie is a different case, part of his phenomenology overlaps with Tyler's. The mother's withholding her engaging-engagement plus the uncooperative father has left Maxie circling in an extraterrestrial space for too long. Maxie used his hallucinations as an autistic retreat (Aulagnier, 1985), a world away from the shared world of reality. Alternatively he would resort to clinging to the surface of bi-dimensional objects. At other times he could show quite clearly some ability to aim projections *into* their inside and introjecting his objects into his inner world. For instance, he could project into his analyst the experience of being dropped and identify with the internalized removed mother or father.

Tyler and Maxie helped me to illustrate the distinction between phantasy world, which is expressed in play and imagination and is a bridge with reality, from hallucination as an invention of a non-existent world that the self can retreat into.

Both children had some ability to phantasize and to relate to the world. But their behavior strongly suggested that their abilities were severely compromised for the lack of exercising the function of attention, that in Maxie's case was not sufficiently called for, while for Tyler paying attention was just not tolerable. What remains to be seen is the extent to which some of the interest in the external world can be recuperated or enhanced.

Notes

1 The notion of unconscious phantasy (spelled with a "ph" to differentiate it from the conscious "fantasy") is probably the major theoretical theme of all the scientific discussions. When translating Freud from German into English during the 1920s it had already been necessary to adopt a term that would distinguish the unconscious character of "phantasy," which Freud used relatively rarely, from its conscious aspects. Susan Isaacs discussed the notion of "unconscious phantasy" in her first and most important paper, "The Nature and Function of Phantasy," read on January 27, 1943 to the British Psychoanalytic Society in what is known as The Freud-Klein Controversies. For a detailed history of the term *phantasy* with a "ph," see Riccardo Steiner's (2003, pp. 1–66) scholarly introduction to the book *Unconscious Phantasy*.
2 My emphasis.
3 Notice the theatrical expression.
4 My use of the gerund is purposeful, as the reader will soon notice.
5 Personal comment.
6 I am grateful to Dr. Marsha Silverstein, who has allowed me to use a portion of her case material.
7 Spiderman is in the cartoons a "good one," Maxie had said at other times.

References

Alvarez, A. (2016). Personal comment.
Aulagnier, P. (1985). Retreat into hallucination: An equivalent of the autistic retreat? In D. Birksted-Breen, S. Flanders, & A. Gibeault (Eds.), *Reading French psychoanalysis*. The New Library of Psychoanalysis. London and New York: Routledge. [First published in French under the title Le retrait dans l'hallucination. Un équivalent du retrait autistique? in *Un interprete en quête de sens*. Paris: Ramsay, 1986].
Bell, D. (2012). Unconscious phantasy: Historical and conceptual dimensions. *Paper given to conference "Unconscious Phantasy Today."* University College London, December 8, 2012.
Bick, E. (1968). The experience of the skin in early object relations. *International Journal of Psycho-Analysis, 49*, 558–566.
Bick, E. (1986). Further considerations on the functioning of skin in early object relations: Findings from infant observation integrated into child and adult analysis. *British Journal of Psychotherapy, 2*, 292–299.
Bion, W. R. (1962a). The psychoanalytic study of thinking. *International Journal of Psychoanalysis, 43*, 306–310.
Bion, W. R. (1962b). A theory of thinking. *International Journal of Psychoanalysis, 43*, 306–310.
Bion, W. R. (1963). *Elements of psycho-analysis*. London: Heinemann.
Bion, W. R. (1965). *Transformations*. London: Heinemann.
Bion, W. R. (1967). *Second thoughts*. London: Heinemann.
Bion, W. R. (1970). *Attention and interpretation*. London: Tavistock Publications.
Breuer, J. (1893). Case histories: Case I Fraulein Anna O. In S. Freud, *Studies on hysteria, the standard edition of the complete psychological works of Sigmund Freud volume II (1893–1895)* (pp. 21–47).
Bronstein, C. (2015). Finding unconscious phantasy in the session: Recognizing form. *International Journal of Psychoanalysis, 96*, 925–944.

Freud, S. (1900). *The interpretation of dreams. The standard edition of the complete psychological works of Sigmund Freud, volume IV (1900): The interpretation of dreams* (first part) (pp. ix–627).

Freud, S. (1916). The history of the psychoanalytic movement. *Psychoanalytic Review, 3,* 406–454.

Freud, S. (1916–1917). *Introductory lecture 23,* S.E., 16 (p. 368).

Grotstein, J. (2008). The overarching role of unconscious phantasy. *Psychoanalytic Inquiry, 28,* 190–205.

Meltzer, D. (1975). *Explorations in autism: A psycho-analytical study.* Strath Tay, Scotland: Clunie Press.

Meltzer, D. (1986). Psychotic illness in early childhood. In *Studies in extended metapsychology* (pp. 122–135). Strath Tay, Scotland: Clunie Press.

Oelsner, R. (1979). La Contratransferencia del Analista frente al Paciente que no puede Soñar (The countertransference of the analyst towards the patient who cannot dream), II Symposium and Annual Conference, Buenos Aires Psychoanalytical Association. Unpublished.

Oelsner, R. (1983). Algunos mecanismos psicóticos presentes en la encopresis (Some psychotic mechanisms present in encopresis) V Symposium and Annual Conference, Buenos Aires Psychoanalytical Association. In *Revista de la Asociación Escuela Argentina de Psicoterapia para Graduados, 15,* 1988. Buenos Aires: Revista de la Asociación Escuela Argentina de Psicoterapia para Graduados.

Oelsner, R. (1985). De la Identificación Primaria a la Identificación Delirante (From primary identification to delusional identification). XXXIV IPAC, Hamburg, 1985. In *Revista de Psicoanálisis,* APA, *42*(5).

Oelsner, R. (1987a). Variaciones sobre el Tema del Autismo. El Paciente Nonato (Variations on the theme of autism. The unborn patient), XXXV IPAC, Montreal, 1987. In *Revista de Psicoanálisis,* APA, *44*(5) – Segunda Parte.

Oelsner, R. (1987b). Vulnerabilidad y Fenómenos Autistas (Vulnerability and autistic phenomena), IX Symposium and Annual Conference, Buenos Aires Psychoanalytic Association. In *Revista de Psicoanálisis,* Buenos Aires Psychoanalytical Association, *11*(1), 1989.

Oelsner, R. (1991a). Sobre la Muerte Psíquica y el Delirio (On psychic death and delusion). XXXVII IPAC, Buenos Aires Sobre la Muerte. In *Revista de Psicoanálisis,* APA, *48*(1).

Oelsner, R. (1991b). Psicosis Infantil (Infantile psychosis). Keynote paper at the Annual Psychoanalytic Conference in Rosario, May 1991. Unpublished.

Oelsner, R. (1998). De la tormenta emocional a la catástrofe mental (From emotional storm to mental catastrophe). Keynote paper at the XX Symposium and Annual Conference, Buenos Aires Psychoanalytical Association, October 1998. Unpublished.

Oelsner, R. (1999). Die Funktion des containenden Objektes in der Umformung des psychotischen Erscheinungsbildes eines achtjärigen Jungens, presented at the Psychoanalytic Forum in Munich, Germany, February 23, 1999. In E. T. Bianchedi, R. Oelsner, R. Antar, L. Pistiner de Cortiñas, S. Neborak, & M. Martinez de Saenz, *Bion conocido/desconocido.* Buenos Aires: Editorial Lugar. Published in English, The function and structure of the containing object: Modulation of a psychotic picture in an eight-year-old boy. *Fort Da, 9,* 13–31, 2003.

Oelsner, R. (2002). Alice in Wonderland and analyst in awe. Presented at the Conference TRANSFORMATIONS IN O: The Further Edge of the Work of Wilfred Bion, September 21, 2002, organized by PINC and NCSPP, San Francisco, CA. Unpublished.

Oelsner, R. (2003). Perfume or the ambivalent struggle to (not to) become human. Paper presented at The Psychoanalytic Center of California, LA, May 17, 2003. Unpublished.

Oelsner, R. (2007). Early trauma and its self perpetuation. Western Branch of the Canadian Psychoanalytic Society, Vancouver, May 5, 2007. Unpublished.

Oelsner, R., & Steinberg, C. (2016). Little Hans went alone into the wide world: Or beta-elements in search of a container for meaning. In D. Blue, & C. Harrang (Eds.), *From reverie to interpretation: Transforming thought into the action of psychoanalysis.* London: Karnac.

Segal, H. (1994). Phantasy and reality. *International Journal of Psychoanalysis, 75,* 395–401.

Spillius, E. B. (2001). Freud and Klein on the concept of phantasy. *International Journal of Psychoanalysis, 82,* 361–373.

Steiner, R. (Ed.). (2003). *Unconscious phantasy.* London and New York: Karnac.

Winnicott, D. W. (1975). Primary maternal preoccupation. In *Through paediatrics to psycho-analysis. The international psycho-analytical library* (pp. 300–305). London: The Hogarth Press and The Institute of Psycho-Analysis.

Chapter 18

Fantasy and trauma

Arlene Kramer Richards

The concept of unconscious fantasy was constructed to solve a clinical problem. Freud believed that mental illness was caused by infantile trauma, particularly the trauma of seduction by a parent or parent surrogate until 1897 (Masson, 1985 pp. 264–266). That theory involved an infantile experience that was reawakened in adulthood when it caused hysteria. He gave up the idea that traumatic sexual seduction was the *only* basis for later pathology after 1897 and substituted the hypothesis that fantasies of traumatic sexual seduction were ubiquitous and by themselves led to pathology just as actual seduction did. He called this the Oedipal Complex because he believed that the fantasy of killing father in order to marry mother as Oedipus did in the drama was universal. So his new idea was that either real or fantasized trauma led to pathology. Psychoanalysts have been thinking and arguing ever since about whether infantile trauma or fantasies of trauma cause later mental illness (Sulloway, 1979; Masson, 1984; Blum, 1991; Simon, 1992; Good, 1995; Laplanche, 1997).

Traumatic deprivation and loss leaves people with a sense of loss, sadness, and a need for repair. The intense need for reparations and for apology is passed down through the generations. This exacerbates both Oedipal pathology and narcissistic pathology. It elicits both guilt and shame. My hypothesis in this chapter is that the inevitable losses and damages of infancy (Viorst, 1986) act as the kernels of fantasy. Wishes for restoration, protection, love, revenge, and nurturance are elaborated during development and in the form of unconscious fantasy influence perceptions and behaviors throughout later life. It is to the extent that these unconscious fantasies motivate later life that they are important to understand. As Arlow (1991a) put it: "In analyzing a symptom it is essential to be able to place the underlying fantasy in its proper context in the history of the patient," (p. 136) To the extent that they impede functioning and leave the person unsatisfied, they need to be made conscious. Making them conscious by putting them into words enables a person to avoid self destructive behaviors.

Trauma and fantasy

Loewenberg (2015) explained the complexity of trauma this way:

> Freud definitively rejected the linear causation of simple developmental time with his concept of Nachträglichkeit (deferred action or après-coup). By Nachträglichkeit Freud meant a deferred or much delayed reaction to a trauma when at a later time it has been reignited or reawakened by new experiences, stimuli, or traumas. The later event stirs up the previously unconscious memory and associated affects, giving them new life and significance (Green 2009, pp. 10–11). This is one of the reasons that every historical period requires a new confrontation with the past, just as every cultural age needs to create its own translations of the texts it wants to comprehend.
>
> (p. 771)

This description of recall or reawakening of memories of trauma receives support from an exhaustive study of recall of trauma in dreams and in behavior (Brenneis, 1997) showing that nowhere in the research literature or in clinical presentations is there a literal copy of a trauma. Instead, transformations and metaphoric representations of recorded traumata and traumatic situations are found. This supports Freud's change of mind when he stopped believing that all symptoms are the result of sexual trauma in early childhood and chose to see, instead, a transformed picture of early events that distorted or metaphorically depicted wishes, fears, and moral values in addition to the external events that precipitated trauma.

The complexity of the discussions about trauma start with the use of the term itself. I propose that we distinguish between an event, a reaction to the event, and a lasting outcome of the event. If an event causes a lasting psychological impairment like nightmares, frigidity, irrational fear or the like, that event has had a traumatic effect. What makes the event traumatic is the person's perception which is always shaped by the current psychological state, including fantasies. In turn, what makes fantasy is experience elaborated into story. When looked at this way, the complex interaction of event, perception, and lasting effect do not require choosing between trauma and fantasy in the etiology of neurosis.

The new idea that has come out of my thinking on this complex issue of whether mental conflict comes out of trauma or out of fantasy is that the inevitable potentially traumatizing events of infancy and childhood are the breeding ground of fantasy. But not everyone can find the strength or resilience to overcome trauma by creating a useful fantasy. As Bachant (2014) put it:

> Mutual influence between biological and social systems is supported by many different kinds of studies and researchers are positing that when we interact, we influence each other's biological state as well as the long term construction of each other's brains (Cozolino 2006).
>
> (p. 76)

The useful fantasies are those that, like Shakespeare's creation of Hamlet after his own father's death, enable the person creating the fantasy to feel powerful enough to overcome the shame of the powerlessness of trauma; this creativity may be inhibited when the shame aroused by the trauma is reinforced by parental and/or social shaming. The shaming by parents and/or society can be crucial in determining whether the initial event is traumatic and whether the reawakening causes neurosis. The support of an attentive audience like that Shakespeare had may even determine whether it can be overcome. At the same time, whether an event causes trauma is determined by how the person's unconscious fantasy construes the event. The four interactive variables of brain function, prior unconscious fantasy, social support, and intensity of traumatic event contribute to the complexity and resistance to amelioration and recovery. If the unconscious fantasy is that a cruel monster mother hovers nearby, and that she cannot wait to betray the father with her lover, having the father die can be traumatic. It can prevent the person from acting in his own best interest. It can even cause the destruction of his entire world, killing everyone, or almost everyone, and leaving the world to a marauding conqueror from another country as it did to the character in the play *Hamlet*.

Case from China: an example of a Hamlet fantasy[1]

1 Basic information

The patient Y is male, 45 years old, married with no child and with non-religious belief. He got college bachelor degree in engineering. He has been a worker in a factory for nearly 20 years and lost his job about 10 months ago.

2 Which problems and complaints did the patient mention in the first interview?

The patient Y don't know how to make eye contact and is afraid of eye contact with the strangers. He believes that there would be an unfamiliar pedestrian who will spit at him and give him a psychiatric label with contempt. The psychiatric diagnosis is OCD made by psychiatrist. He takes medication as follows: fluvoxamine 200 mg/day, aripiprazole 15 mg/day.

3 A short note on the first impression of the patient

The patient is medium height, neatly dressed, wearing glasses, decent, rational. Words are brief and emotion is insipid.

4 Early life background

The patient Y has an older sister and a younger step brother. Y was a posthumous child, his father committed suicide during the Cultural Revolution. His mother was a teacher of the junior high school in hometown. His mother remarried and was pregnant again when Y was 8 years old. Then, Y and his stepfather left their home town for another province because of the Cultural Revolution.

In 1977, his stepfather was a teacher of a primary school. His stepfather is introverted and coward, had no experiences with taking care of child. Once, Y was framed by his classmates, his stepfather didn't know the situation, severely hit Y, and said that a child shouldn't tell a lie. His stepfather was diligent and often come home late. Y often did some cooking by himself. During three years in which they lived together the overall feeling was happy; Y often played with his classmates.

From primary school to high school, Y always made an outstanding academic record, studied hard and almost had no entertainment. In Y's memory, his mother was grumpy, and Y was often beaten and scolded by his mother. On one occasion, the score of an English test was not good, mom tweaked his ear from one end of the playground to the other side. Although often beaten, Y still think that mother is good for him, do not feel unhappy now. Actually, his parents nearly have no communication with him. Y went to college successfully although the college acceptance rates in those days, were low.

Therapeutic process

At the beginning, the patient Y described his sufferings in his college dormitory. It was quite difficult for him to keep good relationships with his roommates. There were four roommates: A, B, C, and D.

When he met roommate A for the first time in the dormitory, Y told A that you looked so old that you must be one of the administrators of our college dormitory and you couldn't be my roommate. Y can't understood why A was so angry when Y told that he looked older than the age he said he was.

One day, roommate B asked Y to buy a ticket for vocal concert for him. Y agreed to buy a ticket for B. But when the concert would be performed 5 hours later, Y had not bought a ticket for B because he was afraid that B wouldn't pay the money for the ticket. Y only bought one ticket for himself. Roommate B was angry about Y's breaking a promise.

One day roommate C invited Y to ride around on bike. When they rode in the campus, there was an accidental collision with others. C argued with them. Y was afraid that there would be a fight and he just stood far away so that he looked like an onlooker.

The patient Y gradually found that his roommates didn't like him. His roommates talked and laughed and helped each other. It seemed that He was excluded from his dormitory. When he walked into his dorm room, he felt unhappy and alone. He didn't know how to set up and keep a good relationship with his roommates.

One day, he found sputum on his schoolbag. He was angry and thought that there must be someone despised him and spit on him deliberately. He concluded that he must be a "psychotic patient." Gradually, the patient Y became afraid of eye contact with the strangers. He didn't know how to operate "eye contact" naturally. He believed that there would be an unfamiliar pedestrian who will spit at him and give him a psychiatric label with contempt. About 25 years ago, the patient Y had come to the hospital and accepted medication treatment for one year. The treatment effect was very poor and the patient Y felt sad and hopeless. Then he secluded himself from others and moved out of the dormitory. During his college life, he was in a state of depression.

When the patient goes home, he finds that his eye contact with familiar people is spontaneous. But when he goes out, he feels nervous and keeps alert. He is afraid that someone will make out that he is a psychotic patient through "his abnormal eye contact." He believes that there would be an unfamiliar pedestrian who will spit at him and give him a psychiatric label with contempt. These symptoms impair his social function.

He got married 8 years ago. His wife always blames and complains that the patient Y never know her heart. Both his parents and his wife haven't find any psychological problem with Y. For the past 10 years when patient Y goes out, the left upper abdominal pain will appear. The pain can't remit until he concentrates on playing computer games for 30 minutes.

After 6 months of medication treatment and 30 sessions of psychological therapy, eye contact-related symptoms have improved greatly. When he goes out, he still feel nervous and still believes that there must be some problem with his eyes, his left upper abdominal pain will emerge and can't relieve until he plays 30 minutes' electronic game.

Before the patient was born, his father suicided for political reasons. His mother had to raise two children alone. It was difficult for his mother to present herself as Winnicott's "good enough mother." There were problems of separation-individuation. During Oedipal stage, father was absent. He could not succeed in achieving a compromise of competition and identity could not be internalized successfully. The major father attachment style is avoidant. The process of internalization of "good" mother and father is difficult. Grumpy mother usually use scolding and beating as educational mode. The mentalization of the patient hasn't been successfully developed. Many primitive psychological defense mechanisms have been revealed, such as: splitting, projection, somatization and so on.

The report went on:

1   How to carry out the work on the left upper abdominal pain?
2   Is the dynamic psychological treatment suitable for the patient with dismissive–avoidant attachment style? Could you give us some advice?

What was most important to me in hearing this case was the great contrast between the patient's early life and his life from college to the present. What happened at that juncture? One way of looking at it is this: He left home. In his description, it was an abusive home. So he now had to provide his own abuse. He needed to be able to feel the care and concern his mother showed in her beating him. He needed to feel the painful love of his mother's dragging him across the schoolyard in front of all his teachers and classmates. So his difficulty in separation was that he could only keep his inner picture of his mother by reproducing her abuse of him.

Another way of seeing his situation is that he needed to shame himself and make himself the object of public abuse to keep an image of his father alive in his mind. His father had likely been treated as others were during the Cultural Revolution. Then he would have been shamed and spat upon. We do not know whether his mother or other relatives told him about this or whether he heard about it from others in their town, or whether he heard about it being done to others during that time. But his description of his fear that it would happen to him has two important parts. First, he fears that someone will spit on him; second, he fears that he will be verbally abused. His symptom is acting as if this is really happening to him; he lowers his eyes as if he is being shamed.

By acting badly to his college dorm-mates, he may have provoked them to act as if they were the shaming crowd around his father. This is a way to keep his longed-for father alive. This fits with the seeming paradox of his description of his time in a distant town living with his stepfather. On the one hand, he says his stepfather did not know how to take care of a child. He says he had to cook for himself. On the other hand, he calls the three years they lived together as the happiest time of his life. At that time he had a father. He was able to play with the other children. He did not bear the shame of his biological father. If people in that town did not know what had happened to his father, they could think his stepfather was his real father. He would then have been free to think of himself as the son of this man and feel protected and cared for by the man who took him away from the people who knew of his family shame.

In this scenario, going to college would again deprive him of a father. Without the presence of his stepfather, the ghost of his father would return to haunt him. The unconscious fantasy that he could resurrect his father would replace the presence of his stepfather. The idea of his father being shamed and spat on would come rushing back to dominate his affective life. He would be drawn into re-enacting the shaming and psychic murder of his father.

Therapy that gives him an interested witness to his suffering helps. Contact with a person who respects him is reparative. Therapy that makes him aware of his need for being shamed helps more. Helping him to become aware of the details of his unconscious fantasy can help even more. In other words, the witnessing (Poland, 1996) helps; the relationship (Mitchell, 2006) helps; the awareness of affect helps (Fenichel, 1941; Hall, 1998): and, learning the creativity of his symptom (Etchegoyen, 1991) helps. All of these aspects of therapy can enable him to create a new narrative for his life that makes sense. Having this narrative in mind will show him that he is not psychotic in a demeaning sense, but creating a means to mourn the loss of his father and to survive. My hope as a therapist would be to help him to find a meaning in his survival so that he can participate in the more nurturing society of present day China.

What was unconscious about this fantasy was the connection between his fears and his father's experiences. His fears of his own suicide were unconscious as well. The scenario of spitting and shaming was already conscious, but the links to his mother's memories of his father and his identification with his father were not. Unconscious fantasies can be partly or entirely unconscious. Repression can make the scenario unconscious; isolation can make the affect unconscious; and either defense can make the links between past and present or current reality and past trauma unconscious.

Fantasies are distilled from the earliest traumas, wishes, and the earliest prohibitions; they grow and develop throughout life, changing as they are affected by traumas and development and yet retaining the earliest wishes as the basis of mental life. Derivatives of the early wishes are subjected to defenses that change their manifestations in daydreams, but the behavior motivated by unconscious fantasy remains manifest in symptoms and acting out (Arlow 1991b). Fantasies are intermediate between traumatic experience and formation of symptoms, dreams, jokes, works of art, and everyday behavior. We call a person masochistic when she understands an event to be a beating she deserved because of her bad behavior even though the thunderstorm that was the actual current event had nothing to do with her behavior.

Implications for treatment

One implication for therapy is that shame and guilt need to be named and explored in order to be sufficiently mastered to allow the person who has experienced trauma to create the kind of fantasy that supports adaptation and promotes self-esteem. The therapy may serve to reawaken old traumas and, in the presence of benign attentiveness, may enable the person to create a new fantasy that allows modification of the crippling effects of severe or repeated trauma. An empathic therapist can be that Horatio; that audience. The therapist reacts to the patient's behavior and statements, makes an imaginative leap, creates a fantasy of what the patient feels, tells the patient what she thinks he feels, and listens for his corrections of her fantasy.

But the therapist needs to interact with the patient in telling him what she thinks the feeling may be that he cannot name, telling him this is a hypothesis and she needs him to correct it, linking the feeling to other feelings he has had in similar situations, times when he had the same feeling in different situations and thereby expanding the web of associations so as to form a coherent story that enables him to actively master the trauma.

The following very brief and simplified account of an analytic treatment conducted in this way shows how important the elaboration of a fantasy can be in changing a person's life.

A patient told me in our first meeting that he was coming for treatment because he was warned at work that he was about to be "flushed." This brought the idea to my mind of a toilet flushing. I thought that in fantasy he saw himself as a turd. Both disgust and shame had entered the room. As we talked he became aware his compulsive house cleaning, his fascination with the exhaust systems of cars, and his history of causing pain to others and himself added up to an anal sadistic character that rested on this fantasy. The fantasy had been the context available to him when his boss at work told him that he was not performing up to expectations. Shame at not doing well enough mingled with guilt over causing pain to himself, his family, and his work colleagues. A detail of the fantasy that his mother had toilet-trained him by showing herself squatting on the toilet passing a stool placed the fantasy as an anal regression from a phallic trauma. The traumatic image of his mother's vulva with a stool emerging had been elaborated into the idea that babies were born of a cloaca. He thought he was born that way. A later set of experiences elaborated this fantasy further. He mourned the loss of a baby he had conceived with a girlfriend when they were in high school. His parents' insistence that the infant be given up for adoption meant to him that it was of no value, "a waste." That bolstered the idea that he was "waste." After years of analytic work he achieved a unique position in the field of solid waste disposal. Both the underlying fantasy and the anal character had remained, but he was now able to use these in an adaptive way. What had been a symptom became a strength. He no longer needed to punish himself for his fantasy but elaborated it in a satisfying way.

Thinking of unconscious fantasy derived from infantile trauma rather than instinct or drive as the motivation for both libidinal and aggressive behavior, verbalization and thoughts privileges the individual experience. It matches up with Green's (1983) description of the effects of the trauma experienced by a child when his mother became depressed in his infancy. The loss of the previously attentive mother created an empty, deadening affect, a fantasy of death as coldness and emptiness. The implication is that the child would wish to join the mother and fear joining her as well. Bergmann (2011) believed that this way of understanding a death wish and death fear was superior to the assumption of a death instinct because it allows for an understanding of the particular circumstances in the patient's life rather than stopping the inquiry about masochism and self-punishment at the presumption that the person has reached unanalyzability. While Bergmann derived his conclusion from a different source, his idea is complementary to that of Arlow and Brenner (1975) in that it replaces instinct with infantile experience. Unconscious fantasy, in my view, is based on infantile experience.

The emphasis on the concept of unconscious fantasy seems to me to have begun with the work of Ella Freeman Sharpe (1949). She says: "In analysis one would say that the assimilation of knowledge of the unconscious mind is an essential part of the psychical process" (p. 18). She compares dreams and poetry as both being constructed according to the same processes. Simile, metaphor, synecdoche, onomatopoeia, parallel, antithesis, and repetition are ways of conveying meaning behind the straightforward logical meaning of the narrative.

Freeman Sharpe explains the psychoanalytic project of interpreting dreams in this way:

> The dream has a two-fold value; it is the key to the understanding of the unconscious phantasy and it is the key to the storehouse of memory and experience. The unconscious wish and phantasy have at their disposal all experiences from infancy. As an approach to the mechanisms that make the manifest dream out of latent thoughts and the unconscious store of experience and impulse I have detailed the principles and devices employed by poetic diction, since these principles bear so directly the impress of the same origin as dream mechanisms. I have indicated the help to be obtained in elucidating dreams from the simple fact that the bridges of thought are crossed and re-crossed by names, that the basis of language is implied metaphor and that we all learned our mother tongue phonetically.
>
> (pp. 38–39)

Freeman Sharpe describes the patient eliciting of detail that characterizes analysis of a dream. Such work requires the time and the willingness to endure pain and boredom, the tediousness of hearing variations on a theme until the underlying theme becomes apparent and the overcoming of the censorship that deletes those aspects of the story that are too difficult to bear.

When I first read her book during my own analysis with Dr. Arlow, I told him that I thought her idea about unconscious fantasy was the same as his. But he replied that it was different because the Kleinian model that Freeman Sharpe was using included early infantile phantasy while he was talking about Oedipal level fantasy. He emphasized that even the spelling was meant to differentiate the two. But the use of the poetic means to understand the manifestations of the unconscious fantasy and the aim of educing it from speech, dreams, and other behavior is essentially the same as what analysts use in the elucidation of dreams, jokes, slips of the tongue, and symptoms.

This way of thinking makes the unconscious fantasy a *sine qua non* of psychoanalysis. It makes the reconstruction of infantile experience (Blum, 1996) compatible with analytic process even when the reconstruction is of something no longer remembered. The unconscious fantasy unites Freud's early topographic theory of psychoanalysis with the later structural understanding of the tensions and conflicts embodied in fantasy. In this sense, it is the return of what has been suppressed in psychoanalysis. It makes psychoanalysis a painstaking and therefore long process. Even long and detailed analysis can change only a little bit of a person's character, but paying attention to unconscious fantasy can make that a crucial change.

Note

1 Recorded verbatim from the Chinese report.

References

Arlow, J. (1991a). Conflict, trauma and deficit. In S. Dowling (Ed.), *Conflict and compromise*. Madison, CT: International Universities Press.
Arlow, J. (1991b). Fantasy symptoms in twins. In J. Arlow (Ed.), *Psychoanalysis: Clinical theory and practice*. Madison, CT: International Universities Press.
Bachant, J. (2014). Complex developmental trauma. In *Wuhan psychotherapy program publication*. Wuhan, China: Wuhan University, Wuhan Psychotherapy Hospital.
Bergmann, M. S. (2011). The dual impact of Freud's death and Freud's death instinct theory on the history of psychoanalysis. *Psychoanalytic Review, 98*, 665–686.
Blum, H. P. (1991). Sadomasochism in the psychoanalytic process, within and beyond the pleasure principle: Discussion. *Journal of the American Psychoanalytic Association, 39*, 431–450.
Blum, H. (1996). Seduction trauma. *Journal of the American Psychoanalytic Association, 39*, 513–535.
Brenneis, C. (1997). *Recovered memories of trauma*. Madison, CT: International Universities Press.
Brenner, C. (1975). *The mind in conflict*. Madison, CT: International Universities Press.
Cozolino, L. (2006). *The neuroscience of human relationships: Attachment and the developing social brain*. WW Norton & Company, New York.
Etchegoyen, R. (1991). *Fundamentals of psychoanalytic technique*. London: Karnac.
Fenichel, O. (1941). Problems of psychoanalytic technique. Albany, NY: Psychoanalytic Quarterly.
Freeman Sharpe, E. (1949). *Dream analysis*. London: Hogarth.
Good, M. (1995). Karl Abraham, Sigmund Freud and the fate of the seduction theory. *Journal of the American Psychoanalytic Association, 43*, 1137–1167.
Green, A. (1983). The dead mother. In *On private madness*. New York: International Universities Press, 1986.
Hall, J. (1998). *Deepening the treatment*. Northvale, NJ: Jason Aronson.
Laplanche, J. (1997). The theory of seduction and the problem of the other. *International Journal of Psychoanalysis, 78*, 653–666.
Loewenberg, P. (2015). Time in history and in psychoanalysis. *Journal of the American Psychoanalytic Association, 63*, 769–784.
Masson, J. (1984). *The assault on truth*. New York: Farrar, Straus & Giroux.
Masson, J. (Ed. & Trans.). (1985). *The complete letters of Sigmund Freud to Wilhelm Fleiss, 1897–1904*. Cambridge, MA: Harvard University Press.
Mitchell, S. (2006). The seduction hypothesis axis. In M. Good (Ed.), *The seduction theory in its second century*. Madison, CT: International Universities Press.
Poland, W. (1996). *Melting the darkness*. Northvale, NJ: Jason Aronson.
Shakespeare, W. (2011). *The complete works of Shakespeare* (Kindle Locations 80961–80970). Latus ePublishing. Kindle Edition.
Simon, B. (1992). Incest – see under Oedipus complex. *Journal of the American Psychoanalytic Association, 40*, 955–988.
Sulloway, F. (1979). *Freud, biologist of the mind*. New York: Basic Books.
Viorst, J. (1986). *Necessary losses*. New York: Free Press.

Chapter 19

Searching unconscious phantasy

Rogelio Sosnik

Unconscious Phantasy, the central object of the psychoanalytic activity, is one of the most important theoretical and clinical concepts of Psychoanalysis. Unconscious phantasy is at the core of what Freud defines as "psychic reality." Psychic reality consists of the reality of our own thoughts, of our own personal world, a reality that is as valid as that of the material world. When Freud introduces the concept of "psychical reality" in the last lines of *The Interpretation of Dreams* (1900) which sums up his thesis that a dream is not a phantasmagoria, but a text to be deciphered, he says:

> Whether we are to attribute reality to unconscious wishes, I can not say.... If we look at unconscious wishes, ... we have to conclude, not doubt, that psychical reality is a particular form of existence which is not to be confused with material reality.
>
> (p. 620)

So there are therefore three kinds of phenomena or realities in the widest sense of the word: material reality, the reality of intermediate thoughts of the psychological field, and the reality of unconscious wishes, and their true complex and more easily shifting Phantasy. Searching unconscious phantasy is how we as clinicians locate the Unconscious in our daily clinical practice.

Methodological difficulties in our search

As analysts we have as well our conceptions and models about how to reach the Unconscious, models that both aid and at times mislead us. I want to cite Laplanche and Pontalis (1968) regarding our subject in order to show the difficulties that we are facing. I quote:

> Since we encounter fantasy as a given, interpreted, reconstructed, or postulated, at the most diverse levels of psychoanalytic experience, we have obviously to face the difficult problem of its meta-psychological status, and first

of all, of its topography within the framework of the distinction between the unconscious, preconscious and conscious systems.

(p. 11)

This will trigger our interventions depending on what we consider the therapeutic action of our interpretative activity. Again, I cite Laplanche and Pontalis (1968): "by making a theoretical transposition, which seems inevitable in practice, between the fantasy as it presents itself for interpretation and the fantasy which is the conclusion of the work of analytic interpretation (S. Isaacs)." Freud would thus have been in error in describing by the same term, Fantasy, two totally distinct realities. On the one hand, there is the Unconscious Phantasie, "the primary content of unconscious mental processes" (Isaacs, 1948, p. 81) and the other, the conscious or subliminal imagining, of which the daydream is the typical example. The latter would be only a manifest content, like the others, and would have no more privileged relationship to unconscious than dreams, behavior, or whatever is generally described as "material." Like all manifest data, it would require interpretations in terms of "Unconscious fantasies" (p. 11).

Our interpretative activity that depends on the conception of the mind based on the models that we hold in our conscious interventions also is supported by the way that we hold fragments of theories that exist in our pre-conscious as Sandler and Sandler demonstrate (1983). Those theories are going to be used by us during our "free floating theorization" (Aulagnier, 2001) that is part of our "free floating attention."

The theories that we hold in our pre-conscious, ready to be used by us at the moment that the clinical situation in its evocative quality triggers them into our consciousness, are also our response to the clinical moment in which we are participating. We are an active part of it with the different levels in which our mind works: conscious, pre-conscious, and unconscious.

Theory

There are three dimensions of the Unconscious Phantasy that I want to consider. Two of them belong to the two different levels that the Unconscious possesses as Freud described in *The Ego and the Id* (1923): the Structural and the Dynamic Unconscious. The first level refers to the structural dimension of the Unconscious, and I would like to mention two approaches in the conception of the Structure of the mind and the characteristic of the unconscious in it. Within the French School, we have the structural conception of Lacan that defines the structure of the unconscious as a language. In it the signifier, a term that comes from linguistics, is the support of the "fantasme" that comes as a secondary formation after the relationship with the "Other" as a separate being is established. In this regard, unconscious phantasy belongs to the level on the "Imaginary," and also to the "Real," that is forever un-apprehensible. Also we have the work of J. Laplanche (1987) that introduced the concept of the "enigmatic message" as the organizer of the sexual dimension of the unconscious and the unconscious itself, in the relationship between the mother and the newborn.

In the Kleinian School, S. Isaacs (1948) extended the meaning of Unconscious Phantasy to become the core of the mental structure from which the Id, the Super-ego, and the Ego are defined. For the Kleinians, since the Unconscious Phantasies are the basic elements that conform to the internal objects composing the psychic reality of the Internal World, Freud's structural dimension of the Unconscious is organized by the relationships that exist between the internal objects within the mind and their relationship with the external object that belongs to material reality. The role that they are going to play depends on the processes of introjection and projection based as they are, in the economy of the basics instincts, Life and Death Instinct.

The second dimension of the Unconscious that Freud described belongs to the Dynamic Unconscious, that implies the inter-systemic level and the communicative aspect that unconscious phantasies possess, in their role of connection between internal reality and external reality with all the vicissitudes that take place in it: pleasure and pain, regulated by defensive mechanisms, as a way to sustain psychic equilibrium and internal balance.

Concerning this dimension, there are important differences between schools of psychoanalysis regarding the way that unconscious phantasy originates and the role that it plays in the structure of defensive mechanisms. It is my contention that those differences reside in the way that they conceive the role of the object, in the earlier relationship between the mother and the baby. This relationship determines the structure and the timing of the formation of the psychic apparatus itself.

Nowadays there is an increased interest in pre-mental states, based as they are in the findings of neurophysiology that confirm that embryonic mental states exist before the baby passes through the caesura of birth. This reaffirms Freud's intuition that: "There is much more continuity between intra-uterine life and earliest infancy than the impressive caesura of the act of birth allow us to believe" (1926).

This interest is centered on unrepresented states of mind, and also in the existence of embryonic mental states (Bion, 1989) and the way that they manifest themselves during the clinical situation. This new research deals with what resides beyond the level of unconscious phantasies and opens a new door to the unknown beyond the unreachable level of the unconscious that resides beyond the primary repression. Our current version of the two-person psychology follows the model of the mother–baby relationship. In it, there is still the controversy on how and when unconscious phantasy is created, and what is the role that the external object plays in it and when.

The third dimension that I want to include is the relationship that the Unconscious phantasy has with the experiences of pleasure and pain, physical and mental pain, not only by expressing them but in the way that pleasure and pain determine the way that mental organization is shaped by them. It seems to me that within this discussion, the place that the body has is central, as is the conception of aggression and sexuality. Following P. Aulagnier (2015) I think of the body in its two dimensions: the biological and the psychological. The biological body is the place where the origin of the impulses resides that generates the exchanges between physical tensions and the exchanges with the external world of objects, with the result of the instinctual organization, as Freud, Klein, Isaacs conceive it. In this conception, this is the way that the psychological body starts to be formed. The other conception on how the psychological body is formed sustains that it is born out of the exchanges with the environmental influences. In it the place of origin and organization of the impulses reside in the exchanges with the external agent, as Lacan, Mahler, Winnicott, Laplanche, and Aulagnier conceive it.

Practice

When we work, we offer a space within which we become the other actor of the scene while assuming the role of the narrator and warrantor of the truthfulness of the experience that is taking place. This space is a space where the presence of the past, the historical past of the patient will emerge, a past that will involve us without knowing it. Repetition compulsion will open the work of building the past history with the patient. Also there is a new experience of the present that will be emerging out of the activity of the psychoanalytic method. Free associations, free floating attention, interpretations, the analytic process evolves within the analytic frame, which has timelessness as one of its dimensions.

My interest in the place that the body has during the experiences of satisfaction and pain regarding mental organization was triggered by the clinical case that I am presenting. I hope that the reader will have a chance to see how my search of the unconscious and unconscious phantasy help me to organize my approach to my analysand.

Clinical case

Miss A is 37 years old. The oldest of two siblings, she is followed by a brother two years younger. They belong to a particular family configuration that was slowly emerging during her four times a week analysis, in our work of building her personal and familial history. Father and mother, both successful academics are part of a small Armenian-Jewish community in a closed traditional society. My patient's father's mother died when he was 5 years old, and being the youngest of five, he was taken care of by his aunt and his father's father never remarried. A's mother lost her mother when she was 2 years old, being the only child in her original family. Her father remarried an acquaintance who had come to America in the same boat of Armenian-Jewish emigrants during the Nazi occupation of Europe. Many family members on the mother's side were murdered by the Nazis during the World War II. Most of these events were partially disclosed, discovered, and clarified during A's analysis. Secrecy was an important aspect of A's family culture. It appears that one of the causes of the secrecy was the fact that the members of the family that migrated had money to pay for their freedom, while the rest of the family went into concentration camps where they were murdered. Miss A's parents became involved in their late adolescence, and A's mother joined the father's sibling family organization. This sibling configuration had the shape of a clan composed of very bright members very well respected within their community. Miss A was named for her mother's mother, a fact that she learned when she was 11 years old when she also discovered that her mother was an orphan, and the woman she knew as her grandmother was not the real grandmother. This was one of the many secrets that her parents kept from their children. At that time, prior to her menarche, she put on weight, an issue that became central for her. She locates in it her sense of shame, of "not fitting" with her peer group. By locating in her body image her entire self, she felt that this became a demonstration of her lack of internal boundaries that she was exposing in her social environment, and obviously betraying in this way, her family double culture of fitting in and secrecy.

The fact that she was and still is very physically active and enjoyed sports did not modify the place that her body size and appearance continue to occupy in her mind. For her, her body reflects her sense of self-regulation in which her emotional states can be seen from outside. Her emotional states varied from manic to intensely depressive. Many times she experienced states of acute anxiety that she tried to calm down by uncontrolled eating.

She felt that in addition to being overweight, she was unsuccessful in romantic relationships; that men never got involved with her because of her size; that relationships always evolved into a kind of friendliness where she became the good listener. She felt lacking in any seductive quality, and did not know "the game" that her girlfriends knew in a natural fashion. She had experienced crushes with boys that never evolved into an intimate, lasting relationship.

From her past history, I understood A. was a happy and active child who suffered skin allergies and some visual difficulties that needed early attention. She had worn glasses since pre-school; an allergic condition that started when she was an infant added to her sense of body fragility.

A started to put on weight at the end of her primary school, in the beginning of her puberty. This was a time when she enjoyed sports and a social life within a very close circle of friends. After high school she went to university feeling uncertain about her vocation, and in the first year she dropped out because she felt unfit. After a year she started her real vocational choice as an architect. During the year of change she was very depressed and gained a lot of weight. In the process of her new self-definition, she looked for help and started psychoanalysis with a woman analyst to whom she became very attached. What she valued the most from her experience of analysis was that she started to recognize and find a name for her feelings, a new experience for her, in contrast with her family culture where orders, admonitions, and facts predominate in their exchanges. She succeeded in her profession and after graduation became part of the faculty of her university school.

When she came to see me to continue her analysis, she was still working with her analyst in order to feel "ready" to migrate to New York City where her friends lived. In the first consultation she expressed concerns about her weight, her deep depression, and her tendency to suffer physical accidents. During the first two years the style of her communication with me was peculiar: she was always on time, was very "chatty," and offered a narrative centered on details of her daily life, her work, and her family life. This was the free association process that she knew. Little by little an atmosphere of "secrets," specifically what belonged to the family life, to their habits and connections, started to emerge and the disclosure of the family history resulting from our work gave her relief and triggered her curiosity. That led her to start to research about the past of her family and to put together for the first time her family history.

While my work during the sessions was to try to convey the meaning of her connection with me within the transference situation, her responses to me were always of a superficial agreement followed by a hypomanic current of association detached from my interventions. The strong persecutory anxiety and terror of proximity and connection with me during the analytic hour made that connection impossible for her. The material was fragmented, the rhythm was manic, and I had no idea what happened with my interpretations, since all the time her response was a "yes," and then there was no connection with what I had said.

I felt alone during the sessions, trying and failing to communicate with her, while on the surface we were "doing" the task as if we were "in" analysis. I experienced the projection of her sense of hopelessness in being understood. She tried to relate to me by bringing dreams every session, dreams that she had written down as that was the way she "understood" how to behave while in analysis. Also since she is a visual person, having dreams is something common for her.

I thought that this was part of her previous analytic experience that for her was the first time to learn how to make sense of how her mind works. In other words, it was part of a repetition of her previous experience, a pre-formed transference, while at the same time an avoidance of a real connection with me. For her, in this new experience, with a man, I was a violent and self-imposing persecutory object. She "lamented" how big a burden she was becoming for me to tolerate: the heavy weight of her depressive mood, her complaints of her sense of failure in her social life, the guilty feelings that she had related to the concerns of her parents about her single status, and the need that she felt to overcome her feelings of despair of any possibility of being closer to a man. Her appearance and her body size played a major role as a rationalization of her destiny as a "spinster." She suffered the weekends because of her depressive moods and sense of isolation. She also needed this time to be alone and recover her energy and psychic stability, but felt guilty about it by not pursuing social encounters in order to "meet a man."

During the separation of vacations, she experienced a state of loss of internal equilibrium. I understood this as the lack of the support system provided by the sessions that became a component of her self-regulation. I thought that she made a stronger connection with the space of my office than with me and interpreted this. I saw her attachment to the analytic situation as a way to "belong," instead of creating a more specific object relationship to me. I thought that the container function of the analytic setting with me included in it as a partial object satisfied her primitive need to reconnect with a maternal object who would take care of her need to keep her physical and mental development evolving. In this context the heaviness of her moods and of her body were felt as too big for her infantile baby self to be attended to.

Listening to my descriptions of the variations of her moods and the recognition of her mental states started to have an effect on her, while she still had great difficulty sustaining a closer relationship with me. The connection with me had a formal quality in which avoidance and idealization predominated.

After two years she started her first romantic relationship. For the first time she was very active trying to build "a relationship," suffering the man's reluctance to make a serious commitment. There were timid references to a frustrating sexual relationship. At that time, the session was the place where she tried to recover better feelings about him, and to preserve "the relationship" since her frustration and anger were taking over her loving feelings. My role was to be the modulator of her anxiety about losing him and her fears of facing again a sense of failure, being alone and rejected.

The sessions that I am presenting belong to the period after she broke up with him, after suffering from the sadomasochistic quality of the relationship and occur during one week. I want to show how, by following the dreams material, I was able to show her mental states at that time and the relationship that they have with the evolution of the transference.

Monday session

After a weekend that was surprisingly satisfactory for her, visiting a family of relatives with children that lived outside New York:

P: ... I dreamed last night, I woke up three times to go to the bathroom, and one of my dreams was about Carl, that we talked, and in the dream he was aloof, like out of my reach, and in that dream you told me that it wasn't wrong if I decided to go back with him, and I got anxious, and thought that I had made a mistake in analysis, and what was I going to do now. And then I dreamt about my schoolmates from my town, and there was a fabric exhibit, like a market, with a lot of fabrics, and a very important old man was there, and it seems that I had some type of connection with him, but I can't remember well what it was. In another dream, Mary was there with her mom, and it seems that Mary's father had died, and they were gathered there, and I went to see them, or to the funeral, something like that, not very clear. Mary is my friend from California who got divorced. Yesterday I went to the park with my friend Sara, and we sat down and watched a group of people next to us who were dressed in black from head to foot, with black hair and eyes, we were struck by them, they looked like those Greek people one sees in the movies.... Sara is having troubles with her husband and she says that she is contemplating divorce.

A: So your dream about me and Carl seems to have to do with the fact that somewhere in your mind you don't know whether you broke up with him because of what your experience was like, because of what your relationship was like, or because I told you to do so. It is as though you are not clear, perhaps confused and suspicious about your true reasons.

P: Yes, I think I'm not sure yet, and yesterday when the plane was flying over the Long Island Sound, and it was such a beautiful afternoon, and I was watching the boats, I thought of Carl and remembered that the last summer we were sailing there.

A: The other dream, about your school, seems to be related to the fact that somewhere you still have a kind of connection, not clear yet, with a man that bears some weight, in the middle of this atmosphere of divorce, Mary, and mourning, the Greeks? And your friend Sara also talking of a future divorce, everything within the context of this weekend, when I think you felt strongly moved because you felt close to a different side of life.

P: I had a very pleasant surprise with them, their children, the style of life that they have ...

Tuesday

(Arrives on time.)

P: What's happening now is that my mind is full of things connected with the weekend, and even though I worked really hard yesterday, they are still in my mind ... (*Brief silence*)

A: What are the things that are in your mind?

P: ... something like images of the weekend that get mixed up with work issues ... and yesterday I was late to work, and also I feel like that today, that I will be late to work. And yesterday at the end of the day I felt tired, and I thought if after two days with three kids I lose my cool and can't keep calm, then what would it be like if I had to work and also had children, and I wonder whether I would be able to do that, and this weekend I looked at Susan's pregnancy pictures, first fat and then thin again, and it made me think that physical changes turn me off so much, and I'm 37 years old and I don't know if I will be able to have children, I can also adopt, and I don't think it's that bad ...

Yesterday I dreamt that I was watching a TV show, and they talked about AIDS, and the symptoms, and I was looking at my skin to see if I had spots on my skin ...

A: So today you are feeling anxious again, with many fears that are difficult to define, not having a calm place within yourself, and at the same time you have a confusing feeling of guilt and fear of being close to me.

P: I was thinking that since I arrived on Sunday I didn't have time to think, everything is mixed up in my mind. And I started to receive phone calls from my posting in Match.com, and I don't feel ready yet to start to think about them.

A: So right now you don't have much room for me inside you, as if today's session happened too soon, and you expect me to help you to calm down instead of facing new things about yourself.

P: It's true, although yesterday's session was very useful, and afterward I thought about it, and today I feel so different, I feel overwhelmed.

Summary of Wednesday session

She came anxious, apologizing for being late, which she was not. Then she started to complain of feeling blocked, disconnected from her feelings, as if "floating over things," detached, and not capable of thinking. She was feeling her attention was directed only to external events, and experienced this state of mind as increasing her anxiety while in the session. Last night she had dreams that she did not remember, and had the sense that she was blocking the closeness with me, that increased her anxiety state.

Thursday

She came after a meeting in her work place, feeling very frustrated.

A: I noticed the anger in your voice, which I think may be connected with your frustration for feeling that you are not being listened to, or that your point was not taken.

P: I'm not angry, I feel that you criticized me, and in the end they accepted my suggestion to call someone from outside to help us do the reorganization, and Phil told me that he realizes that he has to listen more because he doesn't listen to what others have to say.

A: Perhaps that is what is going on here today, that is that you are having a hard time believing that I am listening to you.

P: You see, you're criticizing me!!!!

A: I'm calling your attention to something that perhaps is part of your uneasiness today.

P: Last night I was home talking on the phone, and I saw that somebody had slipped a piece of paper under the door. It occurred to me that it was a neighbor who was complaining because I was speaking too loud, and it was a menu from a Chinese restaurant.

A: So now you are connecting what happened to you last night with what happened here this morning, the fact that you expected me to scold you, a criticism or reproach that you continue to aim at yourself.

P: Well, you know that when I was fat I kept scolding myself, much more than my dad did, or anybody else, and I'm thinking of all the things I must have done as a girl, especially with my parents, so that they wouldn't scold me. I remember that episode I told you about, when I was in second grade and I forged my mom's signature in a disciplinary note, and the teacher caught me and told my parents, so they did scold me.

Yesterday I had several dreams. In one of them I was in a country I didn't know, Israel or something like that. I don't know what city it was, and I was driving a convertible that I think belonged to David's dad. I drove very fast, and as I drove, I was scared because I was going through places I didn't know, and I didn't have a map, nothing, and I was scared because I was driving like a madwoman without knowing the road. Then I had another dream, I was in Florida, on a beach where I used to go and that I know very well because I went scuba diving there several times. I saw that the sea was very calm, and I thought it was very nice, very pleasant, and I walked on a sort of sandbank, and suddenly, I made a turn and found myself in a rough sea, with a strong current, and I didn't know it was there.

And I wasn't alone, I was with some friends from my office, and we had to jump into the water and let the waves carry us, and I was scared of letting myself be swept away by the waves without knowing where they would take me and of relaxing and letting myself be carried away. And in my office, Phil who is very athletic, and runs triathlons, told us an experience that he had of a man who was participating in the competition and had to let himself be carried away by the current. In that case you have to save energy and he had to wait several hours until the waves slowly brought him back to the shore, and this is the way that you have to do it, to keep your energy safe, is the only way to do it. And it reminds me what we did with Francine when we were at the beach.

You know, I realize that this is the place where I can see the sky, and feel good, and really like it.

A: It's true, even though at the same time you are telling me how difficult it is for you to relax and let yourself be swept away by the waves, being able to open up trustfully to feel and examine with me the various feelings that you experience in the session, because you are more concerned with the direction that it will take us, and for that reason you are telling me how sensitive you are to any movement that is beyond your control.

P: Yes, it's true that it's hard for me. At the same time, it's true that this is the only place where I can feel calm and see the sky and stop for a while.

A: Yes, and also have the chance to look inside and let yourself be swept away by the waves of how you feel during this process.

P: You know that my friend Frieda who teaches computer classes had the chance to teach an analyst and although she didn't have enough money she never called her because she had a very bad experience with an analyst that she had seen in consultation and she didn't want to have anything to do with analysts or be near them.

A: Frieda is a part of you, a part that can't let itself be carried away by me trusting that I will take you in the right direction and thus be able to open up to a wave of self-observation and understanding without knowing in advance where we're going, even though, at the same time, through your dream you convey to me your fear of going too fast, or following too fast a mental pace without clear direction.

P: You see, with so many years of analysis I didn't realize that my dream had to do with that. I'm still not aware of my own things.

A: So now the scolding is back, and you're the one aiming it at yourself.

P: Yes, that's right. Tonight my friend, Lisa, is coming to my place for dinner, and I am hoping she will help me solve the problem with my coats, I like both, but keeping both is too much money for me.

Final comments

In the earlier phase I referred to a more acute level of confused anxieties and more primitive material with the quality of part object relationship predominating. At that time unconscious phantasies played a central role in the defensive maneuvers to keep her mental equilibrium and not to feel flooded by her anxiety states. In contrast, the sessions I chose here demonstrate the moment of change in which the transference neurosis was more firmly established, opening the door to explore the unconscious phantasy within the analytic relationship.

Summary

1   Trauma: for A being named after her real grandmother acted as a signifier (Lacan) of the unconscious phantasy of a "dead mother" that was implanted on her and was part of unresolved mourning of her mother and father's earlier losses. I also think that the discovery of her mother as an early orphan added to the trauma that she suffered.

2   A's body became the "depositary" (Pichon Riviere, 1965) of what was implanted in her. The fragility and heaviness that A was feeling regarding her body and the pressure of her anxiety states that determined her constant fear of falling apart were the result of that implantation.

3   As a result her sexual development became arrested.

4   We can see in these sessions that her body still was used by her to express her more basic anxieties: a mixed state of depressive and persecutory

anxieties: her fear of pregnancy, her fear of her capability to deal with children, her sense of body fragility, her allergies, and her dream of HIV. Later her body started to play a more relational role when she began to feel more sexually competent and her connection with men included expectations of their constructive capabilities. The primitive phantasies at the base of her feelings of being in a prison with the primary figures evolved into a more mature relationship with them, inside herself and in the external reality.

5   The analytic activity of discrimination and differentiation between subject and object created the conditions for her to open a mental space where meaning of her emotional experiences had a place.

6   Within the analytic situation, I observed that what appears as a melancholic disposition of A was in reality the result of the implantation of her parental environment where she lacked an internal space to become a new member of a different family configuration.

7   The exploration of the unconscious phantasies in their double aspect, as a way to evacuate basic anxieties and as a way to communicate with me and become more conscious of her personality traits, made it possible for A. to continue her process of mental development. This took place because by naming and recognizing her emotional experiences, she started a process of de-identification from her primary objects. That allowed her to change her relationship with her body and with her body needs, by including her sexual needs and recognizing the aggression that her states of frustration trigger on her.

8   A became more open to legitimize her own experiences of desire and need for an "outside object" different from the primary figures. In the beginning it was me when the transferential neurosis was more firmly established. This gave us the opportunity to start to work with the unconscious phantasies and emotions within the transference with a whole object, a step previous to a meeting with an external real object.

9   The week that I chose shows my work in trying to amplify the free association process. It is only in the here and now of the transference neurosis that we can explore with the patient the unconscious phantasy as it becomes organized and provides the sense of conviction required to produce psychic change.

10   Dreams offer a place for finding unconscious phantasy in the here and now.

With A, in the first two years, her capability to produce and bring dreams was key to understanding what was going on during the sessions since the evacuative and avoidant nature of her communication and the fragmented material was blurring my chance to make sense. As the connection with me became more symbolic, I had more freedom to use free floating attention, and provide interpretations.

To conclude: In the beginning of this chapter, I said that the unconscious phantasy is the central object of psychoanalysis. I hope I have conveyed to the readers my way to search and to use the concept in order to make sense of my clinical experience.

References

Aulagnier, P. (2001). *The violence of interpretation*. Philadelphia: The New Library of Psychoanalysis.

Aulagnier, P. (2015). Birth of the body, origin of a history. *International Journal of Psychoanalysis*, *96*(5), 1371–1401.

Bion, W. R. (1989). *Two papers: The grid and caesura*. London: Karnac Books.

Freud, S. (1900). *The interpretation of dreams*, S.E., 4–5 (pp. 1–723). London: Hogarth.

Freud, S. (1923). *The ego and the id*, S.E., 19 (pp. 3–63). London: Hogarth.

Freud, S. (1926). *Inhibitions, symptoms and anxiety*, S.E., 20 (pp. 77–175). London: Hogarth.

Isaacs, S. (1948). The nature and function of phantasy. *International Journal of Psychoanalysis*, *29*, 73–97.

Laplanche, J. (1987). *New foundations for psychoanalysis*. (D. Macey, Trans.). Oxford: Basil Blackwell (1989).

Laplanche, J., & Pontalis, J. B. (1968). Fantasy and the origins of sexuality. *International Journal of Psychoanalysis*, *49*, 1–18.

Pichon Riviere, E. (1965). Personal communication.

Sandler, J., & Sandler, A. M. (1983). The second censorship, three box model and some technical implications. *International Journal of Psychoanalysis*, *64*, 413–425.

Index

Spillius, E. B. 94, 125, 183
Spitz, R. A. 58
splitting 94
Stanislavski, C. 23
Steinberg, C. 184
Steiner, J. 99, 100, 101
Steiner, R. 6–7, 22, 72, 183–4, 196n1
Stern, D. B. 11
stories 1
Strachey, J. 41
structural unconscious 210–11
Sulloway, F. 199
superego 6, 44, 47, 48, 50, 61, 72, 211
symbolized/symbolization 2, 13, 19, 22,
  28, 71–2, 170

testimony, as a paradigm for therapy of
  extreme traumatization 178–80
therapeutic action 35–42, 183
thinking, birth of 184–6
thought identity 184
timelessness 13, 44, 45, 57–8, 61, 62–3,
  70, 212
transference 1, 4, 6, 7, 8, 9, 10, 11, 14, 15,
  16, 17, 18, 23, 28, 36, 38, 39, 40, 42, 95,
  168, 182, 185; see also
  countertransference; specific case
  studies
trauma 1, 2–3, 6, 9, 10–12, 23, 30–1, 36–7,
  38, 39, 130, 168; early childhood see

Bohleber, W., case study by; Cairo, I.,
  case study by; event, perception and
  lasting effect 200; intergenerational
  175–7; re-enactment of see re-enactment
traumatic blackout 30–1, 174–5
two-person psychology 17–18, 211
Tyler see Oelsner, R.

unconscious 5, 88, 95, 170, 182, 210;
  dynamic 210, 211; structural 210–11
unconscious dramas 33, 183
unconscious fantasy 65–6, 157–8;
  conceptual history of 4–7; early stages
  of development of 182–98
unsymbolized 2, 22, 23, 36, 41

Verhaegue, P. 130
Viñar, M. 67

war 10; Yom Kippur War 176–7, 178–9
Williams, P. 93
Winnicott, D. W. 95, 163, 164, 171, 177,
  184, 212
wishes 2, 23; forbidden 5
witnessing 7, 11–12, 16, 37, 54, 56, 57,
  179–80, 204

Y case study see Richards, A. K.
Yom Kippur War 176–7, 178–9